The Broadway Song

The Broadway Song: A Singer's Guide

Mark Ross Clark

OXFORD
UNIVERSITY PRESS

OXFORD
UNIVERSITY PRESS

Oxford University Press is a department of the University of Oxford. It furthers the University's objective of excellence in research, scholarship, and education by publishing worldwide.

Oxford New York
Auckland Cape Town Dar es Salaam Hong Kong Karachi
Kuala Lumpur Madrid Melbourne Mexico City Nairobi
New Delhi Shanghai Taipei Toronto

With offices in
Argentina Austria Brazil Chile Czech Republic France Greece
Guatemala Hungary Italy Japan Poland Portugal Singapore
South Korea Switzerland Thailand Turkey Ukraine Vietnam

Published in the United States of America by
Oxford University Press
198 Madison Avenue, New York, NY 10016

Library of Congress Cataloging-in-Publication Data
Clark, Mark Ross, 1951– author.
The Broadway song: a singer's guide/Mark Ross Clark.
pages cm
Includes bibliographical references and index.
ISBN 978-0-19-935167-1 (hardcover: alk. paper)—
ISBN 978-0-19-935168-8 (pbk.: alk. paper)
1. Musicals—Instruction and study.
2. Popular music—Analysis, appreciation. I. Title.
MT956.C63 2015
782.1'4143—dc23 2014018544

1 3 5 7 9 8 6 4 2

Printed in the United States of America
on acid-free paper

This book is dedicated to the memory of my parents,
Dorothy Ross Clark and Ray L. Clark Jr.,
and to the three women in my life:
Lynn, Samantha, and Joanna Clark

With gratitude and love

Mark Ross Clark, October 2014

CONTENTS

FOREWORD

KRISTIN CHENOWETH

When you start to study a song, you begin a journey that includes asking a lot of questions that take time to answer. Answers are revealed throughout your life. Even if a young singer is singing a song out of the context of the show, especially in a study situation, it is important to know as much as possible about the song, including where it comes from in the show and who wrote the music and the lyrics.

It is not only imperative for any young singer to understand the lyric and melody to perfection of any song; it is also the way that each role should be approached—even if it is a role you will never play. It is the process of exploration which is important to every singing actor. For example, when I was younger, I studied the role of Violetta in *La Traviata.* I didn't know if it would be a role I would someday sing, but I understood every word Verdi wrote and why he wrote it. I also understood as an actress how she died during the nineteenth century, when so many died of consumption.

If you want to sing about making pies out of human parts, as Mrs. Lovett does in *Sweeney Todd,* by no means should you try this at home. However, all of the research that you do on each character will only help you prepare for the next role as you continue to explore.

As you go on through life, songs become more relevant and relatable to your own life. You begin to better understand what you are singing. Any research that you can do about a composer is only going to be advantageous to your study and to your growth as an artist.

It would be a shame and a missed opportunity for any young singer not to know the composer and lyricist of the piece and what other works they have given us. When I moved to New York I didn't know a lot about Sheldon Harnick and Jerry Bock. I did know that they wrote *Fiddler on the Roof.* What I didn't know was that they also wrote *The Apple Tree,* a show I would come to know I was born to perform and probably should have known earlier. It ended up being the best experience of my career.

Stephen Sondheim is another great example of a composer to study: everything is sung, but it's sung, in my opinion, as a contemporary opera.

Also, it is important to study melodic lines, to see what sounds familiar to you. Why does a melody line go up instead of down when you're not asking a question? Why does it go down when it feels like it should go up? I always say it, and I mean it: we sing because we can't speak it anymore. The second that becomes false for you, it's false for the audience.

All of the important points I have made above are addressed in this book, *The Broadway Song: A Singer's Guide*, which is a helpful aid for the aspiring singer-actor.

ACKNOWLEDGMENTS

I would like to thank those who made this book possible.

Thank you for the encouragement and valued feedback from my wife, Lynn V. Clark, PhD, whose love for musical theatre is based on her talent on stage as well as her appreciation that comes from regular pilgrimages to Broadway; I also wish to thank editor Norman Hirschy of Oxford University Press for remaining positive and highly professional throughout this three-year-plus process. I would also like to acknowledge significant contributions from editors Lisbeth Redfield and Joellyn Ausanka and copy editor Ben Sadock from Oxford University Press. Thanks also for further contributions of reading and support from Dr. Welton Gaddy, Dr. D. H. Clark, Scott Higginbotham, and Daniel Zeagler. Finally, I must pay tribute to those who contributed to the interviews in the book. Of the literally hundreds of interviews I sought, those composers, lyricists, directors, and singing actors who graciously and selflessly offered words of wisdom inspired me because of their desire to pass on their experiences and knowledge to music theatre students. I learned that it is all about respect for the craft and the love for this extraordinary art form.

The Broadway Song

Introduction

How to Use the Book

This book is designed as an aid for the young singing actor to begin (or continue) the journey of study, self-discovery, and application to performance. Research for its own sake is only an exercise of going through the motions, and it is not useful unless it is applied and practiced in the spirit of experimentation and process toward self-discovery. For it is in process that we discover new things that work, and discard those which do not. In the process of trying new ideas, which can have countless applications to performance practice, the student will work with the mirror, video, audio recordings, voice teachers and coaches, peers and colleagues, in studio classes and workshops—to receive honest feedback in order to evaluate ideas. The evaluation feedback that we receive must not be mistaken for an evaluation of our talent, though it is difficult to remove ourselves from that need to know whether we have what it takes. For now, we need to realize that we are here, accepted by a program of study and working with a fine teacher—because we have auditioned for an institution or a studio and our talent has already been evaluated as worthy of investment, which conceptually goes both ways (for teacher *and* student). While *your* energy, time, and resources go into study toward a career, the institution and/or studio is making the same investment. They believe in you, and that should be enough as you embark on your journey. That advice is easier said than practiced, but for you to study, discover, and apply, you cannot be caught up in the trap of always needing to know that you are worthy. This need can pull your focus from what is more important. Not only is your vocal and dramatic talent in your favor; you also have a creative spirit, which performing artists need to nurture and exercise. It can be subjugated in study programs to the wills of teachers and directors who can easily snuff out the creative spirit, because it is *their* ideas that will occupy much of your time and energy. However, the young singing actor needs to take the initiative to flex the muscles of the imagination to apply their own ideas to practice and performance. This is necessary because, to have a successful performing career, performers must develop imaginative and worked-through ideas (while remaining flexible to suggestions coming from the production's creative team) before arriving at the first stage rehearsal (and the preceding audition). Not only do conductors and directors feel this to be crucial; it is almost universally required in the professional world. Our teachers and directors have much information and wisdom to impart. And the *craft* of our art must be learned first—that is true. But the *craft* is not the final goal, because the *craft* is about acquiring the tools to use in achieving our goals.

The questions that we need to answer on our journey are these: What is it that we are trying to achieve in our performances—what are our goals and objectives? Especially if it is clear that no two people have the same opinion in evaluating performance? And how do we go about applying ideas to performance practice?

First of all, we need to think about what it is exactly that we are striving for; if we think back to what we feel is our optimal performance, it may well be a memory of a performance in which we are in total control of what we want to do with our voices and our will, *and* our body feels free from tension. We also will feel energized, inspired and *empowered.* It is not mere coincidence that when we feel technically in control we also feel that we are inspired, energized, and free from tension and worry. The integration of the intellectual ideas and analysis, or right-brain knowledge that we must have for reading notes and rhythms properly, and for understanding the way the voice works technically so that we can sing our high tones with requisite support and so on, is important. By the same token, the imagination that it takes to feel and understand our character's thoughts and feelings is also crucial to the goal of powerful and free performance. In addition, we will discover a loss of dreaded self-consciousness and self-judgment and midstream self-editing if we take the focus off of ourselves and place it upon the character, the music, the composer and lyricist and book writer, and all of the creators who we can figuratively work with in this process.

If there is one shared truth that I learned in my telephone discussions with John Kander, Charles Strouse, Jerry Herman, Stephen Schwartz, Harvey Schmidt, John Bucchino, Frank Wildhorn, and many others in the course of writing this book, it was this: each and every composer, even if one person was responsible for both music and lyrics, recognizes that their creative art of writing music and lyrics for the theatre was only one part of the collaboration between *all* the members of the creative team, which in their opinion includes the actors. Was the music written for an artist they had in mind? Was the casting following the composing of music and lyrics? It didn't matter, because each artist contributed in their own important way, which was acknowledged repeatedly by the composing team. I also observed that virtually all of the composers had an awareness of, and a humble respect for, those creators who came before them, laying the creative groundwork of musical theatre. And they also had an enormous respect and an honest heartfelt love of singing actors and their art.

In order for the entries of this book to be applied to your work, the most important thing is to realize that each entry is not "complete." One thousand words for each song is just the very beginning, but my sincere hope is that, through reading these entries, the book will be a "spark" and open a door to self-discovery, which is the most important discovery of all. I believe that it is true that an idea that sprouts from your own imagination and experimental applications—whether it be in the practice room, studio, or stage—or even from performance, and that self-discovery with the assistance of your mentors and making your performance your own is more exciting and *real* than anything you will be told to do in directive or instruction. It is my wish that an inspiration or germ of an idea found in this book will be an entrée to opening more doors and lead to the discovery of more ideas, possibilities, *truths*. This book does not attempt to do the work for the student. That work is yet to come. The template begins the important process of analysis, dissection, and deconstruction, while the interview represents only one artist affiliated with the song—whether it be composer, lyricist, book author, director, conductor, or singing actor. It is admittedly only a snapshot of their thoughts about the song and how it fits into the show.

I have designed a template for each song for a consistent approach. The first part of entry will tell you what you may already know or can find out easily, but in a format which puts all of the information together about the song: the *character* who sings the song, *duration* of the song, *range* and *tessitura*, the *original production team* and *year* of Broadway premiere, derivation and *source material* of the show, and the *classification* of the song. In classifying the songs, I recognize that, like classifying opera arias, there are different opinions about what type of voice should sing this aria or that song. When a show has a greater history, many different types of voices may have sung the role. However, I have done my best to classify what "type" of song it is, which usually falls into the classification of up-tempo, "belted," or lyric, according to purpose or function. I should mention at this point that one of the reasons I wrote this book was to give young singing actors a catalogue of songs available for them to choose to study for eventual performance, allowing them to make thoughtful choices based not solely on what they are hearing their friends sing, but laid out in print so they can see what is available to them. And I might add at this point that, again, this is only a sample of what is available; however, I have endeavored to include samples of many types of songs covering many different styles and genres of the musical theatre repertoire.

So I may have left out some of your favorite songs (some of *mine* were omitted). I only wanted to include as many representative choices taken from as many voice classification divisions and types as I could.

Next in the template for the song entries, the *plot* will describe in brief what the show is about, and then moves to *character* of the person who sings the song. Again, this is a thumbnail sketch, gleaned from the script and descriptions that come from the score. The character description is a jump-off point, and even when a traditional character meets a singing actor with new ideas and imagination, a remarkable new take on a song is possible; for example, see Justin Bohon sing "On the Street Where You Live" with a courageous, imaginative, and deliciously funny take on the character and song. Justin talks about his journey toward this performance in the book. The all-important *context* part of the template tells you where the song lives in the show, which can teach us the purpose and function of the song. This is important to know, even if the song is sung as a stand-alone performance, as this understanding of function can give your performance more intensity and power as the character understands its purpose and meaning. As the director Jack O'Brien said to me, every song in musical theatre needs its own purpose, or reason to sing.

The *content* is simply what is there on the written page. Yes, it is obvious, in black and white, in the music. However, how many times do we *not* observe the markings in the music? There are dynamics, tempo changes, and articulation markings, and often they are not observed. The correct learning of pitches and rhythms is crucial to performing a song successfully, but so much more power and understanding comes from observing each and every marking in the music. And most importantly, it is not enough to be *correct* in following the directions in the music; it is the *meaning* or *intention* that the character, composer, and lyricist have in mind using this musical language in providing clues toward a powerful performance. And we must focus on the *why*—Why *these* markings that have been chosen by the composer and creative team? As Brian Stokes Mitchell told me, in a discussion of the character of Don Quixote, it is asking the question, *not* knowing the answer, which is important. If we ask *why* this marking exists, then we can come up with our own answer, which often gives us the prized Stanislavsky "What if?" Then our imagination is stimulated. And that is why I have included in the content section the song's many markings which are clearly written on the music page, which I have pointed out in each song's entry, with the intention of drawing a connection between the composer's clear markings in the music to character, text, and situation. Again, this is sometimes my own interpretation, and is an example of my own "What if?" At times, I will admit that in a particular case the markings seem to have an obvious purpose, but I believe that pointing out the obvious still focuses our attention on a feature the composer and lyricist include for a reason, and that focus needs to be spotlit at that moment. Another important component of content is the structure (form) of the song. In the course of analyzing a song, students will often relegate the form of a song to the back burner, or pay no attention to it at all. However, in talking with composers of these great musicals represented in *The Broadway Song,* I found composers are well aware of the importance of form in *building* the song, and what form and shape can mean to a great song. Understanding the creative team's intentions in song construction can and should be taken into account by the singer for powerful performance, even if the overall effect is one of spontaneity and momentum.

The section on *voice* is my own take on some of the technical minefields and challenges that exist in the song, and what can be done to overcome some of the pitfalls. This section is interpretive in nature, and comes from my thirty years' experience teaching many of these songs to young singers in the studio. Some of the challenges deal with range and tessitura issues. What is obvious to many teachers, but often is a pitfall, is the importance of singing with good intonation, simply singing the song in tune. A number of years ago I was adjudicating auditions for the Metropolitan Opera at a high regional level. As one of the three judges, I was tasked with choosing the second aria the contestants would sing. While the other guest judge chose the most "rangy" and florid, challenging arias to sing, the official judge from the Met chose the simplest and least (technically) demanding aria. I asked her why she chose that piece, a slow Mozart aria, a piece almost anyone could sing. She responded, "I just want to know if she can sing a beautiful line—in tune!" It seems obvious that all singers at a high level of study will always sing in tune, but, faced with a slower tune of narrow range, we may not be able to accomplish that, which is an obvious flaw in performance in any genre.

My favorite portion of each template is the *interview.* These were daunting to collect, because it is not always easy to track down contributors. It took the skills of a detective to find these composers, lyricists, singing actors, conductors, and directors. When I sought performers, I wanted contributions from the actors who originated the roles, and it was not easy to establish communication with these people. However, when I was able to talk with original cast members (Arabella Hong in *Flower Drum Song*; Bill Hayes in *Me and Juliet*; Jo Sullivan in *The Most Happy Fella*; Robert Morse in *How to Succeed in Business without Really Trying,* for instance, from the 1950s and 1960s), the interviews were enlightening, stimulating, and full of insights—which often included stories of exchanges with the composers and directors of the show. This is true as well with the composers, all of whom shared lucid memory and interpretive ability to reach back to reminisce and analyze. All of the interviews in the book were conducted by the author via telephone or e-mail communications between 2012 and 2014. I feel fortunate and blessed to have had these rare opportunities, to have a glimpse into history made in the golden age of musical theatre. That being said, I only wish that I could have known at age twenty-five in Los Angeles that I would one day write a book about Broadway repertoire. For it was at that time, in 1977, that I was singing songs written by Frederick Loewe with orchestra in Palm Springs for the composer himself. What questions would I have asked him? Or later in that year, when I sang in a concert with the Los Angeles Philharmonic in the Hollywood Bowl for seventeen thousand people who came to hear the star of the performance, Ethel Merman. What questions would I have asked her? And even later, when I was a part of a production crew at Indiana University which planned an award ceremony for Betty Comden and Adolph Green. I was backstage with them, awaiting the cue to send them onstage to receive their award. What could I have asked? Was this a lost opportunity? Or did it plant the seed of interest that kept me on task in 2011–14 persistently seeking answers to questions I knew would be of common interest to singing actors, teachers, and the Broadway-loving public?

I am pleased to present even this small offering of information for the benefit of students, teachers, and directors, as a part of the history of that uniquely American art form, the American musical theatre.

Mark Ross Clark
May 2014

PART ONE

Soprano/High Mezzo

Falling in Love with Love

The Boys from Syracuse

"She's trying to put a bright face on her sadness."
—Soprano Rebecca Luker

CHARACTER: Adriana

MUSIC: Richard Rodgers

LYRICS: Lorenz Hart, as adapted by librettist George Abbott

BASED ON: William Shakespeare's play *The Comedy of Errors,* which was loosely based on a Roman play, *The Twin Brothers,* by Plautus

SETTING: Ephesus, in Ancient Greece

BROADWAY PREMIERE: 1938

CLASSIFICATION: Lyric soprano

RANGE: 

TESSITURA: High on staff

TIME: 3:05

PLOT: Identical twins are separated in a shipwreck as youngsters. Their servants are also identical twins, also separated. When one set of master/servant twins from Syracuse comes to Ephesus, where the other twins reside, a comedy of mistaken identities ensues, when Adriana and her servant, who have married the other pair, mistake the two men for their husbands.

CHARACTER: Adriana is a young woman between the ages of eighteen and twenty-eight. She is described as a wife who is not very satisfied, and she complains that her husband never stays home. She is married to Antipholus of Ephesus (not to be [but soon to be] confused with Antipholus of Syracuse—the twin). Her husband is a disagreeable man, much different than his twin brother in Syracuse. Adriana is well-liked and kind, but she can also be short-tempered and suspiciously jealous. Her problem is that she has married the wrong man!

CONTEXT: "Falling in Love with Love" is sung by Adriana in act I, scene 2, with the Ladies. She is impatiently waiting for her husband to arrive for dinner. "Is there anything more pathetic and foolish than to be a neglected wife?" she asks. "I won't stand it much longer," she declares. She continues in a lively monologue that has some edge and humor to it: "There's some who say it was a sword's point [shotgun] wedding," she says. She goes on to recount his pursuit of her affection, "night and day." He would tell her "dull stories" about "how wonderful he was in war" and would recite a poem about her beautiful feet. She is tired of waiting for him, and she begins to weave her tapestry with the ladies. She begins the verse of the song in rhyme couplets, while weaving in order to relieve the tedium of waiting for her husband: "Merry wives can sew and sleep; wives can only sew and weep," she observes.

CONTENT: The refrain of the song is set to a waltz meter (moderately, in 1), but the lyrics (and the circumstances) remind us of Lorenz Hart's acerbic wit. The refrain is sung with a lively delivery, while the accompaniment is very light with staccato flute arpeggios above the vocal line. The melody is not doubled in the accompaniment. The classic melody, quite lyric and classically lovely in its phrasings, belies a number of the lyrics, such as "Falling in love with love is falling for make believe." Adriana wants to believe in love, but Hart's cynical lyrics resist that sentiment. She questions whether she married the wrong man when she says that she fell in love one night "when the moon was full," and adds that she "was unwise with eyes unable to see." Basically, the melody is sung through twice. After the first refrain, there is an instrumental repeat of the melody for sixteen measures, before the refrain repeats, "a shade slower," in a higher key. Perhaps, at this interlude and slower repetition of the refrain, Adriana is in full reminiscence of that time ("when the moon was full") and she fell in love. At the conclusion of the final chorus, at the final cadence, the line ascends to F at the top of the staff, basically a leap up the octave from the first time it is sung.

VOICE: The song needs to be sung with a soprano voice that can easily move between the soprano high register voice and the lower- and middle-chest voice with flexibility. For example, there are sustained notes in the lower chest register (middle C) that jump to the high D, sustained, on the word "fool." The text is wonderful, and needs to be delivered with clarity, but it is also a classic, well-known melody, which continues to sweep up to the top of the staff by the conclusion of the song (*coda*). It is important that the quality of the voice is even from low to high, and lovely in quality. There is a little interlude as Adriana ponders and feels the waltz rhythm, before repeating the chorus to the concluding cadential phrases.

BEHIND THE SCENES WITH THE ARTISTS: SCOTT ELLIS, DIRECTOR, AND REBECCA LUKER, SOPRANO

Scott Ellis, director of the 2002 Broadway revival, recalls that the version that he directed was a rewrite of the original 1938 script, this time refashioned by Nicky Silver. While keeping the core of the plot and characters, the new script brought to the stage contemporary language for 2002, since the original creative team intended their vocabulary in 1938 to be current. These up-to-date sensibilities made it easier to play for the actors in 2002. All in all, the production was sleeker and more streamlined, Ellis observed. The director is known for his work on Broadway, but he is also well-known for his work in television as a creative director and producer. He told me that directing actors on Broadway and on television, besides the differing pace of schedule, is the same as far as directing style is concerned. He still asks the actors the same questions (What do you want? What's in the way?), and they still explore character, situation, and intent together.

The way soprano **Rebecca Luker** approaches this classic song is as both an "I want" and an "I have" kind of song. "Adriana recalls the great love she had and still has for her wayward husband, while at the same time, she has regret and she longs for their old flame to be rekindled." As a singer, Rebecca comments, "The song for me is a joy to sing. The introduction—'I weave with brightly colored strings'—does indeed belie her irritation. She's trying to put a bright face on her sadness," she observes. "But the song has longing in it. The long held notes are the longing to me. And when Adriana recalls when she fell in love singing, 'I was unwise with eyes unable to see,' and then she also sings, 'I fell in love with love, with love everlasting, but love fell out with me,' that, to me, is the ultimate longing phrase." Rebecca continues: "And though the song is written in a major key, it has such a minorness about it, a longing."

Rebecca loves to sing this song. To her, it is like an aria, showing a great amount of personality and vocal inspiration. "At the end of the song, she sings this long-held triumphant note, and in a way, she *is* triumphant. She will go on with her life, no matter what happens. I think this song shows that Adriana has grown up a little bit, and of course her husband sees this (because he also realizes in the course of the story that he loved her all along)."

Waitin' for My Dearie

Brigadoon

"The given circumstances and the Scottish temperament combined to create a character who was strong and sassy."
—Meg Bussert, Fiona in the 1980 Broadway revival production

CHARACTER: Fiona MacLaren

MUSIC: Frederick Loewe

LYRICS: Alan J. Lerner

BASED ON: Loosely based on a German folk tale about a mythical village

SETTING: A mythical village in Scotland

BROADWAY PREMIERE: 1947

CLASSIFICATION: Lyric trained soprano

RANGE: 

TESSITURA: Upper staff

TIME: 3:50

PLOT: A mythical village in Scotland comes to life only once every one hundred years, but to the villagers the passing of the century is but one night. If any of the residents leave the town, the village will cease to exist. The town materializes in front of two American tourists, Tommy Albright and Jeff Douglas, on a hunting trip to the Scottish highlands. Their visit has lasting repercussions. As they enter the town, they realize that a village wedding is about to occur.

CHARACTER: Fiona is about twenty-four years old and possesses a strong character. She has a dream about who she is going to marry, and "there's no compromisin.'" She is sure that she will find him, but she is happy to wait, even though her younger sister, Jean, is about to be married. These are unusual ideas in the village, to be content to wait for a husband, where it is traditional for a girl to get married in her teens and be happy about it.

CONTEXT: American tourists Tommy and Jeff, lost on a game-hunting hike, begin to hear the repeatedly sung word "Brigadoon," and notice a village in a valley that does not show on their map. They remain hidden from view to observe their new, fantastical surroundings. Everyone they see is dressed in traditional Scottish costume. The MacLaren family enters with daughter Fiona. They are preparing for the wedding of younger sister, Jean. One of the other girls of the village asks Fiona when she will get married. She would prefer to wait to find true love, rather than risk marrying the wrong person.

CONTENT: The form of the song is traditional, following a three-measure introduction after a sustained chord (fermata). There is a twenty-measure "setup" in verse form that shows Fiona is strong in her convictions, with a quarter-note rhythm on each downbeat, sung with conviction and deliberate confidence. The song starts in the key of C major, but the second eight-measure phrase of the verse modulates to the key of E major (she is not a predictable girl). Although Fiona is strong of character, the verse is sung with lyricism and playfulness. The dynamics are marked "mezzo piano" and "piano." The vocal line is doubled in the accompaniment. After a four-measure transition that goes back into C major ("Foolish ye may say" . . . [fermata on the word "say"], "Foolish I will stay" [fermata rest]), the song goes into the lilting refrain, sung in cut time (two beats per measure). The melody continues to be doubled in the accompaniment. There are short one-measure "interludes" between phrases. At the text "Though I'll live forty lives till the day he arrives " there is an eight-measure bridge that indicates that she will not grieve, even if she has to wait for the mythical "him" a long time, because she believes that there is someone out there for her, and therefore the final repeat of the end of the refrain is sung (again) confidently, but is marked "piano." What follows is a musical interlude in which her village girlfriends question Fiona about her conviction to wait (for her "dearie"), and she answers patiently with wit and warmth. There is a new section (*più mosso*), a sixteen-measure interlude of "question and response" up to a high A, a strong declaration at the words: "when the lad's not right," followed by a final refrain (tempo I), which has now modulated into the higher key of D major. Another repetition of the chorus includes the voices of the girls in ensemble support-singing chords underneath Fiona's melody to the ending.

VOICE: The song requires charm and lyricism mixed with strong doses of confidence. Fiona's strong character need never be angry or strident. She is not defensive or apologetic about her philosophy, even though her younger sister is about to be married. Fiona needs to be true to herself. The song is not so high to sing in tessitura, but the performer should be careful at the F-sharp and E on top in the phrases singing the bright *i* vowel in the words "dearie, he," for instance, because the vowel can sound too "chirpy" or pinched without jaw space at the higher pitch level as the pitches are negotiated. Her final sustained note, sung on the word "me," also falls into that category. The other high pitches, on high A, for example, "When the lad's not right," with the high note on the word "lad's," also needs jaw space at the top of the vocal range. When Fiona sings syllabically on quarter-note rhythms throughout the piece, some space in the jaw is wise, so she does not "chew" the words, which can result in stridency of tone. Articulate the text with the tongue, lips, and teeth during the beginning/final consonants, and keep the breath support strong.

BEHIND THE SCENES WITH THE ARTISTS: MEG BUSSERT, FIONA IN THE 1980 BROADWAY REVIVAL

Meg Bussert revived the role of Fiona in a very successful revival of *Brigadoon* on Broadway in 1980. British director Vivian Matalon helped shape the role for Ms. Bussert, especially in her opening song, "Waitin' for My Dearie," in the MacConnachy Square scene. Rather than label Fiona as a dreamy, doe-eyed innocent, the director steered Ms. Bussert's portrayal of Fiona in a different direction. The show was "Scots in flavor and poetically Irish" in tone, Meg told me. "The given circumstances and the Scottish temperament combined to create a character who was strong and sassy. The given circumstances are this: there are no grown men in her immediate family, the women of the village do not approve of her strong disposition, and she sings 'Waitin' for My Dearie' to get the girls in the village off her back. She is the wedding planner, organizing the impending marriage of her little sister. Her romantic future at that point is not in question; it is hopeless, and she is fine with it. Spinsterhood could be in her future. She is running the household alone." This made sense to Ms. Bussert, and it also made the sudden appearance of Tommy, the American lost on a hunting trip stumbling into the timeless mythical Brigadoon, very amusing. 'Who is this guy?' was Fiona's take on their first meeting." Ms. Bussert goes on to explain that it also was emphasized by the director that the romantic relationship between Fiona and Tommy that developed was designed from the beginning to be without touching, including their first duet in act I, "The Heather on the Hill." The result was more of a childlike, innocent playfulness about their initial affection for each other.

If I Were a Bell

Guys and Dolls

"Before singing this song, Sarah needs to understand the text and their relationship (as Sarah would truly like it to be). Even though she has been drinking, she still possesses nerve, spunk, and courage."
—Jo Sullivan Loesser

CHARACTER: Sarah Brown

MUSIC AND LYRICS: Frank Loesser

BOOK: Jo Swerling and Abe Burrows

BASED ON: "The Idyll Of Miss Sarah Brown" and "Blood Pressure," two short stories by Damon Runyon

SETTING: New York

BROADWAY PREMIERE: 1950

CLASSIFICATION: Soprano/mezzo up-tempo

RANGE: 

TESSITURA: Middle of staff, not high soprano

TIME: 2:24

PLOT: *Guys and Dolls* is a classic American musical which has a rich history of performance and revival. In act I, we see the hustle and bustle of New York City, originally detailed by writer Damon Runyon in his short stories. The focus here is small-time gamblers betting on horse races. Contrasted to this underbelly of hustlers in the city are the band members of the Save-a-Soul Mission, which is a sendup of the Salvation Army movement. The mission's goal is to save as many souls as possible, by getting them to give up the evils of gambling, drinking, and lying.

CHARACTER: Sarah Brown is a prim and proper young lady who has devoted her life to saving souls for the Save-a-Soul Mission in New York City, where there are many sinners—especially gamblers. She is smart, pretty, and does not let her guard down. She has a strong personality and is not afraid to speak her mind. She is idealistic about saving souls, but begins to lose her confidence when Colonel Cartwright of the Save-a-Soul Mission threatens to close the mission because of the lack of "sinner interest."

CONTEXT: The smooth-talking Sky Masterson, a high-rolling gambler, falls for Sarah. Sky is willing to bet on anything (when he knows he will win), and Nathan Detroit, Sky's friend, bets Sky that he cannot get Sarah Brown to accompany him on a quick flight to Havana, Cuba, for dinner. Sky lies to get in her good graces, going to Sarah's mission and declaring that he wants to be saved. He also promises to deliver a dozen "genuine sinners" to the mission if Sarah agrees to go to Havana with him. Sarah recognizes the intent of his advances and turns him down, describing (in song) the kind of man she is looking for. She sings "I'll Know," and he, too, sings his own version. He kisses her, resulting in a slap. As the story unfolds, Sarah (under pressure from her superiors) must deliver more sinners to the mission or it will be closed down. Honoring her agreement made with Sky to deliver sinners, Sarah goes to Havana with Sky, where he introduces her to "Cuban milkshakes," called *dulce de leche*, a sweet rum drink. She doesn't realize that there is liquor in her milkshake, but it is clear that she is letting down her hair. Sitting by a fountain, Sarah tells Sky that for the first time she is having a wonderful time. Dropping her guard under the influence, she sings "If I Were a Bell."

CONTENT: The song is in two verses. It needs to "swing," as if Sarah has lost her inhibitions. The song will move, and it should not be sung too slowly in a controlled manner. This song needs to have a feeling of abandon. In the first verse (opening), the music is marked "ad lib" to bar 5, when it is "a tempo." This means that the opening measures are "free," without swing, but go into the swing tempo after the caesura in bar 4. The words are very clever: "If I were a banner I'd wave," and "If I were a goose I'd be cooked."

VOICE: The range of "If I Were a Bell" is not characteristic of the other music that Sarah sings in the show. For example, in "I'll Know," all of the pick-up tones, unaccented, are F-sharps at the top of the staff, which need to be sung without strain in a light and uninflected lyric manner. In "If I

Were a Bell," the singer should enjoy the chest-voice tones (sustained on the B-flat below middle C) that are a major part of the song's delivery. She should also enjoy the fact that this is perhaps the first time she has let herself go. The transition between chest voice and soprano voice can sometimes shift roughly, but it is consistent with the situation, since Sarah is "under the influence." In the shift to the soprano register to sing: "Ding, dong, ding, dong," starting on the D, the best effect when singing these "ng words" is to go directly into the "ng," closing and vibrating the tone for a bell-like effect (except for the last note, sustained on high E-flat for three measures), which should sustain the vowel longer. But be careful—to get the most "ring" from the tone, keep the jaw free, and close to the *ng* with the tongue behind the top front teeth for the most resonance and "spin."

BEHIND THE SCENES WITH THE ARTISTS: JO SULLIVAN LOESSER, WIDOW OF THE COMPOSER, FRANK LOESSER, AND GUIDING FORCE BEHIND REVIVALS OF HIS MUSICALS

"Before singing this song, Sarah needs to understand the text and their relationship (as Sarah would truly like it to be). Even though she has been drinking, she still possesses nerve, spunk, and courage." Jo Loesser advises the young soprano not to sing this song "over the top" (drunk, sliding and slurring). Sarah is "a little high," more happy than drunk. The text is important; it is a terrific song that Sarah enjoys singing, and the point is that the drinks give her courage and function more as a truth serum, giving her the ability to show the sunshine and youth in her personality that she possesses deep down.

I Have to Tell You

Fanny

"It was a challenge because...she bursts out onstage and sings what is essentially an aria."
—Florence Henderson, the original Fanny

CHARACTER: Fanny

MUSIC AND LYRICS: Harold Rome

BASED ON: Marcel Pagnol's trilogy of plays *Marius, Fanny,* and *César*

SETTING: Marseille, France

BROADWAY PREMIERE: 1954

CLASSIFICATION: Soprano lyric

RANGE: 

TESSITURA: Upper-middle staff

TIME: 1:45

PLOT: Set in Marseille, France, in the 1930s, *Fanny* is a romantic tale about a young woman who marries a wealthy older man she does not love to give her newborn child legitimacy and a "good" name. Fanny is a young woman whose love, Marius, leaves her to go to sea for five years. His father, Cesar, a tavern owner, disowns him. After Marius leaves, Fanny discovers that she is pregnant. Under familial pressure, she marries an older man who wants an heir and is willing to keep the secret of the child's illegitimacy. Marius returns from sea on the child's first birthday, and while he expects to claim Fanny (and his child), he is spurned by the family. Fanny sings the song "I have to tell you" before Marius is turned away.

CHARACTER OF FANNY: She is "an attractive young girl, the daughter of Honorine, a poor fishmonger in the port of Marseilles. Fanny is a young woman who is well meaning, innocent, good to her mother, and loyal to her family. "Fanny and Marius are not erudite, educated people. They feel more than think," remarks Leslie Caron, who portrayed the role of Fanny in the movie version in 1963, based on the play.

CONTEXT: Fanny's true love, Marius, has gone away to sea for five years. Fanny discovers that she is pregnant after he leaves. After she marries Panisse, a wealthy and generous older man she does not love, he prefers to keep the child's illegitimacy a secret. On the child's first birthday, Marius unexpectedly returns. He expects to claim Fanny (and the child), but he is turned away, even though Fanny still loves him.

CONTENT: The song is brief and is built on a three-note quarter rhythm motive, which is deliberate in its emotional weight, and is repeated at different pitch levels to the top of the staff, as the refrain unfolds. The refrain is then repeated, as indicated in the score. "I Have to Tell You" is turbulent, passionate, and dramatic. The given circumstances are all-important. While ending the relationship, Fanny is still telling Marius that she loves him and will always need him. Perhaps it would be easier to fabricate anger to dismiss him, but she cannot do that—she must reveal her true feelings for him. She tells him at the end of this brief encounter to "now forget it, unless you feel the same way, too." These are conflicting signals, and they underline her youthful passion, her youth, and her struggle to break off the relationship for the sake of the child. Fanny has probably rehearsed this scene in her mind a number of times, but she must mine deep emotions without onstage opportunity to build emotions to the song. She doesn't want to hurt Marius, but she can see that he is stunned and in pain.

VOICE: The young singer should not be too polished vocally, and must imagine the facial reaction of Marius in singing this song. "I Have to Tell You" is built on three-note motives that are haltingly repeated a number of times (it is difficult for her to reveal her feelings) at different pitch levels as the melody ascends into the soprano range. As the vocal line rises through the *passaggio* (the passage from chest resonance into head resonance), the song continues to build in crescendo with active accompaniment. After the initial, emotional expression, Fanny sings, "I've said it, I've told you" in her lower range, detaching a little from her previous emotional delivery. The singer will require a genuine soprano range that can support higher, sustained tones and expressive vocal emotions. At the same time, the text must be emphasized, and the words cannot be distorted, even in the high range.

The words that are chosen for the singer to sustain are singer-helpful, using the words "start" and "heart," but at the end, with the phrase "Maybe you do," it is difficult to crescendo on the F at the top of the staff on the *u* vowel without opening (freeing) the jaw and rounding the lips too. Otherwise, the *u* vowel can be constricted if the jaw is not free. Likewise, at the climactic phrase of the song, when Fanny is singing, "love you, need you, want you," all on quarter-note rhythmic values above the staff, the jaw will instinctively want to help articulate the words, but should not. Allow the jaw to be free, and articulate the all-important and emotional text with the lips, teeth, and tongue, continuing to keep the jaw free as described before. At the same time, the breath support is crucial to keeping the larynx anchored. A high larynx may constrict the throat. It is easy, when one becomes emotional, to feel those "big" emotions in the throat, but it is very important for the singer to take a deep, low breath, distanced from the larynx, and use the entire body to support the tone and the commitment of diction.

The singer should determine how the repeat of the refrain will be sung. A repeat should always have a musical/dramatic variety to it, whether the performer is singing classical or Broadway/musical repertoire. Is Fanny more determined the second time she sings? Is it perhaps sung with more voice? Or less? Is it a little faster tempo (with the heart rate possibly faster, or trying to get it over with quicker?). These are the questions that must be asked in rehearsal, and then answered in performance.

BEHIND THE SCENES WITH THE ARTISTS: FLORENCE HENDERSON, THE ORIGINAL FANNY

Florence Henderson remarks that she saw in the character of Fanny "a sweet, innocent young woman who was very helpful to her mother and desperately in love with Marius." She further remarks, describing leading up to the song, "I think she knew Marius was going to sea and wanted to express her love for him." Ms. Henderson recognizes the challenge of Fanny's singing the song in the show, "because she bursts on stage and starts singing what is essentially an aria."

Somebody, Somewhere

The Most Happy Fella

"It is a difficult role to play: she has no jokes, and she is not an innocent young kid."
—Jo Sullivan Loesser, the original Rosabella

CHARACTER: Rosabella

MUSIC, LYRICS, AND BOOK: Frank Loesser

ADAPTED FROM: "They Knew What They Wanted," by Frank Howard

SETTING: Napa Valley, California

BROADWAY PREMIERE: 1956

CLASSIFICATION: Soprano lyric

RANGE: 

TESSITURA: Middle of the soprano voice

TIME: 3:50

PLOT: *The Most Happy Fella* is a stylistic combination of opera, operetta, and American musical theatre that comes from an organic mix of characters from Texas ("Standing on the Corner," "Big D"), and the Italian culture ("Abbondanza") that is set in California's Napa Valley. Some of the songs are in standard song form; others are snapshots of passionate emotion that capture the mood but do not always follow traditional show song structure for form's sake. Tony is the mature, Italian-born owner of the Napa winery who observes (unnoticed) Rosabella in a San Francisco diner he is visiting. He is entranced by her, but too insecure about his age and thick Italian accent to approach her. At the winery, Tony writes love letters to Rosabella and sends her a picture of one of his younger, handsome ranch hands, Joe, because Tony is afraid that she will not write to him if she knows that he is an older man. Rosabella falls for Tony (Joe) through his charming, heartfelt letters, and she comes to the ranch to meet him. Despite her shock at Tony's deception, she ends up feeling sorry for him when Tony has a serious car accident on the way to meet her at the train station. Rosabella, in defiance of her own feelings for Joe after he tries to charm her, instinctively marries Tony. However, she is unable to resist Joe, and has a brief relationship with him at the end of act I, the night of her marriage to Tony.

CHARACTER: Rose is a waitress in a diner in San Francisco. She has a friend from Texas who also works at the diner, but Rose is lonely and tired of her dead-end waitress job. She is well-meaning, sincere, and good spirited. She is also lonely and needs a change of scenery. She would like to meet a man and settle down.

CONTEXT: Rose has just received a letter in the mail from Tony, an admirer she has never met. She sings this song as she contemplates the picture that she has just received. She thinks that the picture is of Tony, but actually it is the younger worker, Joe.

CONTENT: The opening eight measures of introductory material, or "set up," are marked "molto espressivo e con colore." The "forte-piano" marking and the off-the-beat vocal entrance-realization, "That's what it is" after the eighth rest, gives the phrase an excitement and energy. This section is also indicated to be sung two beats to the measure, and moves to the melody-chorus after expressive dynamics and slowing (marked "rubato") with fermatas in the voice and accompaniment. The refrain/chorus is marked "lamentando" and is two beats to the measure. The half note is marked "60" (each quarter note is one second in duration). The song is sung with some excitement and movement. Basically, Rosabella has been lonely, and this song is a realization that *someone, somebody, somewhere* is interested in her. The song alternates between a daydream quality of suspended hopes and a need to do something—anything—to find her love to release her from her dead-end existence. The rhythmic note pattern, ascending to the top of the staff, with clear tempo markings and dynamics, brings the song to life and captures Rosa's emotions at this time in her life. The last line, "That's very wonderful to know," sung in the middle range, has a secure and sincere warmth that comes with a realization that there is someone out there for her.

VOICE: It is important not to sing the melody too slowly. Motion is important, so that the performer does not have to take a predictable breath every two measures. If the song is sung with motion and momentum, even with the sustained notes at the end of each phrase, the singer can manage a four-measure phrase when needed to keep the momentum of the song flowing. The song builds in powerful expression of excitement as Rose moves the line forward with more energy (marked "accelerando") at the text "That's very wonderful to know." She then returns to tempo I at "somebody lonely" before another build to the E-natural on the phrase "To notice him there," after which she returns to the refrain melody: "Well, I want to be needed . . ." Rose once again builds toward the climactic moment, marked "largamente," at which point the song broadens to twice as slow (a half note now equals 30) to the high, sustained G at the top of the staff (fermata). Since the word sung on the top G contains the bright *i* vowel ("me"), it is wise to give the jaw some space, so that the tone is not too bright or strident. Thankfully, the word changes to the more open vowel of "and . . ." (sustained by the fermata marking, as the line descends to an octave below) "that's . . ." as it suddenly pauses—caesura—and continues "very wonderful to know" as the orchestra crescendos in the final chord, sung on a sustained middle G to the cutoff release.

BEHIND THE SCENES WITH THE ARTISTS: JO SULLIVAN LOESSER, THE ORIGINAL ROSABELLA

Ms. Sullivan told me that she recalls that, before rehearsing *The Most Happy Fella* onstage, the cast was instructed to learn and memorize the music in advance of blocking the show, which was not a usual sequence in rehearsing Broadway shows. This was perhaps because the creative staff recognized that the music was challenging to sing and had to be learned and memorized before stage movements could be rehearsed. Ms. Sullivan told me that her vocal lessons and resultant technique were very important to her as a performer, and even today she has continued to study voice, with daily practices and vocal exercises. She loves to sing and has learned how to sing correctly. She learned right away that the challenging role of Rosabella also needs to be acted well in the show. "It is a difficult role to play: she has no jokes, and she is not an innocent, young kid. She is a nice girl, but she is tough. She is working in the city as a waitress, and is probably sharing an apartment with her Texas friend Cleo. Rose is looking for stability, she is tired of working, and she is lonely. 'Somebody, Somewhere' comes at a good spot in the show," Ms. Sullivan observes. "This is a chance to get to know our heroine. We have to want her to make it, so she has to act and sing it well."

Warm All Over

The Most Happy Fella

"Rosabella doesn't know how to say, 'I love you.' She doesn't have the courage to come right out and say it."
—Jo Sullivan Loesser, the original Rosabella

CHARACTER: Rosabella

MUSIC, LYRICS, AND BOOK: Frank Loesser

ADAPTED FROM: "They Knew What They Wanted," by Sidney Howard

SETTING: Napa Valley, California

BROADWAY PREMIERE: 1956

CLASSIFICATION: Soprano lyric

RANGE: 

TESSITURA: Middle of the soprano voice

TIME: 2:05

PLOT AND CHARACTER: See "Somebody, Somewhere."

CONTEXT: Tony's sister Marie continuously reminds him that he is not young and that time has passed him by. She is also critical and judgmental by nature. Rosabella feels sorry for him in scene 3, from which the following stage directions are excerpted: *In the vineyards, a month after Rosabella's entrance into Tony's life. We see that the vines in the distance have grown much higher and greener. Into the scene come the boys and girls of the younger set of workers, dancing and cavorting with youthful abandon.*

TONY appears in the wheelchair pushed on by the DOC. [On the day of Rosabella's visit Tony is in a car accident and badly breaks his arm and leg.] *He is in better shape now with only a sling in which to rest his left arm and a small cast on his foot replacing the huge one that covered the entire leg. TONY beams appreciatively as he watches the antics of the YOUNG PEOPLE.*

Everyone loves Tony. He is an endearing, genuine character. He has many friends and loyal employees at the winery, and one of his most charming qualities is his broken English. During the song "Young People" Rosabella dances with the young folks at Tony's insistence. As she dances offstage, Marie, Tony's judgmental sister, mentions that young folks feel sorry for old folks that cannot get around, and "old people gotta get left behind." After her comments, Marie leaves Tony, who has a look of doubt and sadness on his face. Reentering, Rosabella notices his mood and with concern approaches him. "Where's that happy face, that glow, that I depend on?" she begins to sing.

CONTENT: After a four measure introduction with thoughtful arpeggiated chordal patterns (marked "tenderly"), Rosa begins to sing the setup before the chorus. She asks why he is no longer cheerful, with a smile that she has grown to depend on... The smile that makes her "warm all over" as she begins the refrain (in stricter tempo). The vocal line is doubled by the accompaniment. The melody unfolds with no repetition except the words "warm all over," and its rhythmic motive, which frames the words. The melody remains in tempo to the conclusion of the song. The one sign that the song is concluding is the caesura—the meaningful pause after the final declaration of the words "warm all over," followed by her concluding thought, singing, "with a tender love" to finish the piece. Rosabella finally confesses that she sincerely loves Tony in this song.

VOICE: The melody that Rosabella sings is simple and sincere, but with a vocal line that has many accidentals to carefully negotiate. She is not sure, she has her doubts, and she is confused by her simultaneous feelings (that she tries to deny) for the younger Joe. Perhaps her confusion is reflected in Rosa's trying to find her way melodically (and emotionally)-before she finds the refrain. The singer should also observe that the song has few places to pause/rest. She is not giving Tony a chance to respond.

BEHIND THE SCENES WITH THE ARTISTS: JO SULLIVAN LOESSER, THE ORIGINAL ROSABELLA

"Rosabella doesn't know how to say, 'I love you.' She doesn't have the courage to come right out and say it," says Jo Sullivan Loesser, the original Rosabella. "Because it is a tentative expression, the range is quite a bit lower than Rosabella's other song in the show, 'Somebody, Somewhere.' 'Warm All Over' has sustained notes around the middle C, but also has notes at the top of the staff, needing a large, flexible range. If the lower notes are sung too heavy and 'belted,' the upper notes will not be connected to the rest of the voice. And Rosabella needs both extensions of her range and connection to her breath support to sing with 'one voice.'"

My White Knight

The Music Man

"The song for Marian is both a lovely moment with her mother as well as an honest outpouring of her desires for the kind of man she wants in her life."

—Rebecca Luker, Marian in the 2000 Broadway Revival

CHARACTER: Marian Paroo

BOOK, MUSIC, AND LYRICS: Meredith Willson

BASED ON: A story by Meredith Willson and Franklin Lacey

SETTING: 1912, Mason City, Iowa

BROADWAY PREMIERE: 1957

CLASSIFICATION: Soprano lyric

RANGE: 

TESSITURA: Middle of the staff

TIME: 4:50

PLOT: The story is about a small Iowa town in 1912 and a lone salesman who comes into the town on July 3. His intent initially is to fleece townspeople, but he instead ends up changing them profoundly, which in turn ultimately changes him. The prim and proper librarian Marian Paroo is also a piano teacher and lives with her widowed mother and younger brother. Harold Hill, the salesman, who recognizes that Marian is skeptical of his credentials and his plan to sell the townspeople band instruments, uses all of his salesmanship to win her over. He ends up genuinely falling in love with her, and Marian reluctantly falls in love with him. When she has a chance to turn him in as a fraud and prove that in fact he has false credentials, she aids his escape instead.

CHARACTER: Marian has been on her own for a while. Although she is an unmarried librarian still living with her mother and little brother and has the reputation of being a strict and straight-laced piano teacher and librarian, she has a mind of her own. She is an educated young woman who loves books. In fact, her passion for books and music and her caring for others have led to a substantial contribution to the library by "Miser Madison," as the late gentleman was not-so-lovingly labeled in his later years.

CONTEXT: The song "My White Knight" is placed toward the end of the first act. It occurs immediately after the fast-talking salesman Harold Hill tries with no success to woo the skeptical Marian. He has already charmed most of the townspeople (and Marian's mother), but Marian is much more suspicious of his motives. The song "Marian the Librarian" concludes with all of the school kids in the quiet library being whipped into a dancing frenzy by Harold Hill. Marian is of course irritated by Hill's actions. The song culminates in a stolen kiss answered by a slap that he manages to avoid, perhaps from experience.

Later that evening on Mrs. Paroo's front porch, Marian has just been talking with her concerned mother. Mrs. Paroo doesn't want her daughter to end up a spinster in the small Iowa town, continuing to work in the library without husband or family. Marian describes her vision of who she will someday marry, singing "My White Knight."

CONTENT: After a single measure of a fermata-sustained tremolo in treble between octave A-flat, the song begins with the refrain, a sweeping melody that is not doubled in the orchestra. "All I want is a plain man," marked "poco mosso," begins the B section, and the key modulates up to D from D-flat. The section builds to the words "more int'rested in me," followed by a dramatic caesura, which is followed by two more phrases, both delineated by a caesura and a quarter rest. As the usually firm-minded Marian wanders (again) to the key of D-flat, the song goes into another section: "And if occasion'ly he'd ponder," marked "poco lento" for three measures, further slowing, before the recapitulation of the refrain. The triplet rhythms in the melody tend to naturally broaden the vocal line, but as the melody reaches the final notes, the music is marked "very broadly" and "molto lento" to the final cadence, marked "crescendo." This beautiful song is a lyric, classic romantic love song. However, Marian is talking to her mother, not dreamily singing to herself. She is telling her in song that she is not "shooting for the stars"; she is shooting "low" and doesn't much expect to find a man she could love. In fact, it is possible, that if she could actually talk with this mythical companion about the arts and books, that would be icing on the cake, but it would not be the most important thing in the relationship—and certainly not expected!

VOICE: The song requires a lyric soprano who can sing a beautiful vocal line simply and genuinely, expressing it with real emotion, without false pretense. The opening chorus of "My White Knight" is quite low for the lyric soprano, and so it is important for the singer to mix more of the chest resonance into the voice so that the lyrics are sung with some deliberate confidence and the tone is not too lightweight and hollow. The strongest performance of this song will build emotionally and vocally from the initial opening phrases, as if Marian is haltingly unsure of who this man could be, to the last chorus, when she is confident that she knows who he is, and he is out there somewhere. With the final high notes (F at the top of the staff to optional high A-flat), she is energized and inspired by the thought, as the orchestra builds in textured fullness and the rhythm seems to beat a little faster, just like her heart. In the middle section ("All I want is a plain man, an honest man"), Marian moves the line with more momentum and less vocalized attention to tone. The singer has to think of the text more, and then leap up to an F-sharp at the top of the staff, then ("I would like him to be more interested in us than in me") before returning to the final chorus. Has Harold Hill awakened her heart?

BEHIND THE SCENES WITH THE ARTISTS: REBECCA LUKER, MARIAN PAROO IN THE 2000 BROADWAY REVIVAL

Ms. Luker sings "My White Knight" in a way that conveys vocal beauty and captures an essential moment in Marian's life. "Marian, up to this point in the play, didn't have very many vulnerable moments. She suspects Harold Hill from the beginning and fiercely protects her family. Of course, she also senses something different and attractive in him, so there's a war inside her." Rebecca chose not to fully vocalize the opening phrases of the song. In fact, music director/conductor David Chase had the idea to lower the opening of the song so that the key was lower and more in line with Rebecca's speech/pitch level, before moving to the original key with the words "Please dear Venus, show me how." She worked long hours with director Susan Stroman to find the "simple truth in the song," following "natural inflections and phrasing" without overthinking. Her process was to dissect the song, line by line, but ultimately the song was thought of as a whole scene that needed to flow naturally."

Rebecca describes her thought process and inspiration while singing the song this way:

"I had a story in my mind that I played out every night as I sang the song. The story made it real for me. I also had my husband in my head as I finished the song. To think about the person I loved most in the world helped me end the song in the most intense way."

Love, Look Away

Flower Drum Song

"The integration and coordination of dramatic and vocal technique became possible through coaching and practice."
—Arabella Hong, the original Helen

CHARACTER: Helen Chao

MUSIC: Richard Rodgers

LYRICS: Oscar Hammerstein II

BOOK: Joseph Fields and David Henry Hwang (2002 revised version)

BASED ON: A novel by C. Y. Lee

SETTING: 1950s, Chinatown, San Francisco

BROADWAY PREMIERE: 1958; 2002 (revised)

CLASSIFICATION: Alto lyric

RANGE: 

TESSITURA: Upper middle staff

TIME: 2:54

PLOT: The show is based on C. Y. Lee's best-selling 1957 novel, a serious novel that focuses on a wealthy refugee from China who settles in San Francisco's Chinatown. The musical (more light-hearted than the novel) shifts the story to focus on his son, Wang Ta, who is torn between traditional Chinese values and the American culture. The original show was directed by the actor Gene Kelly on Broadway. The newer version (2002 Broadway revival) retained most of the original songs, but centers the story on the romantic relationships.

Wang Ta, the son, trying to break from his father's strict set of traditional Chinese values, is more interested in the American culture. He goes on a blind date with the Americanized Linda Low (a singer at a club), telling her he is going to law school, and asks her to marry him. When the father finds out, he is not pleased, and Ta is humiliated. Trying to comfort Ta in act II is his childhood friend Helen Chao, whose romantic affection for Ta is not returned.

CHARACTER: Helen Chao is first introduced in act I, scene 3, in the Wang living room. Helen, a seamstress who works at the same nightclub as Linda, is making a graduation gown for Ta. She reveals that she has known Wang Ta since he was "a little fellow," and she plans for the gown to be a gift for his graduation. Additionally, she has grown fond of him. The first impression of Helen is that she has a kind and serene, calm quality about her, even when the high-strung nightclub owner Sammy Fong is present.

CONTEXT: The first time the song is heard is in act I, after Ta reveals that he is in love with Linda, which humiliates and hurts his father. Linda tells Sammy Fong that she is quitting the club to marry Wang Ta. Helen's heart is broken as she sings the song "Love, Look Away" in act I. The opening of act II (scene 1) takes place in Helen Chao's room, which is described in the script as a modestly furnished room with an open kitchenette, a bed, and a door to the bathroom. There is a sewing machine and a telephone. In the center of the room is a table with two chairs, and a bottle of tiger-bone wine on the table. Ta is angrily pacing the room after the events of act I. He remarks that he has made a fool of himself, and she is calmly reasoning with him. How is he going to face his father? He appears to be drunk, and Helen tells him to lie down and rest awhile. She will call a taxi and wake him when it comes. It is morning as Helen is preparing breakfast. Ta comes out of the bathroom and says that he must leave. She ties his tie and tells him that she would "love to go out with him." He says, "We'll do that sometime." He looks at his watch, remarks that he has to go, and says he'll call her. She gives him her business card. He puts it on the bed as he grabs his raincoat and leaves. Realizing he has left her card behind, she begins to follow him down the stairs. Helen realizes just how pathetic the futility is of pressing her attentions on a man who is obviously not interested. She walks downstage, letting the card drop from her hand, as she begins to sing.

CONTENT: The act II reprise of the song "Love, Look Away," begins with Helen singing dreamily on the middle B-flat, "I have wished before." She is finished with wishing. The song is marked "lento." After an instrumental interlude of four measures, she moves directly into the lovely refrain of "Love, Look Away," as she addresses a personified "Love" and tells Love to fly away from her. "No good am I for you." She dreams too much, she cries too much, she tells Love. She repeats the "Love, look away" refrain ("Call it a day"), this time with more emotional insistence and orchestral support, though there is no doubling of the melody in the orchestra, which accompanies her throughout in rich block chords. The song builds and ascends as she sings, "Go away, and set me free." The bridge ("Wanting you . . .") is only eight measures long, serving more as a transition than a full section. The gentle syncopated rhythm in this section keeps the momentum of the song moving. She then recaps the main musical phrase of the song, this time with full brass and orchestra doubling/support. "Look away," she repeats three times to a climactic cadence—"from me!"

VOICE: Singing this song requires a strong middle range on sustained tones with some upper soprano extension at the top of the staff, especially for the climactic ending, to the optional high A-flat. Helen's emotional state, given the circumstances, needs to be reflected in the singing of the song, especially the opening. The song needs to be built and shaped to reveal these "hidden" emotions which she now shows. Singing this song also requires good vocal control, as the opening (on B-flat in the middle of the staff) is marked "pianissimo." Helen reveals through the song a careful control, besides the dynamics, of the careful attention to rhythmic values with the frequent combination of the dotted quarter followed by two sixteenth-note rhythms many times in the piece. This device, when the rhythms are strongly defined, gives the vocal line forward propulsion and momentum to the tones at the top of the staff, including the (optional) A-flat at the conclusion of the song, on the *e* vowel ("a-*way* from me"), as she can no longer control her emotions.

BEHIND THE SCENES WITH THE ARTISTS: ARABELLA HONG, THE ORIGINAL HELEN

Ms. Hong told me that she felt honored that the song "Love, Look Away" was written for her by Richard Rodgers and Oscar Hammerstein, who she felt were particularly attached to this song and her performance. There was concern that with Ms. Hong's extensive opera training, her performance of "Love, Look Away" would be too operatic in delivery, but Ms. Hong told me that her dramatic work onstage is rooted in method acting and the association of her characters' situation with her own life experiences. This "substitution," as she called it, was especially possible during the time of the show, when, she told me, she was trying without success to have a child. That desire and longing became a strong emotion to draw on when looking into the lights and focusing on her needs and obstacles. Ms. Hong further explained that her many years of vocal training allowed her to channel strong, deep emotions without concern that beauty of vocal tone would be sacrificed. The integration and coordination of dramatic and vocal technique became possible through coaching and practice. I asked Ms. Hong about the final A-flat. "If they were concerned that your performance would be too operatic, then why add the high note?" I asked. She laughed before telling me, "The shifting of scenery right before the song ended created some noise distraction for the audience, and singing the high note helped to conceal the noise of the scene shift!"

When Did I Fall in Love?

Fiorello!

"In act II, when Thea sings this song, we learn that since they have been married, she has fallen very much in love with her husband."
—Sheldon Harnick, lyricist and book writer

CHARACTER: Thea Almerigatti

MUSIC: Jerry Bock

BOOK AND LYRICS: Sheldon Harnick

BASED ON: *Life with Fiorello* by Ernest Cuneo

SETTING: New York, 1915

BROADWAY PREMIERE: 1959

CLASSIFICATION: Lyric soprano

RANGE: 

TESSITURA: Middle of the staff

TIME: 3:50

PLOT: Fiorello LaGuardia was the mayor of New York City after World War I. As mayor, he reformed city politics by helping curb a strong political machine.

Thea Almerigotti, an attractive young woman, is arrested for leading the women shirtwaist workers on strike. Under the guidance of young lawyer Fiorello LaGuardia (who is infatuated with the beautiful Thea), the women win the strike. Released from prison, Thea forms a political bond with the lawyer. By the end of the first act, after Fiorello goes to war and subsequently returns, Thea agrees to marry him.

CHARACTER: Historically, Thea met Fiorello in 1915 while working as a dress designer in the garment district. Born in Trieste, Italy, she was the opposite of the five-foot-tall Fiorello in appearance: tall with blonde hair and porcelain skin. After their marriage in 1919 they had a child, Fioretta. The child was born in poor health, and Thea had a difficult recovery from childbirth. Thea and the child soon contracted tuberculosis. Fioretta died at age one, and Thea died six months later, at the age of twenty-six. In the musical *Fiorello*, Thea lives for eight more years.

CONTEXT: At the opening of act II LaGuardia (in flashback) runs for mayor after he and Thea are married. Thea, home from a visit to the doctor, sings of her love in "When Did I Fall in Love?"

CONTENT: In the opening of the song (introduction), Thea is asking some questions of herself. She wonders when it was exactly that her feelings for Fiorello changed from respect into love. She muses how strange it is that a touch that once meant nothing now is filled with meaning. After a four-measure interlude, in which the key modulates from B-flat major to C, she continues to ask questions as she sings the refrain: "When did I fall in love? What night? Which day?" she insistently asks herself. Thea continues to ask more questions, and she adds the expressive triplet rhythm for variety. The range is even wider in the next measures ("How could the moment pass?") as she sings an A below middle C, and in the next line ("Where was the crashing chord?") she soars up to a D at the top of the staff. The next section is the repeated melody that cadences in "I love him now," with a fermata indicated on the word "him" before the B section, or bridge ("moderately fast"). In this section, there is some ambiguity of key reflected in written accidentals in melody and accompaniment, as Thea is unsure of herself, and surprised that she misses him when they are apart. At tempo I, Thea again sings the chorus verbatim, warmly and low in the range (middle C), modulating toward a climactic, extended ending on the highest pitch, G at the top of the staff. The accompaniment at the conclusion is fuller, richer, and a stronger support to the end of the song.

VOICE: This is an emotional song, sung with a lot of expression. A suggestion is that the performer, when beginning the refrain on the middle C, should *not* sing these lower, quieter passages off of the breath support in a breathy, "crooned" voice. If that is done, then when the singer switches gears suddenly to the top of the range with power, passion, and fullness, the voice will not sound as one instrument, and it is also not healthy for the voice. Another suggestion is that when singing at the top of the staff and the text needs to be understood and enunciated, the diction should be clarified by the supported initial consonants, and careful use of the articulators (teeth, lips, and tongue). Keep away from diphthongs—they can tighten the jaw—and make sure that the throat is open for good, healthy, free, powerful, expressive vocal sound.

BEHIND THE SCENES WITH THE ARTISTS: SHELDON HARNICK, LYRICIST AND BOOK WRITER

"From the time Fiorello is a lawyer and helps her win the strike, Thea develops great respect and admiration for him. However, when he proposes to her, she's not certain that what she feels for him is enough to warrant marriage." Sheldon continues by describing a story that furthers their relationship. "Thea is deeply upset that Trieste [where she was born] is under Austrian, rather than Italian, control. When LaGuardia goes off to fight in World War I, he extracts a kind of mock promise from her that if he manages to restore Trieste to Italian control, she will marry him. At the end of the war, Trieste *was* restored to Italian control. In a very emotional scene at the end of act I, when LaGuardia returns to New York, he gives Thea what he says is the 'key to Trieste' and proposes to her again. This time she accepts him. In act II, when Thea sings this song, we learn that since they have been married, she has fallen very much in love with her husband."

Ice Cream

She Loves Me

"The song, to a certain extent, requires a virtuoso performer."
—Sheldon Harnick, Lyricist

CHARACTER: Amalia Balash

MUSIC: Jerry Bock

LYRICS: Sheldon Harnick

BOOK: Joe Masteroff

ADAPTATION OF: The play *Parfumerie*, by Miklos Laszlo

SETTING: Budapest, 1930s

BROADWAY PREMIERE: 1963

CLASSIFICATION: Character song for soprano

RANGE: 

TESSITURA: Lower half of the staff during the narration, then at the polka C-sharp to E at the top of the staff

TIME: 3:06

PLOT: Act I takes place in Maraczek's Parfumerie, and many of the characters are employees of the shop. Georg Nowack is the shy manager, but as the show opens and Georg enters the shop, he is upbeat and happy. A nervous young woman, Amalia Balash, comes into the shop, hoping to interview for a job at the store. The initial meeting between Georg and Amalia is not friendly, and when Amalia is hired at the shop, the two argue constantly. As the play unfolds, we find out that they both have secret romantic "pen pals," who turn out to be each other.

CHARACTER: In the script, Amalia Balash is described as "attractive, intelligent, and at her entrance in the show, very nervous." She is nervous because she is entering the shop to apply for a job as a sales clerk at Maraczek's Parfumerie. It is an early morning, in summer. She is told emphatically that although she has excellent references, there is no position open for her. Amalia ingeniously (and perhaps desperately) shows her talent in sales by showing Mr. Maraczek that she can be highly successful in the shop by independently approaching a customer in the shop and making a successful sale.

CONTEXT: Act II, scene 2. The script describes the setting: "An attractive one-room apartment. The window shades are drawn to keep out the daylight. Amalia, in pajamas, is asleep in her bed. After a moment, there is a knock at the door. It is Georg. After getting out of bed, "rather unsteadily," she puts on a bathrobe. She tells him that she is not well and is not planning to go to work. She thinks that Georg is suspiciously checking up on her to see if she is really sick." "With mounting hysteria," she looks for her hat, her shoes, to get ready to go to work.

Georg carries a brown paper bag. Inside is a container of vanilla ice cream. It's the best thing in the world when you're sick, he says. She has been writing to her "friend," who has written lovely letters to her as a "secret admirer," and she does not yet know his identity. Through correspondence, they agree to meet, but Georg from the shop (the secret admirer), loses his nerve at the last minute, and Amalia's meeting with this mysterious admirer does not take place. Amalia, alone in her apartment, is upset about being stood up by her admirer as Georg looks in on her to see how she's doing. She is reading the novel *Anna Karenina* (which she has been reading throughout the show), and Georg suggests that she take some time off from work to finish the book. She says that she has finished it. "It's remarkable how it stays with me," she says. "Every train platform—is Anna's platform. And I can see her come out of the crowd and walk slowly toward her death. I've even tried to stop her some times." Georg exits, and she writes another letter to her unknown admirer as she sings "Ice Cream."

CONTENT: The beginning (set up), with no introduction, is marked "lento" and is in 3/4 meter, as the same repeated motive in the treble of the accompaniment is played ten times as she searches for the words to write. Amalia begins by half-speaking the words of her letter, begun with the salutation "Dear Friend" as the accompaniment begins to repeat an arpeggiated chord pattern in the treble. She begins to fully vocalize the text, explaining that the meeting she suggested was perhaps ill-advised, and she lightheartedly remarks that someday the two of them will laugh about the date that never happened. Her thoughts then turn toward thinking about Georg, as she murmurs, "Ice cream . . . he brought me ice cream . . . vanilla ice cream . . . imagine that!" as the song moves toward a different key accompanied by a polka rhythm. Her heart beats faster with the words "ice cream." The melody is sung softly at first with intense excitement, then the tempo accelerates little by little as the range ascends to D, and the dynamic is forte for only three beats in the accompaniment before it is piano again. The accompaniment in the bass is marked "staccato" as the tempo reaches allegro. "Will wonders never cease," she sings, and then the same phrases sequence up a step higher and get louder, and the tempo moves faster (to allegro) as she gets more excited, noting (surprised) that he (Georg) was friendly, and she is puzzled because that isn't like him. "It's been a most peculiar day!" She has called in sick, had an unexpected, normally disagreeable visitor, and now she can't stop thinking about him and his unusual gift. At this place in the song, her reverie stops, and she gets back to her letter and her pen pal. This is more a comic recitative, halting as she edits herself. Then once more, the slow polka begins again as her thoughts return to Georg. "A man that I despise has turned into a man I like!" Of course, it's not about the vanilla ice cream but the unexpected surprise that it represents, and that excitement allows a mini-cadenza to a high B-natural to the ending, a sustained E at the top of the staff. Each section needs a change of focus stimulated by the *idea* in her head before beginning.

VOICE: "Ice Cream" requires a comic's sense of timing, an actor's believable text delivery, and a trained soprano voice with coloratura ability. Some of the sections will benefit from rehearsing the lyrics in speech for inflection and understanding, *then* singing. For example, practice speaking the lines that contain the words "fat" and "bald." (to keep Amalia from feeling badly about being stood up, Georg makes up a story about seeing a fat, bald man in the vicinity of the proposed meeting the previous evening). These words should be heavily inflected for best effect. Some of the pickup notes (e.g., "*will* wonders never cease") are set with the pickup note E on "will" at the beginning of the line, and Amalia should be able to sing this lightly, as a true unstressed pickup, meaning that these upbeats should not have weight or tension. At the final cadence, there is a true, traditional, opera-like cadenza sung up to a very high B-natural above the staff. At the words "ice" and "cream" the E natural is sustained for seven measures, marked "presto," as the accompaniment plays four beats per measure, quickly. The cadenza here is not just for showing off the voice. It is to demonstrate Amalia's excitement and her delight.

BEHIND THE SCENES WITH THE ARTISTS: SHELDON HARNICK, LYRICIST

In act II, as the result of plot complications, Amalia is sick in bed, and Georg has come to visit her bearing ice cream. He knows that his behavior on the previous evening is the reason that Amalia is feeling under the weather. Sheldon saw that this situation could lead to an effective song. "I thought it would be interesting to have Amalia start to write a letter to 'Dear Friend' about the unfortunate events of the previous evening and then veer away from writing the letter as she marvels at what has just happened between her and Georg. Not only has this man whom she dislikes so much brought her ice cream; he has also turned out to be a charming and sympathetic friend!" Sheldon goes on to explain what the song requires from the singing actress to be successful: "The song, to a certain extent, requires a virtuoso performer. To make the song as effective as it can be, whoever plays Amalia must be a fine actress, able to realize all of the dramatic nuances in the lyrics. And she must have a good comic sense to capitalize on the humor inherent in the dramatic situation. And, finally, she must be a capable soprano with a high B in her range. If she has all of these qualities, then she'll make 'Ice Cream' a showstopper!"

Far from the Home I Love

Fiddler on the Roof

"The song needs to be sung through the text, not the melody."
—Julia Migenes, the original Hodel

CHARACTER: Hodel

MUSIC: Jerry Bock

LYRICS: Sheldon Harnick

BOOK: Joseph Stein, based on *Tevya and His Daughters* and the theatrical adaptation, *A Family Portrait in Five Scenes,* by Sholem Aleichem

SETTING: Czarist Russia, 1905, in a village called Anatevka

PREMIERE: 1964

CLASSIFICATION: Young soprano lyric

RANGE: 

TESSITURA: Middle of staff

TIME: 2:33

PLOT: The story revolves around Tevye; his wife, Golde; and his three daughters. Tevye, a poor "self-employed" day worker trying to scratch out a living for his family, is a Russian Jew and a traditionalist. He is unable and unwilling to acknowledge that a new world will touch his small village and affect his family and traditions. He grew up in a strict religious household, and he expects that his family will follow that path, though he fears that this is not going to happen.

CHARACTER: Hodel is the seventeen-year-old middle daughter of Tevye and Golde. Growing up in a small Russian village and in a strict Jewish-traditional culture, the three girls are expected to have successful marriages at a young age arranged by the matchmaker. Tevye is appalled that his daughters have minds of their own in these matters, especially his head-strong daughter Hodel. She is in love with an "outsider," Perchik, who comes into the village. He is a young Marxist scholar who agrees to tutor Tevye's two younger daughters in exchange for food.

CONTEXT: In act II, the young man leaves for the city of Kiev to work for the revolution. Hodel courageously decides to join him there, even though Perchik has not asked her to do so. When the couple brashly tell Tevye that they are engaged, the shocked father refuses permission for their union. Hodel and Perchik tell him that they are not asking for permission, just for his blessing.

After Perchik goes to Kiev, a rumor quickly spreads through the village that he has been arrested and sent to Siberia. Without any discussion, Hodel decides to join him there, and Tevye says goodbye to her at the railway station. She explains to her father that her home now will be wherever Perchik is, though she will always love her family.

In the dialogue immediately preceding the song, Hodel explains to her skeptical father that Perchik has not asked (or demanded) that she come to him in Siberia, where he is a political prisoner. Tevye does not understand why she wants to go, and she sings the song in reply.

CONTENT: The four measures of instrumental introduction is haunting in its weaving "modal melody." She begins to sing the song, the melody written in a minor key with a raised fourth, which is sometimes known as Ukrainian Dorian mode, because of its association with Ukrainian folk music. This lends the melody a folk-like ethnicity. The singer needs to realize that the melody is not doubled in the accompaniment. Since Hodel cannot follow the melody in the accompaniment, she is "self-powered," both musically and figuratively. She is trying to make her father understand why she is going away. Hodel underlines at the end of every verse the home she loves that she is both leaving and will hold in her heart. The song is not all somber: she recalls that once it was enough for her to be happy in the town. She is not in denial—she knows that it will be a difficult road to travel, leaving her home. At the concluding verse she moves to the major key when she talks about "her heart," which leads her—with hope—to be near Perchik.

VOICE: Although the song is most beautifully sung in a youthful, pure soprano voice, the melody is written in the middle-staff range, and in fact descends four times down to land on the middle-C tonic pitch (written in the key of C minor). Although the opening four measure introduction is written to be counted in four, the melody as Hodel begins is notated in cut time, in two. In other words, this song must not be sung with too much angst and sorrow. She is on her way to be with Perchik, and she needs to make her father, Tevye, understand her feelings for Perchik as soon as possible before the train arrives to take her far away from Anatevka. It should be sung in a simple, straightforward manner in this public place (the train station), and it is abundantly clear that Hodel has already made up her mind and is on her way. She should not put too much drama or somber weight into the voice, which will cause the "changing of vocal registers" as the soprano voice goes to chest resonance (usually at bottom line E-flat) to be too marked if heavy and dramatic. The singer needs to be very conscious not to slow too much at cadences to make an already poignant moment overly sentimental. However, the performer should observe all directions in the music, especially the tempo markings. Observe the *più mosso* at "Who could see that a man would come" as her pulse quickens; notice the phrase "change the shape of my dreams" (ritard), followed by *menno mosso* in four, on the words "Helpless, now I stand with him," with "poco ritard" marked at the end on the phrase. Be aware of the meter reverting back into cut time at "Oh, what a melancholy choice this is." The final four measures of the song have four beats to the measure, with a fermata over the word "I'm"(on the D-flat) to the final tonic on C—"home," an octave above middle C. It is important to observe that the final chorus, although moving in 2, is also sung piano, as marked, not as if a belligerent decision is made at that point but to show that Hodel is sad but sure she must go to Perchik, and her mind is made up.

BEHIND THE SCENES WITH THE ARTISTS: JULIA MIGENES, THE ORIGINAL HODEL

Ms. Migenes remembers that, even as a very young singer on Broadway, she had definite ideas about what she wanted to do with rubato at the cadences, namely, a slowing at the end of her phrases, and she was irritated that the conductor was not interested in following her. In speaking of what is important in the delivery of the song, Julia says, "The song needs to be sung through the words and not the melody."

From lyricist Sheldon Harnick: "The song occurs in the midst of a very dramatic scene: a father and daughter who love one another are saying goodbye, knowing that they may never see each other again. Like all lyrics in serious musicals, the lyrics of this song are meant to be a continuation of the drama and, as such, are to be acted as well as possible. When these lyrics are sung honestly and with understanding and, at the same time, the melody is sung beautifully, the result is a powerful performance."

What Makes Me Love Him?

The Apple Tree

"The challenge becomes for the lyricist in determining where and why the songs are inserted into the dialogue of the play."
—Sheldon Harnick, lyricist

CHARACTER: Eve

MUSIC: Jerry Bock

LYRICS: Sheldon Harnick

BOOK: N. Richard Nash

BASED ON: The first act is adapted from *Eve's Diary,* a short story by Mark Twain

SETTING: The Garden of Eden

BROADWAY PREMIERE: 1966

CLASSIFICATION: Soprano/mezzo/lyric

RANGE: 

TESSITURA: C to C octave

TIME: 3:00

PLOT: The first act of *The Apple Tree* is based on Mark Twain's short story *Eve's Diary*. The musical is divided into three distinct parts, each based on different source material. "The Diary" by Twain is simply Adam's day-by-day journal as if it were written in the present day. In the musical, Adam first awakes and names all of the animals he sees; then he meets Eve. She begins to name all of the animals in greater detail. This annoys Adam because he thinks that she believes herself to be superior to him. Adam builds a shelter, and when he sees Eve remaining outside, he invites her in. She immediately begins to redecorate. The arguments continue between the two. Even though Eve is told by Adam not to eat the " forbidden fruit," Eve takes a bite from the apple, as the snake has told Eve that Adam is wrong about the fruit being forbidden. Adam realizes that something has changed in his "Beautiful, Beautiful World."

CHARACTER: Adam labels Eve "the creature with the long hair." "The new creature eats too much fruit," writes Adam. He says that she disturbs him and the garden by imposing her will in many situations. She puts up signs all over the park, Adam says. She "titters and blushes," he writes. Eve's diary, of course, reports things differently. While Adam's entries are filled with descriptions of his activities, Eve notices the stars, the moon, and the beauty of nature around her. Humorously, she remarks that she has taken naming things "off his hands," believing that she has helped him in Eden. She speaks about her emotions, and she is charmingly naïve when exposed to the surrounding circumstances.

CONTEXT: When Adam and Eve leave Eden, Eve has a baby, Cain, and then they have another son, Abel. She sings a very funny lullaby to her children, "Goodnight, Whatever You Are." She tells Adam that she wants to die together with him, or at least she needs to die first, because she needs him more than he needs her. She then sings "What Makes Me Love Him?," a lovely song of musing whimsy that is very charming. She sets up the song by saying to the audience: "I love certain birds because of their song. But that hardly applies to Adam."

CONTENT: The song begins with short, simple phrases, and then unfolds with a beautiful, arching musical shape. The accompaniment plays the repeated figure of four quarter-note rhythms per measure in the same repeated chord progression, which gives the song a music-box feel. The song is humorous and affecting. In the first verse Eve makes a comment about the "quality" of Adam's voice, saying that it is so unpleasant that it "sours the milk." But she goes on to matter-of-factly say: "It's gotten to the point where I prefer that kind of milk." After only a measure and three beats of interlude she begins the second verse, telling us that she does not love him because of "what he knows," because "he knows a multitude of things...mostly wrong." At the end of the second verse, she muses that "he is a good man," and "were he a plain man"—here is a sustained note, with an added fermata on the word "man"—she continues to sing in the final phrase, "I'd love him still." The last verse begins again with the question: "What makes me love him?" and as she goes on to try to find the answer, she cannot figure it out. Sheldon Harnick is subsequently able to rhyme the words "define" and "masculine," with the final word, as she searches to discover the reason why she loves him—it is because, she says, "he is *mine*." There is a lovely countermelody that weaves through the last verse.

VOICE: The song needs to be sincerely and simply sung. It is thoughtful, innocent, and initially childlike in expression, then unfolds in more of a knowing, feminine way. All the notes Eve sings are quarter-note values, except for final half-note rhythms with whole notes in the phrase. While the accompaniment is repeating the same quarter-note rhythmic pattern, there is no doubling of the melody, so with the many accidentals to negotiate, it is not always easy for the singer to negotiate the correct rhythms. However, it is important for the performer to be musically secure and confident in identifying the correct pitches. Although most of the song is set in the middle voice, Eve should be able to sing in lighter vocal colors, and the song should not be sung heavily or belted. The song is sung syllabically, which also lends a childlike quality of innocence to the piece, and allows the audience to clearly understand this wonderful text.

BEHIND THE SCENES WITH THE ARTISTS: SHELDON HARNICK, LYRICIST

Sheldon credits Twain for the lyrics to the song, and certainly for the inspiration and the ideas. However, the challenge for the lyricist becomes determining where and why the songs are inserted into the dialogue of the play. "Toward the end of 'The Diaries,'" Sheldon explains, "not long before Eve dies, Twain has Eve ask herself what it is about Adam that made her love him." This, the lyricist found, was a good place for the song. The rest of Sheldon's work had to do with adapting the ideas into song form, which is an art unto itself. Another adaptation was the use of this line in the song for the show's opening:

He is a good man
But I would love him
If he abused me
Or used me ill.

The word "abused" is Twain's word, and the word in Twain's time (and in the show's premiere in 1966) means something different now, and so it has been adapted since then:

He is a good man
Tho' far from perfect
And on occasion
He's used me ill.

This is just one example of Sheldon Harnick's creative craftsmanship.

Moonfall

Drood or The Mystery of Edwin Drood

"I believe that creating a specific set of values for a character is very important whether those values are good or evil."
—Patti Cohenour, the original Rosa Budd

CHARACTER: Rosa Budd

MUSIC, LYRIC AND BOOK: Rupert Holmes

BASED ON: The unfinished novel *The Mystery of Edwin Drood* by Charles Dickens

SETTING: Music Hall Royale, London

BROADWAY PREMIERE: 1985

CLASSIFICATION: Lyric soprano

RANGE: 

TESSITURA: Upper middle of the staff

TIME: 2:25

PLOT: The cast members of *Drood* do not play the Dickens characters, but instead play English music hall performers performing in the style of Dickens. This allows a light play-within-a-play format, which is out of kilter with the original Dickens novel. In fact, the darker novel that the musical is based on was never finished, which led to much speculation as to how *The Mystery of Edwin Drood* was to end. The creative solution, consistent with the English music hall approach, was to give the audience an opportunity to vote for a variety of endings. The English music hall, which is one of the precursors of American musical theatre, was popular during Dickens's life.

CHARACTER: Seventeen-year-old orphan Rosa Budd is Edwin Drood's fiancée. Their marriage has been arranged by the couple's fathers. Rosa is a sweet girl, but she can be childish. A number of other characters are also enamored of Rosa, including Drood's uncle, John Jasper, the Cloisterham choirmaster, who is Rosa's music teacher and has inappropriate desires for her. Rosa dislikes and fears Jasper intensely. Another admirer is Neville Landless, a man of high temperament. He is the twin brother of Helena, who is a dear friend of Rosa's, and lives in the Nuns' House with her—Rosa's home since she was seven, an orphanage in Cloisterham. The details of the tragic accident which claimed her mother's life are described in the original Dickens source material for the musical, the unfinished novel *The Mystery of Edwin Drood* (1870). "The fatal accident had happened at a party of pleasure." Rosa's mother, "who had been brought home in her father's arms, drowned." Her father's "wild despair" and "bowed-down grief" was such that he "died broken-hearted on the first anniversary of that hard day." Upon marrying Rosa, Drood plans to take her with him to Egypt, where he will become an engineer with the firm in which his father had been a partner.

CONTEXT: Early in the show, Rosa Budd is introduced. It's her birthday, and her music teacher, the choirmaster John Jasper, has written a song for her that he insists she sing at the Nuns' House, but Rosa does not want to sing it. "The lyrics are not proper," she protests, but Jasper insists. The situation and the inappropriate nature of the song cause Rosa to be upset to the point of fainting. Helena comes to help her. Charles Dickens's text offers more information about the relationship of Rosa and her music teacher, as told by the girl herself: "He terrifies me. He haunts my thoughts, like a dreadful ghost. I feel that I am never safe from him." And later Rosa offers more insights into his power over her: "He has made a slave of me with his looks. He has forced me to understand him, without his saying a word; and he has forced me to keep silence, without his uttering a threat. When I play, he never moves his eyes from my hands. When I sing, he never moves his eyes from my lips." She continues her fearful description of their interactions. "When he corrects me, and strikes a note, or a chord, or plays a passage, he himself is in the sounds, whispering that he pursues me as a lover, and commanding me to keep his secret."

CONTENT: The introduction of two measures in the piano accompaniment establish immediately the otherworldly sound of the piece, marked "molto espressivo." There are just two verses to the song, and there are repeated off-the-beat entrances in the melody lines followed by eighth-note rhythms that tie the song together. The song has an eerie sound to it because of the intervals chosen by the composer, beginning in the introduction, which is accompanied by only piano. With the lyrics "and in the moonfall," the violins enter. Rosa is singing this song because Jasper is forcing her to sing it. Her alarm is evident in her voice as she reads the words, hears the harmonies, and sings the melody. The song is extremely romantic, in the sense that there is an expressive ebb and flow, or rubato and accelerando, in the each phrase. Dynamic markings are important, as are observations of caesuras before several of the final phrases. All of the markings have to do with a romantic sensibility that is important to the dramatic situation.

VOICE: The main melody begins on the upper pitches and descends downwards. There are a number of accidentals in the melodic shape (and especially in the bridge, where the harmonic progression takes the singer through a number of different keys, then returns to the "tonic" key). With the significant number of marked accidentals to negotiate throughout the song, the pitches need to be tuned carefully so as not to cause intonation problems. The shape of the descending vocal line adds to the haunting quality of the piece. All attacks (onsets at the beginning of phrases) need to be sung without strain or glottal attack (on vowels), especially at the top of the staff (for example, measure 27, with "between our eyes," where Rosa needs to lightly enter on the *i* vowel of "be-tween" on the high G). Although the song reveals Rosa's sweet soprano tone, and her voice should sound lyric and unforced, there are many words to enunciate, and the setting of text to music is syllabic. It is important that the higher pitches should not be forced, especially since much of the song is not written that high in the soprano's range. However, the song requires the pure tone of the soprano quality, and the final, sustained E is sung on the *u* vowel, which should not be pinched in vocal production. The lower pitches are intended to be sung lyrically, without sounding like a different vocal quality. However, the lower tones can have a caressing, warm quality that is more sensuous in timbre without taking on weight.

BEHIND THE SCENES WITH THE ARTISTS: PATTI COHENOUR, THE ORIGINAL ROSA BUDD

Ms. Cohenour has important insights into Rosa Budd's character: "She was immersed and schooled under strict Victorian standards which were both suppressive and frustrating. This results in her confusion about her attraction to Jasper, who emotionally repulses and attracts her all at the same time. . . . When singing the haunting 'Moonfall,' the imagery of the song exposes her attraction to Jasper even though she knows that these feelings are sinful." Although Rosa is a fragile, naïve young girl, Patti always gives her characters an inner strength. "This is especially true when portraying an ingénue, because a sugar-coated shallow young woman is never as interesting as one who possesses passion and fire." The actress finds the song "Moonfall" interesting and challenging to perform: "The challenge is to believably portray that Rosa is sight-reading the piece while at the same time acknowledging and exposing her deep emotional attraction to Jasper."

Patti offers some excellent advice to young singers studying the song: "I would recommend exposing the textual imagery of the song. Also, it is a technically demanding piece, especially finding where to breathe, and an excellent song to challenge a student on learning breath control." However, she would further caution the soprano that the successfully singing of the song should not solely dwell on mastering the breath control of the piece. "The singer should first focus on the lyrics because the words are key to making the performance of the song more significant, and hopefully in time Rosa should achieve solid breath control as well."

Another Suitcase in Another Hall

Evita

"It is a particularly poignant melody that should play with an audience's emotions."
—Michael Grandage, director of the 2012 Broadway revival

CHARACTER: Peron's Mistress

MUSIC: Andrew Lloyd Webber

LYRICS: Tim Rice

SETTING: Buenos Aires, Argentina

PREMIERE: 1979

CLASSIFICATION: Soprano lyric (pop) with text

RANGE: 

TIME: 2:45

TESSITURA: Upper middle of staff

PLOT: The opening of *Evita* takes place in 1952, upon the announcement of the death of Eva Peron, the beloved first lady of Argentina. The show then travels in flashback to 1934, when Eva is fifteen and she is ambitiously beginning her career as an actress. She ambitiously sleeps her way up the chain of military command to Colonel Juan Peron, who himself is in the process of climbing up the political ladder. After a disastrous earthquake hits the country, there is a charity event for the victims. Peron addresses the crowds with words of hope, and Eva later suggests that she can help him in achieving his political ambitions.

CHARACTER: Director Michael Grandage, the director of the 2012 revival of *Evita* on Broadway, makes the following observations about the mistress and her relationship to Eva Peron. "Peron's mistress is not a character that has an opportunity in the show to be developed. But it is important for the audience to see that this sixteen-year-old girl, who Peron at times introduces to others as his daughter, understands the character of the ambitious Eva and her relationship with Peron. His sixteen-year-old mistress is nothing more than a bedmate, and twenty-four-year-old Eva understands the power of her relationship with Peron that allows her to discard the mistress, even as Eva must feel the insecurity of being the 'older' woman in the relationship. Peron realizes that in Eva Duarte he has a woman with useful talent to him. She flatters him, and encourages his ambitions. In turn, he recognizes that she will be popular with the people [she already is], and that truth will be important for his political ambitions."

CONTEXT: The song occurs in act I, when Eva takes steps to remove Peron's young Mistress from his life, clearing the way for Eva. Before the song, Eva confronts the girl, addressing the Mistress in a rock-inflected musical section, as the girl is removed from Peron's life. "Hello and goodbye," Eva says. "Don't act sad or surprised."

CONTENT: The simple accompaniment of soft strummed guitar in broken-chord patterns is heard in the opening measures of the introduction to the song. The first vocal entrance leads into a pretty, engaging melody, with the opening phrase repeated twice, as the young Mistress asks herself, "What happens now?" and wonders about her immediate future, before going on to say that she will be fine—she'll survive. The second verse has her reflect about this recurring pattern in her life, which leads to hurt. The final verse looks forward more optimistically, and then the song finishes once again with the question, "Where am I going to?" "Don't ask," is the answer. The attractive song is in three verses, with refrain (embellished by a small male ensemble in the show). The last line, sung by one of the ensemble, is "Don't ask anymore." The ensemble also sings (with Che) the words "You'll get by—you always have before," indicating that she is a survivor.

VOICE: With a strong rhythmic accompaniment underneath played by guitar, marimba, harp, and keyboard, a pretty lyric soprano voice is a plus, with a chest voice to show different colors of emotions, along with the ability to sing some of the lower pitches (middle C) on the words "Where am I going to?" There is an underlying coolness, an acceptance, contrasted with an emotional difficulty to deal with the reality of the situation, which leaves her out on the street. The advantage of the possession of a light, agile voice is that the motive "What happens now?" has a sixteenth-beat rhythm sung at the top of the staff (E-natural), which is pitched high to be sung on a difficult-to-sing vowel on an uninflected syllable.

BEHIND THE SCENES WITH THE ARTISTS: MICHAEL GRANDAGE, DIRECTOR OF THE 2012 REVIVAL

I asked director Michael Grandage how he set up this number onstage and what he thought the original purpose was for this character and song. "Tim Rice and Andrew Lloyd Webber were both intrigued by the stories that surrounded the life story of Eva Peron when they began researching it in the mid-1970s. The private life of Juan Peron, in particular, threw up all sorts of complexities, his rumored penchant for young girls being one of the most startling. Rice and Webber decided to feature this in the musical as part of the journey of Eva and Peron's rise to power. It took the edge off a 'fairy tale' courtship and revealed ambition and sleaze beneath the surface. It gave the musical some real backstory and is part of a sequence that involves the introduction (and speedy ejection) of Peron's 'mistress' following the first meeting of Eva and Peron. From a production point of view it offers an opportunity to show the ruthlessness of Eva (Peron leaves it to her to kick the girl out of his apartment). It also offers us a moment to show a wider social context. The young teenager is put out onto the street with nowhere to go, as a chorus sings 'another suitcase, another hall.' She is clearly vulnerable following Peron's rejection, and it allows us to see a city swallow her up. We staged this by having her emerge in just a night dress from the grandeur of Peron's balcony apartment. The audience then watches Eva toss the girl's clothes down onto the street before placing her suitcase beside the mistress and slamming the door in her face. The mistress then descends the stairs singing about her need to move on but constantly asking, 'Where do I go from here?' She picks up her clothes and packs them in the case as shadowy figures move around in the city's catacombs behind her.

"It is a particularly poignant melody that should play with an audience's emotions. The mistress clearly knew what she was doing sleeping with an older man, and yet there is something exploitive about it as well. Eva's bitchiness should be enjoyed by an audience, but they should also be investing in the plight of a young girl's eviction.

"Interestingly, the song gets one of the biggest ovations at every performance. It's partly familiarity (it was released as a single sung by Barbara Dickson along with 'Don't Cry for Me Argentina' back in the 1970s and so is the other big 'known' number in the show), but it's also because the song is entirely self-contained within the musical as a whole. The narrative of this section is so well structured that it is obvious the journey of the mistress is complete by her exit. This allows the audience to invest in a single moment while also learning more about Eva and Peron's character as they move forward in the story."

Barbara Dickson had an enormous hit with this song in the United Kingdom in the 1970s. Here is her story: "I was talking to Andrew and Tim about the role of Evita, but my voice is too delicate in tone for what was required. Think of 'Buenos Aires.' They then offered me the one song NOT sung by the title female character. I don't remember much about the recording process other than Andrew insisting that I sing the song too high for my range to make me sound younger, as the Mistress was a teenager in reality. I never liked the original recording for that reason. The song has seasoned over the years with my singing of it."

It Hurts to Be Strong

Carrie

"She was a nice character to play, with a good heart and high morals."
—Sally Ann Triplett, the original Sue Snell

CHARACTER: Sue Snell

MUSIC: Michael Gore

LYRICS: Dean Pitchford

BOOK: Lawrence Cohen

BASED ON: The 1981 novel *Carrie* by Stephen King

SETTING: A Midwestern high school; the show opens in the gym

BROADWAY PREMIERE: 1988

CLASSIFICATION: Soprano/mezzo character song

RANGE: 

TESSITURA: Upper middle of staff, C and D sustained

TIME: 2:40

PLOT: The musical *Carrie* is based on the novel by Stephen King. The musical was inspired, the show's composer said, by a performance the creative team saw of the modern opera *Lulu* by Alban Berg. The musical, first opening in England and then on Broadway, was at first a monumental failure, closing after a small number of performances and costing eight million dollars to produce on Broadway. Perhaps this was the result of the subject matter, or the fact that the movie *Carrie* is well-known to many people, creating expectations in the story line. Also, because of the critical failure of the first productions, the musical was constantly tweaked and songs dropped and added, resulting in a lack of cohesion and a limited run. The show was recently revamped and revived on Broadway.

CHARACTER: Sue Snell is the "popular girl," as she is experienced in high school romance and dates the most popular boy. At first, Sue taunts Carrie and makes fun of her, like all of Sue's friends, but afterward feels remorse and asks her boyfriend, the popular Tommy, to ask Carrie to go to the prom with him. In this act Sue has good intentions, but her "friends" see the date as an opportunity to play a practical joke on Carrie, which backfires later in the show. Sue witnesses Carrie's rage at the end but, despite that, comforts Carrie during her last moments.

CONTEXT: Act II opens as the boys in the school are going to a pig farm in the middle of the night to gather pig's blood for their act of terrorism at the prom. Back at the high school, Sue is confronted by friends questioning her rationale for getting her boyfriend to ask Carrie to go to the prom. Sue believes that she is doing the right thing, which is not always the most popular thing to do. "You're ruining the prom!" a girl exclaims. "You're spoiling it for the rest of us," another girl says. "She doesn't belong!" Sue stands by her convictions, and sings "It Hurts to Be Strong."

CONTENT: The eight-measure introduction of the song sounds like the setting up of a pop song, attractive in its rhythm and chords (the song is marked "With strong cut-time feel"). Sue talks about her friends at the beginning of the song. She used to think that she knew them, that they were "as close as they could be," narrating simply in a syncopated rhythmic pattern, marked "piano." She wonders what happened to them. Or, she further wonders, "What happened to me?" In the second verse Sue talks about her "perfect" childhood; she never raised her voice, sang along, but "never too loud." "Now I'm all alone in my song," she observes. She sings that she doesn't believe in her heart that she's wrong, as her voice builds in confidence to "It hurts to be strong," which acts as the "refrain hook" at the end of every verse. After two verses, during the B (bridge) section (marked "driving"), she sums up what she knows, the "obvious" known facts, but asks what she should do "when bridges burn" in a high "belted" sustained tone at the top D. The line "You've got to learn, so I'll learn" transitions to the last verse, in which she strongly states that she liked the way that things used to be. But, she sings, "there are a number of things you don't learn in school." The final poignant lines, acting as a coda, are more sensitively sung, as she asks herself if she follows her instincts—what she knows is right—will she ever belong again? "It hurts to be strong," she finally sings, in a vulnerable tone, sung mezzo piano. The song is a terrific character piece, telling

Sue's story, and showing that even a popular girl can have problems. "It Hurts to Be Strong" needs to be strongly sung as Sue stands by her principles—with layers of sensitivity, understanding, and empathy toward Carrie.

VOICE: The song requires attention to text, denying a traditional pop style performance, which is more general in its delivery. This is a "discovery" song, as the character is working through some very important, wrenching problems in her mind and heart that do not seem to have an easy, rational solution. I suggest the singer not belt the line "It hurts to be strong," every time. The refrain's delivery can possess a poignancy, for instance, with the title phrase sung softly the first time, showing vulnerability in Sue, a quality that one may not usually expect of someone so popular. The song is pitched high, with a repeated, sustained E natural, and Ds, which are best sung in more of a soprano head voice mixed with elements of "high belt."

This song is sometimes transposed, pitched a minor third below the key in the score if the Sue who is cast has a lower singing range. However, it makes sense for Sue's voice to be pitched above Carrie's range, so that the two voice qualities are delineated.

BEHIND THE SCENES WITH THE ARTISTS: SALLY ANN TRIPLETT

"When we first performed the show in London my character had a song called 'White Star,' which was about wishing on dreams and about how alone Sue felt at that time. When we got to Broadway the writers wanted to give Sue something that would show she was feisty and capable, so they wrote 'It Hurts to Be Strong.'" The song is about "a young girl finding out about herself and sticking to her guns about something she feels very strongly about, that is, helping Carrie and getting her boyfriend to take her to the prom. She was a nice character to play, with a good heart and high morals."

Anytime (I Am There)

Elegies

"I had to walk that fine line between being too emotional and unable to sing and feel[ing] enough to communicate the lyric."
—Carolee Carmello, the original Monica

CHARACTER: Monica

MUSIC AND LYRICS: William Finn

SETTING: New York City

PREMIERE: 2003

CLASSIFICATION: Musical/art song for alto/mezzo soprano

RANGE: 

TESSITURA: Middle of staff

TIME: 2:59

PLOT: *Elegies* was written in the aftermath of the September 11 attacks of 2001 by composer William Finn. The tragic loss of life that day and Finn's loss of friends to AIDS inspired him to write this beautiful cycle. There is no story line per se, but there are characters, and the work is commonly staged in the theatre with theatrical values, including stage movement and lighting. Each song is a gem of music and lyrics. Excerpted songs can be performed as individual character studies in workshop and performance. There are nonfictional characters, including producer Joseph Papp, composer Ricky Ian Gordon, Quentin Crisp, and the composer's mother. Although many of the songs in the cycle are very strong character narratives, "Anytime" has a strong, uplifting universal message of hope, and the effect of the music synergized with text is inspirational.

CHARACTER: Monica is married to Andy and is a friend of Mark, who is in the hospital dying of AIDS, at that time a disease that was always fatal. Monica and Andy have been in the hospital visiting him. Later, Monica and Andy adopt two children, naming one of them Mark after their departed friend.

CONTEXT: Composer William Finn told me that the song before "Anytime" sets it up. It is the story of Andy, Monica, and Mark. Some friends go to the hospital to visit Mark, who has AIDS. They run into Andy and Monica, who they have "heard about for years." Andy and Monica were planning on going to the opera with Mark, but they are now in the hospital, not aware of the severity of Mark's condition. They are "waiting for Mark to get better," but they are told by the doctor that he will die that afternoon. The doctor comforts them and tells them that they should see him very soon to say goodbye. Mark dies and they become friends with Andy and Monica. They fall in love with Monica, and they become godparents of their adopted children. Suddenly, "out of the blue," Monica is losing her hair and is sick. The doctors tell her that this is due to stress, but she knows what is really wrong. She plans her own funeral, and she wants the composer to write a song that would "make people cry." He writes a song, written from her point of view, "maybe a mother singing to her daughter . . . this is the song I wrote," which segues directly into "Anytime (I Am There)."

CONTENT: The accompaniment begins with a flourish-like motive that is very quickly played in a sixteenth-note figure and repeated three times. Monica sings at the opening with confidence, hope, and, as Carolee Carmello (who first sang the song) delivered it, with a radiant look of love and determination. She does not know why this has happened to her, but she wants her loved ones to know that her spirit will be there to watch over them in everything that they do—she will not be absent from their lives. Her voice becomes more animated and rhythmic with the line "I'll be there on the baseball field," her spirit watching her kids, over four quarter-note chords per measure in the piano accompaniment. The song moves with energy, but there are sustained tones at the end of phrases. The refrain is more lyrical in quality, as she sings "I am there each morning" in a very attractive "hook" melodic phrase that is lovely to sing and hear. After the second verse, going into the second ending, Monica's melody ascends as the climactic phrases require her to sing in a high belt a sustained D toward the top of the staff.

VOICE: The piece requires a singer who knows how to sing with many colors. Higher and middle belt voice with full support is needed in singing an ascending line to the top of the staff (D). Commitment to text is very important, and the singer must manage higher belt tones in varying dynamics. The emotional nature of the song will produce many vocal colors, but during the passages where softer tones are required, the singer will need to continue to define rhythmic values and text for clarity and keep control of the building of the piece, continuing to project courage and strength. This is a difficult challenge when singing such an emotional song.

BEHIND THE SCENES WITH THE ARTISTS: CAROLEE CARMELLO, THE ORIGINAL MONICA

Carolee said that she remembers shedding many tears while rehearsing and performing this emotional song; this made it very difficult for her to sing. She said that when she gets "choked up," it is challenging to find the requisite vocal strength. She does not recall a single time before the opening when she got through the song without crying. "I had to walk that fine line between being too emotional and unable to sing and feel[ing] enough to communicate the lyric," she remembers. The character singing the song is a young mother who dies, leaving behind her children. This especially resonated with Carolee, because, she said, "In real life, I have two children and always related to that scenario in a very visceral way." As the song is intended to comfort the child left behind, she had to stay as calm and collected as possible, a difficult task. The only way she could manage this, she says, was "to think about anything else, just to distract myself from the overwhelming sadness." This was counterintuitive for her as an actor, but "sometimes it's important to stay slightly neutral in order to allow the audience to feel their own emotions." She felt that the lyrics of the song were "incredibly expressive and poetic," without being "sappy... It's powerful. I adore Bill Finn, and I truly feel like it was an honor to originate that song."

William Finn originally wrote this song for a family member who died of cancer. He sang it at her funeral.

Some Things Are Meant to Be

Little Women

"The kite in the scene is a metaphor for Beth's fatalistic philosophy of life—that 'some things are meant to be,' to mean that wherever the wind blows you, that's where you go."
—Susan Schulman, director and collaborative writer of *Little Women* on Broadway

CHARACTER: Beth

MUSIC: Jason Howland

LYRICS: Mindi Dickstein

BOOK: Allan Knee

BASED ON: *Little Women*, the novel by Louisa May Alcott

SETTING: Concord, Massachusetts, 1869

PREMIERE: 2005

CLASSIFICATION: Lyric soprano

RANGE: 

TESSITURA: Middle staff

TIME: 3:39

PLOT: Based on the book of the same title by Louisa May Alcott, the classic story follows the lives of four young sisters, told from the viewpoint of Jo, an aspiring writer. It takes place in Concord, Massachusetts, during the Civil War, while the girls' father is serving as a chaplain in the war.

CHARACTER: Beth was always a sickly child. This frustrates the stronger, older sister Jo. From the book *Little Women* comes this description of Beth at age thirteen: "Elizabeth—or Beth, as everyone called her—was a rosy, smooth-haired, bright-eyed girl with a shy manner, a timid voice, and a peaceful expression, which was seldom disturbed." She was a gentle girl, and "she seemed to live in a happy world of her own, only venturing out to meet the few whom she trusted and loved."

CONTEXT: In the middle of act II, Jo wants Beth to promise that, whatever comes, she will "fight it." "Tell me about New York," Beth asks of Jo. "I'm going to take you there," Jo promises Beth, and paints a picture of what the big city is like. The dialogue continues over the introductory measures of the music, as the breeze swirls around them and Jo lets the kite be carried up into the sky. The director Susan Schulman observes that "the kite in the scene is a metaphor for Beth's fatalistic philosophy of life—that 'some things are meant to be,' to mean that wherever the wind blows you, that's where you go. Beth wants her sister to accept the fact that Beth is not strong enough to live much longer, and Jo should let the string holding the kite go, up into the sky." Jo is quite different. "The older sister will forge her future by the force of her will and desire, and does not want Beth to give up. As different as the two girls are in personality and basic outlook, they are sisters who deeply love each other. When Beth dies, Jo is devastated, and never really recovers."

CONTENT: Jo is trying to get the sickly Beth out of the house in a visible denial of Beth's condition. Beth has come to terms with what the future holds for her, and that results in her words "Some things are meant to be," which Jo does not want to accept. As the two sisters watch their kite sail into the air during their dialogue, the busy piano accompaniment begins, in a repeated pattern of sixteenth- and eighth-note rhythms, tied across the bar for forward momentum. While the accompaniment is constantly moving (is it the swirling breeze?), the vocal line is more sustained, replicating the soaring of the kite in the air. At times during this sustained line, there is a sudden eighth-note-triplet fast rhythmic movement in the melody, which also cleverly mirrors the action of a kite in the air, which at time soars, then dips suddenly and quickly in movement. Jo (always the writer) suggests that they pretend that they are kites flying through the air, and Beth quickly picks up the melody before the chorus. The words "Some things are meant to be" are Beth's, which is her way of dealing with the sickness that will soon end her young life. The words are underlined by the entrance of sustained strings, giving more importance to the line and introducing the chorus of the song. In the same musical motive, she continues, "Some things will never end," and she concludes that hopeful line with the words "the love I feel for you," sung with warmth and comfort. The second verse of the song includes more fantastical imagery—"We'll sleep on stardust, dine on bits of moon"—and this is where the two sisters sing in harmony and simple imitative counterpoint, ending with sustained, descending whole notes. There is a fermata rest, followed by a few short lines of dialogue. "You'll get better," declares Jo, hopefully. "Some things are meant to be," responds Beth, confidently, "no matter what I do," she says, and she concludes with comforting words: "Some things will never die . . . the memories when I am far from you." Finally, Beth asks Jo, "Let me go now." The song has two verses, both followed by the chorus. After some important dialogue (Beth's acceptance of imminent death and requesting Jo's acknowledgment), there is one more chorus, sung slowly and poignantly by Beth as she asks Jo to let her go, with love.

VOICE: This song requires a voice with a range that projects in the lower voice at the middle C area, but also "soars" to a high belt an octave higher, then ascends, sung in a soprano voice to a sustained E-natural at the top space of the staff. Beth is not as assertive or as physically strong as her tomboy sister Jo, and this is reflected in more of a lyric approach as her voice ascends without pushing. Also, Beth is at peace with her destiny, while Jo does not accept it, and continues to hope and push for Beth getting better. In this duet, Jo acts more in support of Beth, rather than an equal musical partner. Jo encourages Beth, and does not want to accept the fact that her dear sister is in failing health. In other words, in a stand-alone solo rendition, it is possible for Beth to sing alone, following her vocal melody line when both are singing, since Jo is embellishing rather than singing a primary melody. When trading off lines, Beth will need to sing Jo's lines as well.

BEHIND THE SCENES WITH THE ARTISTS: SUSAN SCHULMAN, DIRECTOR

Ms. Schulman has heard the song sung by Beth as a stand-alone solo audition piece since the time she directed the premiere on Broadway. She observes that as a solo by the Beth character the song is sung differently. That means that the strong imposing personality that her sister Jo brings to the song, giving the song a "push-pull" feel between the two personalities, is not present in the performance. However, since Beth begins the song with the words "Let's pretend," the performer in stand-alone, out-of-context performance can also pretend that Jo is present onstage with her.

The Light in the Piazza

The Light in the Piazza

"She doesn't necessarily realize that she's growing or flourishing, but she knows there are things within her that were like locked doors that are now opening."
—Katie Clarke, Clara in the original Broadway production

CHARACTER: Clara

MUSIC AND LYRICS: Adam Guettel

BOOK: Craig Lucas

BASED ON: A novella by Elizabeth Spencer

SETTING: Florence, Italy

BROADWAY PREMIERE: 2005

CLASSIFICATION: Lyric (mezzo-soprano)

RANGE: 

TESSITURA: Low at the beginning of the piece, then sustained at the top of the staff

TIME: 3:08

PLOT: A young American tourist, Clara, accompanied by her mother, visits Florence, Italy. She meets and falls in love with a young Italian man (Fabrizio); her mother (Margaret) opposes the relationship for reasons only revealed to the audience in time.

The score has been described as neoromantic, with a heavier orchestration better suited to an opera score than a Broadway musical. Still, the melodic phrases and lyric poetry are consistent with traditional musical theatre stage tradition. It is a very interesting score, with shifting harmonies and complex rhythms capturing the style and mood of the musical play. The neoromantic musical style is also well suited to the fantastical stage mood that is expressed from the opening curtain as the piazza in Florence awakens and comes to life ("Statues and Stories"). The magic of Florence is a wonderful backdrop for this story.

CHARACTER: We do not know very much about Clara as the show begins, but we can see that Clara's mother (Margaret) is for some reason extremely protective of her daughter. Margaret can lack patience with the girl, which further creates a shaky relationship between mother and daughter. We also suspect that there is some emotional instability with Clara, and we find that she experienced a head trauma when she was a child, resulting in symptoms of mental imbalance.

CONTEXT: Act II; Margaret takes Clara to Rome to distract her from her infatuation with Fabrizio, with no success. They return to Florence. Clara accuses her mother of ignoring her needs. Margaret replies that Clara makes things up. The tearful argument escalates to the point that Clara blurts out, "Daddy doesn't love you." Finally, the confrontation between mother and daughter culminates in Margaret slapping her daughter, and Clara's response is to sing and try to express her feelings with "The Light in the Piazza."

CONTENT: The song begins softly, emotionally. The four measures of introduction in the accompaniment have a "shimmering" quality that perfectly captures the elusive, transparent quality of this Florentine light, with arpeggiated repeated figures of treble against bass. Clara does not look at or think about statues or stories, she says. That is not what she sees, but she knows the meaning of the light, as she sings the lovely, repeated melodic phrase "the light in the piazza." She describes the quality of this light as the vocal line moves with more momentum, becoming more active, with greater intervals as her enthusiasm grows and the orchestra responds to her joy with more rhythmic activity. The changes of meter, from 4/4 to 2/4 to 3/8 to 4/8, with wide intervals, lend an unsettled quality to the song. All she knows is that she has something now that she has never possessed before, as she sings an ascending line reminiscent of the opening phrase, but expanded up to sustained D, E, and F-sharp at the top of the staff. "And sad is now happy. That is all I see," she sings, and then she repeats the motivic phrase "the light on the piazza," expressing the text with more enthusiasm to describe it. "It's everywhere," Clara sings and repeats, before she says his name, Fabrizio, in arching, broad phrases sung higher on the staff. Finally, she puts her thoughts together, singing once again the motive—"the light in the piazza. My love," sung softer and slower in the lower register, with an awareness of the powerful feelings that she has discovered inside.

VOICE: This song captures the character and situation of a young girl who is able to articulate the discovery of newfound feelings. It is such an important moment in the show, putting into words and music what Margaret has lost and Clara, the daughter, has gained. Clara has had such a troubled and turbulent past, but all she knows is that she was sad and now is happy. She attributes that transformation, she tells her mother, to the light on the piazza—and Fabrizio. Only these words and the power of music and the voice can capture the moment. The youthful voice must be full of innocence, but also full of wonder and the awe as she discovers the feelings that transform her. As the song builds in range and emotional power, it is important that Clara's voice is not forced or pushed in any way to achieve these dynamic changes. The opening vocal lines, beginning with "I don't see a miracle," are quite low, extending down below middle C to a low A, and cannot be forced in vocal production.

BEHIND THE SCENES WITH THE ARTISTS: KATIE CLARKE, CLARA IN THE ORIGINAL BROADWAY PRODUCTION

Katie's story is remarkable. She was a musical theatre major in a Texas college, then suddenly she was "thrust into a Broadway show," *The Light in the Piazza.* It was "a dream come true," but it was also filled with challenges. "I very much recall a lot of loneliness during that time. I was very green. I didn't know anyone in New York or how to get around the city, much less what eight shows a week felt like," she says. The answer, ultimately, was to learn how to stay "true to what I felt as Katie, and let that translate to my work onstage as Clara. Just as I was learning and growing into a professional actress, Clara was learning and flourishing in Italy. Clara connected to Italy—the beauty of it, the art, the people and culture—and it helped her to open up and grow as a woman, and simultaneously, every night, the Broadway stage was doing that for me." Therefore, her understanding of the role of Clara and the connection to the character was based on a truth that Katie could understand. She was able to "trust that and allow the show to change and vary every night, because I was still being true to Clara," she said. "My director, Bart Sher, told me from day one that Clara is going to be your best friend in all of this, and he was exactly right." In approaching the singing of the song, Katie suggests that it is important to "be as honest and real as possible." Actors must refrain "from 'performing,' per se, and just need to personalize Clara's story. Actors need to know the given circumstances, which are that this is a girl who has never been inspired or encouraged the way that Italy has inspired and encouraged her. She sees deeply, not just what's on the surface, and we as the audience watch her unlock those areas within herself in real time onstage. It hasn't been figured out beforehand; she's discovering it all right before our eyes."

The song "The Light in the Piazza" is another discovery for Clara, one that happens before our eyes, not something she's thought about for days and figured out how to communicate ahead of time. She discovers the truth as she sings. "The moment before is an argument with her mother, and when Margaret slaps her, she's not stung, but more centered. The first chord of the music happens at the same moment as the slap, and Clara can begin to unlock some of the things she struggled to communicate before." It is all new to her. "She doesn't necessarily realize that she's growing or flourishing, but she knows there are things within her that were like locked doors that are now opening. It's very internal and very genuine. When she looks at things it is without judgment or opinion. She simply takes it in, just like a child would. That is what makes her childlike, not the injury necessarily, but the fact that she's seeing and discovering things, quite literally, for the first time."

Will You?

Grey Gardens

"[Edie] just had to use all of her strength to get past the emotional turmoil that she was dealing with."
—Christine Ebersole, the original Edith Bouvier

CHARACTER: Edith Bouvier

MUSIC: Scott Frankel

LYRICS: Michael Korie

BOOK: Doug Wright

BASED ON: The 1975 documentary *Grey Gardens*, about the lives of Edith Bouvier Beale and her daughter, Little Edie

SETTING: East Hampton, New York, set in two time periods, 1941 and 1973

BROADWAY PREMIERE: 2006

CLASSIFICATION: Soprano lyric

RANGE: 

TESSITURA: Middle staff

TIME: 3:20

PLOT: *Grey Gardens* is based on a 1975 documentary about the Beales, the aunt and cousin of Jacqueline Kennedy, set in the family mansion in East Hampton, New York. The show is in two parts, documenting their journey from wealthy, social aristocrats to eventual financial and social decline in isolation.

The composer was attracted to the project in a statement "because of the unique blend of humor, heartache and humanity." When the "real Little Edie" found out about the idea of Grey Gardens being turned into a musical prior to her death in 2002, she said, "I am thrilled about *Grey Gardens* the musical! My whole life was music and song! It made up for *everything*! Thrilled! I have all of Mother's sheet music and her songs she sang. Even with all I eventually didn't have, my life was joyous." The "everything" that Little Edie referred to was the constant struggle between her and her mother, and the challenge of living with her mother after 1952 (following the death of Edie's wealthy grandfather) in poverty.

CHARACTER: Edith (Edie's mother) is forty-eight years old in 1941, and she is described as "American royalty." For Edith, a fiercely attractive woman who sports a blue Japanese kimono and a turban when first seen, times are good. She likes to sing, accompanied by her friend Gould. Her speech is sprinkled with French phrases, and she is witty and clearly delighted with her many opportunities for entertaining in her home. The grounds and gardens around the mansion are lavish.

CONTEXT: Toward the end of the first act, during the time when they enjoyed high financial and social status, there is a terrible fight between mother and daughter. "When I go to New York, I am NEVER coming back!" declares Little Edie. Meanwhile, guests are arriving at the mansion. "Cars are pulling up outside," says Brooks. "That's Grey Gardens for you. Those on the outside clamoring to get in, those on the inside dying to leave."

Edith struggles to regain her composure as she dedicates the song she is about to sing to her daughter. But her daughter, suitcase in hand, is leaving Grey Gardens. She is a free spirit and cannot wait to get away. Meanwhile, Edith is watching her good life in Grey Gardens slip away. Her daughter doesn't want to stay, her husband is gone, and she is in danger of losing everything, including her "friends"—even her accompanist partner Gould. Edith welcomes the guests as they arrive, trying not to show her inner turmoil in response to the present situation. She announces the song as "one of our all-time favorites, 'Will You?'"

CONTENT: The song is written in verses, and is marked at the top "cantabile, in 2." The texture of the piece is homophonic (chords supporting melody), and the accompaniment has a rhythmic pattern that is a quarter note followed by a half note, then another quarter note, which is repeated each measure. The melody is unusual and haunting. After the second verse, there is dialogue spoken over an instrumental verse. As she talks about her daughter, "Little Edie," in further dialogue, her delivery is clearly forced as Edith struggles to keep her composure under the given circumstances. One more verse is sung, with the apt text "When wild geese of autumn fly, will you?" (after the "flight" of her daughter) to the final measures, marked "broader," followed by "rallentando," and then "slower," to a fermata as she sustains the penultimate note, before a caesura, and finally, "Will you?" This question, which is repeated by Edie throughout the song, ties the piece together. Each time it is sung, "you" is sustained.

VOICE: The song is not challenging as far as range is concerned, but the piece is most effective if the voice is a little impassive, not too expressive, even though so much has happened around her. Edith is tightly wound, and it is wise to sing the song trying to keep it all inside, sung with restraint. All of the longer sustained tones in the song are on the *u* vowel of "will you?" which has a haunting sound in itself when sustained and not emoted or forced.

BEHIND THE SCENES WITH THE ARTISTS: CHRISTINE EBERSOLE, THE ORIGINAL EDITH BOUVIER

I asked Broadway actress Christine Ebersole how she thought Edith managed to gather her energy to overcome such stress to sing "Will You?" under the given circumstances. Christine replied that "although Edith knew what the stakes were, she also knew that she didn't have any choice but to push through. Essentially, Edith had no choice. Her back was against the wall. She just had to use her strength to get past the emotional turmoil that she was dealing with."

PART TWO

Mezzo-Alto

Anything Goes

Anything Goes

"She is the center of the wheel and everything swirls around her. And when she comes onstage, you know that something is going to happen."
—Sutton Foster, describing the character of Reno

CHARACTER: Reno Sweeney

MUSIC AND LYRICS: Cole Porter, revised by Howard Lindsay and Russel Crouse

BOOK: Guy Bolton and P. G. Wodehouse

SETTING: An ocean liner (SS *American*), 1930s

BROADWAY PREMIERE: 1934

CLASSIFICATION: Alto belt

RANGE:

TESSITURA: Within the octave

TIME: 1:40

PLOT: The story, a simple one, revolves around complications aboard an ocean liner involving Billy Crocker, a young Wall Street businessman, who falls in love with a girl he meets in a taxi on his way to board the liner to bid bon voyage to his boss. His boss is on his way to a business deal in London. Also aboard the ship is Reno Sweeney, who Billy has known for a long time. He sees Reno as merely an old friend, while she has romantic feelings for him. Also on the trip are gangsters using secret identities along with members of the British upper crust, making for an interesting (and farcical) trip for all.

CHARACTER: Reno is a former evangelist turned nightclub singer. She is brassy and sassy and has not yet met the man who is her match. Although she is attracted to Billy, she ends up marrying Lord Evelyn Oakleigh, a wealthy, stuffy Englishman.

CONTEXT: In act I, Billy Crocker, stowing away, is disguised as a sailor working on board. The crew, however, has realized he is not a sailor and is about to give him up. Reno, helping Billy out, creates a new disguise for him, which includes a "beard" made from clippings from the prized dog of high-society-member Mrs. Harcourt. Reno sings "Anything Goes," summing up the outrageous circumstances.

CONTENT: Although the text is dated, Cole Porter's lyrics are witty, smart, and to the point—consistent with Reno's character. It is important for the singer to look up all topical references and know what Porter is referring to throughout the song, whether or not two verses or more are sung. The song has a swing and a swagger because of the syncopation in the melody. The accompaniment plays a steady and strongly supportive four quarter-beats each measure, and does not double the melody line. The verse each time is in the key of A-flat minor (seven flats in the key signature), while the chorus, marked "relaxed two," is in the key of A-flat major. Following the chorus, Reno moves into a strongly delivered short bridge of nine measures as she sings: "The world has gone mad today," before moving into the final verse-chorus. A "dance break," when all onstage break into a dance section, delineates the song, and if the song is performed as a stand-alone performance, this is where the song can conclude (before the dance break).

VOICE: An even belt (not stronger in one particular part of the range); a variety of dynamics are important in the vocal delivery. Although the performer can display an awesome belting voice in this number (since it does not go too high or too low), Reno's strong character will enunciate the text clearly with a forceful delivery. The singer would be wise not to fully belt all of the phrases but still remain in the chest voice throughout. In parts of the song where the performer chooses not to powerfully belt in the lower range, the text still must be spit out and delivered with attitude. Porter is very clever to voice the many turns of phrases in the lower range with syncopated rhythms, while the repeated phrase, "God knows, anything goes" is in the "high belt" area (with a sustained B-flat) and can be projected fully with strength easily at that pitch level.

BEHIND THE SCENES WITH THE ARTISTS: SUTTON FOSTER, RENO IN THE 2011 BROADWAY REVIVAL

Sutton Foster sees Reno Sweeney "as a fast-talking, brassy girl from the thirties right out of a movie. But she has a heart and desires. She is someone who has seemingly everything: her own nightclub, a fabulous lifestyle, but she doesn't have love. It seems silly, but she doesn't have that one thing—but everyone loves her and knows her. She walks into a room and everyone goes 'Reno Sweeney, there she is!' and she's like, 'Yeah, that's right!'"

Ms. Foster sees Reno as sort of a philosopher in the song, because "she has her own point of view." Speaking of portraying the role of Reno, Ms. Foster observes: "She is the center of the wheel and everything swirls around her. And when she comes onstage, you know that something is going to happen."

While Ms. Foster is fully aware of all of the great performers who have sung this role, including Ethel Merman and Patti LuPone, she made a conscious decision to make the role her own and not view any previous performances. She says that it is never a good idea to try to replicate or copy a great portrayal of the past.

Ms. Foster has taught some students at NYU's Tisch School of the Arts, and she gives students the following advice: "Be yourself, be authentic, and find your own voice. It is hard to do when you are eighteen, nineteen, twenty years old, but don't try to emulate anyone else's career, blaze your own path. Your uniqueness and singularity is your own strength."[1]

Rob Fisher, Conductor of the Broadway Revival, approaches reworking a classic musical by researching the "music of the period, and what was going on in the creator's lives." He says, "The best freshening of old music is finding out what seemed so contemporary when it was written." Rob also comments that he often notices "how people may have diminished the freshness of songs . . . rather than looking for ways to amp it up." For "Anything Goes," students should "know something about Ethel Merman as well as Cole Porter. There is so much valuable information notated right there on the page."

So Far

Allegro

"This show is experimental in its approach to musical theatre, and is reflective in the functions of the characters, like Beulah."

—Susan Schulman, director of the 1994 Lincoln Center Encores! revival

CHARACTER: Beulah

MUSIC: Richard Rodgers

BOOK AND LYRICS: Oscar Hammerstein II

SETTING: The 1920s, before the Great Depression

BROADWAY PREMIERE: 1947

CLASSIFICATION: Lyric mezzo or soprano, lyric

RANGE: 

TESSITURA: Lower middle staff

TIME: 3:50

PLOT: The story of this show follows the main character growing up in a small town, adjusting to an increasingly modern world. At the opening of the show, we witness the birth of Joe Jr. in 1905. The father is Dr. Joseph Taylor. Joe grows in front of our eyes, scene by scene. He meets Jenny and they date in high school. When Joe prepares to leave town to attend college, Joe Sr. hopes that his son will someday return home to help his father with his medical practice.

CHARACTER: Joe Jr. is a smart young man from a small town who has gone away to college. At the college, both Charlie (the popular star football player) and Joe are premed students, and the star athlete clearly needs Joe's help to survive academically at school. This makes Joe indispensable, and

Charlie shepherds Joe into one of the most popular fraternities in the college, Charlie's fraternity house. Because of Charlie's popularity, Joe is eager to do whatever his friend wants. Beulah is an experienced girl that Charlie chooses for Joe for a blind date. She falls for Joe on their double date (with Charlie and his girlfriend), but she becomes angry with him when he falls asleep after they kiss.

CONTEXT: Back home, Jenny's wealthy father encourages her to meet other boys. Away at college, Joe meets other students and makes new friends. He goes on a blind date with Beulah, who is initially enthusiastic about their potential for romance, especially since they are drinking together from his flask. They find themselves alone in the woods: "You're not that type of girl. You're romantic—like me." "Say! I'm just beginning to get you!" Beulah says, and she proceeds to sing "So Far" as they stroll. After the first refrain, Joe goes to kiss his date. However, Joe is unable to keep Jenny from his thoughts, and he draws away. Beulah throws her arms around Joe and kisses him "with such verve that it throws him on his back." As she finishes the song, Beulah realizes that Joe has fallen asleep, humiliating her.

CONTENT: The opening introduction is marked "moderato," and it moves in cut time (two beats per measure) with a syncopated rhythm in the vocal line. This gives a swing feel to the music, and the chords in the accompaniment mirror the quarter-note rhythm of the vocal line. At measure nine the accompaniment will double the voice line. The dynamic in the accompaniment is marked "piano," and the rhythmic pattern is four quarter beats per measure, composed in quarter-note vertical chords in the opening (verse) section. At the refrain, the music is still marked "piano," and the tempo is marked "slowly, in four beats." All four lines of text begin with the same word, "no," as in: "*No* fond recollections" and "*No* scene to recall," meaning that they have no past, and yet, Beulah intimates that they may have a future . . . The refrain melody is straightforward, mostly in quarter-note rhythms sung in a deliberate manner (in 1920s style), in such a way as to leave no doubt that, although this is not a blatantly seductive song or a cute "beating around the bush" song, it is above all, a *suggestive* song. The text "But now I'm face to face with you," marked "pianissimo" and "gradually crescendo and marcato," underlines the suggestive flavor. After the refrain, the song weaves through some chromatic inflections and does not pause before coming to an interlude. Before this interlude, there is literally no pause in the song. After the interlude, there is a repetition of the melody and text (and dynamic markings) to the end, with the last phrases signaled by a caesura after "And now we can look forward to . . ."

VOICE: It is best to deliver the "setup" introduction with rhythm and swing, and there are a number of sustained tones at the upper C and B-flat of the staff, as well as the lower middle C. The refrain, however, requires more of a syllabic delivery, with the performer still "connecting" the melody line with sustained dotted half-note rhythmic patterns. The singer will require a good, strong D at the top of the staff, which is sung in an octave leap from the D below. The D comes suddenly, almost as if Beulah is trying to get Joe's attention. The delivery is sung deliberately by the experienced and confident girl. Observe all markings in the music and the importance of applying *meaning* to each directive, which comes out of character and situation. In the final phrases of "But now I'm face to face with you," the accompaniment dynamic is marked "ppp," "gradually crescendo," "marcato," and eventually "dolce." It is important to think about the *dramatic purpose and intent* for each marking. After an interlude, there is an exact repeat of the last section of the refrain, with the same markings. The song concludes with Beulah singing a final, sustained (for eight beats with fermata) B-flat in the middle of the staff.

BEHIND THE SCENES WITH THE ARTISTS: SUSAN SCHULMAN, DIRECTOR

Director Susan Schulman notes that the show is experimental in nature because of its subject matter, the Greek chorus, and the characters in the play, which do not conform to the traditional functions of musical theatre characterizations. For instance, secondary female and male characters (e.g., Ado Annie in *Oklahoma!*) traditionally are placed in the show for comic relief and are given the upbeat character songs ("I Can't Say No" and "Everything's Up to Date in Kansas City.") Beulah is a character who is secondary and is not the ingénue, but she fits into the story line and sings a poignant song, "So Far." She realizes that there is no hope for the future of their relationship and yet holds out hope for Joe loving her. She knows that she is not going to get him, and so the song is poignant and is tinged with sadness as she tries to arouse him in vain.

An English Teacher

Bye Bye Birdie

"Dick Van Dyke in the original production had a personality that was sympathetically naïve."
—Charles Strouse, composer

CHARACTER: Rosie Alvarez

MUSIC: Charles Strouse

LYRICS: Lee Adams

BOOK: Michael Stewart

BASED ON: Inspired by the phenomenon of Elvis Presley

SETTING: New York and Sweet Apple, Ohio

PREMIERE: 1960

CLASSIFICATION: Alto; lyric with temperament

RANGE: 

TESSITURA: Low to middle of staff

TIME: 2:00

PLOT: The title *Bye Bye Birdie* refers to the mythical pop star Conrad Birdie's being drafted into the Army and leaving to serve at the onset of his meteoric rise to success. Birdie is managed by Albert in New York. Albert is thirty-three years old and manages (and writes songs for) just one artist, Conrad Birdie, and it appears that he may now lose his only client to the draft. In addition, Albert still owes Birdie a $50,000 guarantee on his contract. Before entering the Army, Birdie (loosely based on Elvis Presley) will kiss a girl on the Ed Sullivan variety show as a publicity stunt. The girl, Kim MacAfee, is a young fan from Sweet Apple, Ohio.

CHARACTER: Rosie is Albert's girlfriend. She has been with Albert for many years, as girlfriend, secretary, confidant, and surrogate mother. She is loyal, faithful, and patient (for the most part). She dreams of their future as a married, settled-down couple. However, as the show begins and we see in the dialogue how long Albert has taken Rosie for granted, we can see her frustration with him and understand how she feels.

CONTEXT: The song "An English Teacher" is near the beginning of the show, after the opening production number, "Going Steady," followed by dialogue between Albert and Rosie. Rosie Alvarez is acting as secretary for the now-in-jeopardy eight-year-old business, which is named Almaelou. The name is a combination of the names of Albert; his meddling mother, Mae; and their deceased dog, Lou (Al-Mae-Lou). Rosie had hoped and wished they would have a future together, but at this point she is fed up with working for Albert for almost no pay and waiting for him to make a commitment. The situation is not a happy one, but the lines should be played for laughs to avoid there being too much of a serious tone during their discussion at the beginning of the show.

CONTENT: This song is a terrific example of using music and the articulation of a song to delineate and clarify emotions. After a "furious" introduction of repeated staccato quarter-note rhythms, with the tempo marked "angrily, in two," Rosie begins the song with two verses of clipped words with an energized delivery. An irritated Rosie is sure that once Conrad is drafted Albert will be free to quit show business, with its lack of job security, and get on with his (and their) life. However, Albert reveals that since he is in debt he can't quit the business yet. After two of these verses, punctuated by Albert's weary lines: "It takes time to go into business," Rosie begins a new section, "It was only a sideline" (singing in energized half-note triplet rhythms), reminding him of what he said he intended to do (instead of "becoming a music bum"). The following section (chorus) begins with the lyric line "An English teacher," as Rosie sings of her long-held dream of being "Mrs. Albert Peterson, the English teacher's wife," while the key modulates from D major to G-flat major. Following these lyric lines, she recaps what it has been like over the last years in a recitative-like bridge back in D major to underline her concern and irritation ("It was goodbye, Geoffrey Chaucer; Hello, William Morris"). Then, finally, she repeats the chorus that begins with "An English teacher" (again in G-flat major), once more hoping that Albert will change his mind and listen to her. The truth of the song is that, even though she is being treated badly, she still cares for him, and still dreams of their future together.

VOICE: At the beginning, during the staccato-like delivery, the range is low, and we hear anger and hurt in the voice (low G-sharp and A below middle C). Rosie thought that Albert was going to go to NYU and get a degree, instead of following a different path of writing one hit song and managing Conrad Birdie. The delivery is clipped, none of the pitches are sustained, and the singer needs to appear to be in charge of the rhythmic momentum (not following the pianist). This means that the singer leads the momentum from the entrance of each line. The singer cannot sing the opening section too hard or heavy in the chest voice, because it will sound too different in color, too vocally schizophrenic in its contrast with the lyric sections with the line "An English teacher." When Rosie is singing the lyric sections, the voice takes on more of a warm quality as she dreams of what their life could be. But it still needs to be sung with the same voice, with a different color.

BEHIND THE SCENES WITH THE ARTISTS: CHARLES STROUSE, THE COMPOSER

Mr. Strouse agreed with me that in the opening dialogue between Albert and Rosie, it appears that Rosie has been taken advantage of, and she is basically a "doormat." She has been his secretary for very little pay (and little appreciation), and you would think that she would have left long ago. Also, Albert's strong-willed mother is still on the scene. Mr. Strouse said that while all of this is true, Dick Van Dyke in the original production had the type of personality that was sympathetically naïve, so the scene kept the audience wanting and hoping that he and Chita Rivera would stay together. He was flawed, but the audience liked him.

Is It Really Me?

110 in the Shade

"The song dictates all. It is lyrical, yet makes practical sense . . . just like the character of Lizzie herself."

—Karen Ziemba, Lizzie in the Lincoln Center revival of *110 in the Shade*

CHARACTER: Lizzie

MUSIC: Harvey Schmidt

LYRICS: Tom Jones

BOOK: N. Richard Nash

BASED ON: Nash's play *The Rainmaker* (1954)

SETTING: The town of Three Point in the southwestern United States, 1936

BROADWAY PREMIERE: 1963

CLASSIFICATION: Mezzo lyric

RANGE: 

TESSITURA: Warmly in lower register, pickups at top-space E (lightly sung)

TIME: 2:24

PLOT: It is the Fourth of July in 1936 in a southwestern town that has been scorched by a blistering heat wave for many days with no relief from the heat, and no rain. A "rainmaker," Bill Starbuck, comes to town, and with bold promises guarantees rain within twenty-four hours for one hundred dollars.

CHARACTER: Lizzie is a twenty-seven- to thirty-seven-year-old unmarried woman who is intelligent, witty, and sympathetic. Her family loves to have her around, as she is a fabulous cook and homemaker, but they also know that it is only right for her to have a husband and her own home. At the beginning of the show Lizzie is portrayed as a realist who has come to terms with her lack of romantic effect on men and her limited prospects for a husband. Sometimes she is her own worst enemy in meeting men, because she is a straightforward woman who speaks her truth. The local sheriff, File, a lonely man, is interested in Lizzie, but he is driven away by her straightforward manner. The script says that she "yearns for romance" and has a "courageous approach to search for it."

CONTEXT: In act II, scene 4 in Starbuck's wagon (the "Rainwagon"), there is a scene with Lizzie and the charismatic Starbuck as he encourages her to see herself anew as a beautiful young woman. He is able to bring her to a new level of confidence. They embrace, and kiss. She confides in him, telling a story about when she was twelve. A boy kissed her on a dare, "and from that day on," she says, "I knew I was plain." "Are you plain?" he asks. "No, I'm beautiful," Lizzie realizes, and she then sings: "Is It Really Me?"

CONTENT: After a lovely instrumental introduction under the dialogue, with simple underlying chords of support for two measures, the opening melody is repeated twice. The song moves forward with emotional momentum in a bridge with the text "Moments ago I was alone, hoping that this could be," emphasizing triplet rhythms. When Lizzie comes to the end of the vocal line "And I'm no longer lonely," the chord progression and the tuning of the melody line, transitioning to the final chorus, is compelling, and it should be recognized as special by the performer. The song returns to a recapitulation of the opening phrases. "Is it really me? Is it really true?" she asks. Then strongly, she sings, "Suddenly I'm beautiful, all because of you." This line is repeated, and then the singer takes control of the last line, finishing with a fermata on a B in the middle of the staff, pausing, and leading up to a final D at the upper end of the song's range (upper D).

VOICE: This song requires the singer to show the lyricism and range of her voice while conveying a dramatic transformation in the scene. After all of the doubts and negative feelings she has had about herself, including her failure to find someone who appreciates her and loves her, she wonders aloud if it can it be possible: "Is it really me?" The opening intervals, as she poses her questions, is challenging, requiring managing tricky intervals and some quick register changes between chest and head voice. The song begins at the low A below middle C, and sweeps up to a high E natural at the top of the staff in the first measures. It should also be pointed out that the highest pitch (E natural) is voiced on the unstressed second syllable ("real-*ly*") in the phrase, so it cannot be punched. The uninflected syllables need freedom and must be sung lightly without constriction. With the challenge of singing the wide intervals, especially at the beginning of the song, the singer needs to sing the vocal line evenly and in tune. It is not always easy to keep the voice even at the top of the vocal range. But the performer also needs to voice consonants and not distort the vowels, because textual clarity is important. The words "beautiful" and "you" are difficult to sing at the high range because the *u* vowel (sung on the sustained D at the end of the song) wants to spread open or pinch closed with tension. It is important that the singer be conscious of keeping the jaw free and the breath support anchored while rounding the lips.

BEHIND THE SCENES WITH THE ARTISTS: KAREN ZIEMBA, LIZZIE IN THE LINCOLN CENTER REVIVAL OF *110 IN THE SHADE*

Alluding to the fact that at the beginning of the show it appears that Lizzie has accepted her fate as an "old maid," in this scene, on the contrary, Karen states that "the tables have turned. Someone [Starbuck] has made Lizzie see herself through their eyes, and she now realizes she's a beautiful human being capable of giving love to, and receiving love from, a man. Lizzie may be almost dizzy in a swoon-like state, but the words she speaks are clear and practical as she describes her feelings. The song dictates all. It is lyrical, yet makes practical sense . . . just like the character of Lizzie herself."

Composer Harvey Schmidt explains that in this important love scene, an experience Lizzie has never had before, she looks into Starbuck's eyes and expresses herself in the first positive words she has spoken. "It is evening, and she sings this sweeping, grand melody to him. She was on a journey of harsh disappointment and frustration culminating in 'Old Maid' at the end of act I, and now she has two men interested in her, one who has told her that she's beautiful."

Old Maid

110 in the Shade

"The song has a fabulous arc ..."
—Karen Ziemba, Lizzie in the Lincoln Center revival of *110 in the Shade*

CHARACTER: Lizzie

MUSIC: Harvey Schmidt

LYRICS: Tom Jones

BOOK: N. Richard Nash

BASED ON: Nash's play *The Rainmaker* (1954)

SETTING: The town of Three Point in the southwestern United States, 1936

BROADWAY PREMIERE: 1963

CLASSIFICATION: Mezzo lyric

RANGE: 

TESSITURA: Middle voice, but sustained above the staff at conclusion of the song

TIME: 3:06

PLOT AND CHARACTER: See "Is It Really Me?"

CONTEXT: File tries to sweet-talk Lizzie by using a more straightforward approach. After all, everyone in town knows that she is looking for a husband. He opens up to her in the song before "Old Maid" with the straightforward duet "A Man and a Woman," telling her he believes that a man and a woman can be so close that "they almost become like one." Although he has some romantic ideas that he hopes will woo her, File is more of a realist, Lizzie a dreamer. In response, Lizzie's straightforward comments drive him away as she faces the possibility of a lonely future. She sings the affecting song "Old Maid," which closes act I.

CONTENT: The introduction is simply two bars in the accompaniment, with functional chords played on beats two and four. It is marked "not too slowly—in 4." The song starts very simply, with four quarter-note rhythms per measure and the text syllabically set. The dynamic at the start of each of the beginning two verses is marked "piano." Young singers will frequently dot some of these quarter notes, but the three solid quarter beats per measure gives the piece a weariness that suggests the oppressive heat. "Old maid!" Lizzie exclaims, then sings the words with a sustained cry. She sings two verses, each strophe closing with her own admonishment: "Old maid!" In the verses she addresses the pointlessness of visiting relatives on trips intended to help her find her a husband. She advances through a short eight-measure transition, changing keys ("Be kind to your poor aunt Lizzie," she sings sarcastically). In the next section ("piu mosso—in 2"), she complains that her dress is too tight, her skin is hot and irritated with the heat. It's turning to night; there is no sign of breeze, her clothes seem to be on fire. "Why won't it rain?" she sings, sustaining an E at the top of the staff. "Please let it rain!" Then there is a fermata rest and a break, toward a broad (in 4), arching, sustained high G above the staff: "O God, don't let me live and die alone!" There are syncopated and accented figures in the accompaniment to bring needed momentum to the piece as the notes are sustained by the singer above the staff. The cutoff (blackout) is the punctuation of two abruptly accented eighth-note rhythms.

VOICE: The song begins softly, as Lizzie sings: "Always being one. Never being two," as she builds the song carefully, propelled forward by the text and the circumstances, and aided as well by the marked dynamics, tempo, and articulations. While the text is set more syllabically in the opening of the piece, as the song moves forward to its climactic ending, a strong performance is about driving the momentum of the song forward, negotiating the higher pitches, and the emotional turbulence that must be conveyed. The sustained pitches at the top of the staff are operatic in their demands and passionate expression. All of the frustration, the heat, the small minded townspeople, her family give rise to her need to let loose by the end of act I, vocally and dramatically.

BEHIND THE SCENES WITH THE ARTISTS: KAREN ZIEMBA, LIZZIE IN THE LINCOLN CENTER REVIVAL

Ms. Ziemba told me that "Lizzie is jarred by being dismissed or deserted by her brother, father, and beau-hopeful, File. She finally comes to the realization that she may, in fact, be a spinster for the rest of her life." Karen comments on Lizzie's state of mind: "She is anxious, yet clear-eyed about her plight." The music "is agitated and becomes lush." Karen says about the lyrics and music: "They totally drive the character's emotions." Finally, Karen explained why "Old Maid" is an excellent example of great musical theatre songwriting: "It builds right along with 'Lizzie's' emotions until she breaks down and screams to the heavens 'Oh, God don't let me live and die alone.' It's very simple. The woman has so much to give but keeps coming up empty and is at the end of her rope. It's like a simmer turning to a boil and then exploding. The song has a fabulous arc."

Composer Harvey Schmidt: The song occurs at the end of the first act at a crucial point of the show. Mr. Schmidt gives much credit for the creation of the scene to the writer of the play *The Rainmaker* and the book for the show, Richard Nash, and to the lyricist, Tom Jones. "Tom gave the outline for the spot first, word for word, and we went from there." Lizzie has just had a fight with her brother, who tells her that she is not really a woman in the true sense of the word. The lack of moisture and little hope of rain on the horizon is symbolic of Lizzie's chances of becoming a wife and mother, which are also drying up. Mr. Schmidt vividly recalls that the production team wanted a red sunset as a backdrop, and Lizzie was alone onstage in a red dress. She begins the song in almost a childlike simple musical expression, and then she vocally surprises in a startling outburst that is momentous in its unexpected force. That is the intended effect.

Not a Day Goes By

Merrily We Roll Along

"When Beth sings this song in act I, she is absolutely furious."
—Susan Schulman, director of the 1994 off-Broadway revival

CHARACTER: Beth

MUSIC AND LYRICS: Stephen Sondheim

BOOK: George Furth

BASED ON: The 1934 play of the same name by George Kaufman and Moss Hart

SETTING: Contemporary suburbia

BROADWAY PREMIERE: 1966

CLASSIFICATION: Mezzo lyric "belt" song

RANGE: 

TESSITURA: Low, below the staff

TIME: 3:50

PLOT: Franklin Shepherd, a former composer of Broadway musicals, now is a producer of Hollywood movies. The show starts when he is at the height of his fame, having given up his friends and family to reach his position of status, and moves backward in time.

The show begins with a number sung by the ensemble in a frivolous (but still cynical) commentary on the "journey" of life, "See the Pretty Countryside." Soon the ensemble is singing the praises of Frank, the golden boy. Frank has charisma, talent, and wealth, and also possesses a gorgeous wife, Beth, and a young son. He is perfect: "He's polite and considerate, rain—or shine."

CHARACTER: Director Susan Schulman observes that Beth is a naïve character, especially before she marries Frank. She is very much in love with him but finds herself on the outside of Frank's circle, which includes Chip and Mary.

CONTEXT: While the year is 1974 at the beginning of the show, the year is now 1966 in the story. Frank's wife Beth is divorcing him, and they fight over the custody of their young son in the courthouse. Beth knows that Frank is cheating on her as she sings this song. In response, Frank is consoled by his friends, who assure him that the divorce is the best thing that could ever happen to him. Beth's line before the song begins is: "You won't like what you hear this afternoon."

CONTENT: The instrumental introduction to the song consists of nine whole-note chordal clusters, all sustained (fermata). Beth begins (marked "slowly") to sing tentatively, with the main melodic motive, singing, "Not a day goes by," sustaining the final note of the motive while the orchestra's line moves, which it repeatedly does on the sustained sung tones. When the voice moves, sustained chordal support is heard in the accompaniment. The refrain is repeated: "As the days go by …" The meter changes from common time (4/4) to 6/4 in some of the phrases. She asks herself: "When does it end?" which is followed by repeated triplets of words and rhythm to hammer home this idea of mindless and incessant repetition. The first repetition of triplets is a stream of present participles, each triplet ending with the words "forgett*ing*," "think*ing*," "sweat*ing*," "curs*ing*," "cry*ing*," "turn*ing*," "reach*ing*," "wak*ing*," and finally, "dy*ing*." The sustained phrase "Not a day goes by" is composed on different pitch levels. After a number of these sustained phrases at different levels, the singer returns to the repeated triplet-rhythm patterns once more, this time with the text "day after day" repeated over and over. This pattern again has the effect of an incessant, almost deadening torture of repetition, before the song ends with the slow, repeated, stretched "Not a day goes by," again at varying levels of pitch.

VOICE: This is a very difficult song to sing due to a number of factors. Because of the given circumstances in the scene, the emotions are running high, while the singer needs to sustain tones that are higher in range and also needs to possess vocal control while displaying emotional turmoil.

To shape the musical phrases, the performer must inflect the important syllables in the text. The singer should linger just a little on the word "day" as the phrase: "Not a *day* goes by" so that the word or syllable is inflected, which will give the musical phrase a shape. Each word in the repeated triplet patterns should also be properly inflected. When in doubt where the proper stress should be placed, the performer should practice by speaking the text to see where the natural stress lies. If all syllables have the same stress, the triplets will sound mechanical in their delivery. There is another important feature of the song: since the repetition of the phrase motive ("Not a day goes by") is sung at different pitch levels, these phrases are challenging to sing in tune. The tuning is challenging because the melody is not doubled in the accompaniment, and the pitch, with its composed accidentals, needs to be carefully negotiated to avoid faulty intonation. The last "day after day" triplet repetition can be accelerated as the final repetitions unfold.

BEHIND THE SCENES WITH THE ARTISTS: SUSAN SCHULMAN, DIRECTOR OF THE 1994 OFF-BROADWAY REVIVAL

Ms. Schulman says that when Beth sings the song "Not a Day Goes By," she is absolutely furious. She has been abandoned and betrayed. "She has always loved Franklin, but he has grown professionally and personally without her, while her life has remained stagnant." Ms. Schulman observes that it is a Sondheim convention in a number of his shows to have a special song sung by different characters with different texts and circumstances, which results in a completely different delivery. This song is an example of such a device. In the original Broadway version in 1981, the song is sung by Franklin in act I, and then reprised by Franklin and Mary in act II. In the 1994 version, which was directed by Susan Schulman and remains the current version, Beth sings "Not a Day Goes By" at the end of act I, and the song is reprised in act II by Franklin, Mary, and Beth.

Aldonza

Man of La Mancha

"It's how she reacts to the word 'milady.'"
—Julia Migenes, Aldonza in 1996 revival of *Man of La Mancha*

CHARACTER: Aldonza

MUSIC: Mitch Leigh

LYRICS: Joe Darion

BOOK: Dale Wasserman

ADAPTED FROM: Wasserman's nonmusical teleplay *Don Quixote*

BASED ON: Miguel de Cervantes's seventeenth-century novel *Don Quixote*

SETTING: Spain, late sixteenth century

PREMIERE: 1965

CLASSIFICATION: Mezzo/alto with temperament

RANGE: 

TESSITURA: Low phrases at opening; later lies in high voice

TIME: 3:22

PLOT: The show is designed to be a play-within-a-play as Miguel de Cervantes is awaiting trial by the Spanish Inquisition. The story is about the "mad" knight Don Quixote, who can be described as one of the patron saints of lost causes and is called "The Knight of the Woeful Countenance." The naïve errant knight tells of his adventures. His imagination projects him into a world in which a windmill appears to be a four-armed giant, and he is defeated. Thinking it is because he has not been dubbed a knight, Quixote renames himself, and he and his squire, Sancho, continue their journey. Thinking he sees a castle, the "knight" stops (in reality, it is a roadside inn). There he spots Aldonza, a serving wench in the inn and part-time prostitute. In his imagination Quixote sees her as a lovely, pure maiden. But in real life, she is propositioned, mistreated, and abused. Throughout the play she is taunted and disrespected, and her responses are equally verbally abusive, but to Quixote she is an angel.

CHARACTER: Aldonza is a used and abused young woman who appears to be much older than she is. She projects a weariness in her voice and bearing as she relates her life's circumstances, but she is a survivor. She is not shy and will speak her mind. She's often angry about her condition and circumstances, and sees the world cynically. The song that introduces Aldonza, "They're All the Same" is sung early in the show in act I. Her story includes these telling words: "I have loved too many men, with hatred burning in my breast."

CONTEXT: In act II, at the request of Quixote, she tries to help a group of muleteers, and for her efforts she is beaten, raped, and carried off by the men. When she appears with bruises, Quixote swears revenge on her attackers, but she turns on him in anger, wanting to be left alone. This is the point at which she sings the song "Aldonza," weary and beaten.

CONTENT: The musical form of the song is AABAA in verses, then AAB/tag, with no repeated text. The meter alternates between 3/4 and 6/8, according to the rhythmic inflections of the text. The accompaniment is intended to imitate the repeated rhythmic patterns of traditional Spanish guitar playing.. The melody is not doubled in the piano at any time. Aldonza is frustrated with and weary of Don Quixote's delirious behavior. She is angry, and even though the music is marked "piano" for the opening two verses in the lower range, spitting out the consonants and finding the inflective syllable stresses can help in projecting her anger and frustration. Words like "ditch," "cold," and "scum" are colorful and descriptive words to sing, and they become especially expressive when the consonants are "spit out." In the B section, Aldonza modulates from D-flat major to B-flat major. As she sings the text "So of course I became," she ascends to the top of the staff in her mixed soprano/chest-resonance voice. As she reflects on her "delicate" birth, her pitches are placed lower on the staff while she describes herself as "a casual bride of the murdering scum of the earth," her voice descending below middle C deep into her chest voice. Quixote remarks that she is still his lady, which only stimulates her anger more. In the next two verses she is more graphic in describing her position in life. Her language becomes increasingly harsh. Quixote continues his inflated, formal platitudes, and repeatedly calls her his "Dulcinea." She attacks him in the last section as the key modulates up one half step (to D major), telling him that his words cruelly torture her. The final phrases crescendo to a powerful fortissimo as she exclaims, "I am nothing, no one, I'm only Aldonza the whore!"

VOICE: The singer will need to possess a strong lower chest voice below the staff while projecting text and barely controlled anger at the beginning of the song. An ability to switch gears and sing into the upper range with the D and E-flat at the top of the staff while projecting text is important. This shift into the soprano register is very exposed and brings out a completely new dramatic color, a vulnerability, in this emotionally charged song. The song has six verses, and she has a lot to say as her anger and years of frustration spill out. The performer must think about different ways to express Aldonza's exasperation, frustration, and revulsion as Quixote continues to address her as "milady," while she tries to deal with physical and emotional pain. Each verse should be sung differently. For dramatic choice, consider clues from the dynamics, articulation, and tempo markings resulting in varying vocal colors.

BEHIND THE SCENES WITH THE ARTISTS: JULIA MIGENES, ALDONZA IN THE 1996 REVIVAL

About the character of Aldonza, Ms. Migenes says: "She is powerful, has fighting spirit, and is direct when she speaks." She also "has great emotional strength, but definitely knows she is in the lowest of class and feels herself somehow less intelligent and more a victim of life's circumstances."

Ms. Migenes says further about singing the song: "It all comes from how Aldonza said the line 'I was born in a ditch' [which is how the song begins], and it comes from the emotional tone of the previous dialogue interaction with Quixote. It's how she reacts to the word 'milady.'" Julia explains that the word "desperation" can mean many things, but should never in Aldonza's case be seen as a sign of weakness. She is a survivor, in the sense that "Aldonza's way of survival is to act like a 'she-cat.'" Finally, Ms. Migenes notes an important element about the singing of the song: "Do not forget that she is in terrible physical pain." The delivery of the song should reflect that, as well as her mounting rage.

Cabaret

Cabaret

"All of the tension buildup of leaving Cliff and the denial of the fact that the Nazis were a threat to Berlin and the world, all accumulates to the point where the song accelerates and almost loses control."

—John Kander, composer

CHARACTER: Sally Bowles

MUSIC: John Kander

LYRICS: Fred Ebb

BOOK: Joe Masteroff

BASED ON: John Van Druten's play *I Am a Camera,* adapted from Christopher Isherwood's1939 novel *Goodbye to Berlin*

SETTING: The Kit Kat Club in prewar Berlin

BROADWAY PREMIERE: 1966

CLASSIFICATION: Alto belt

RANGE:

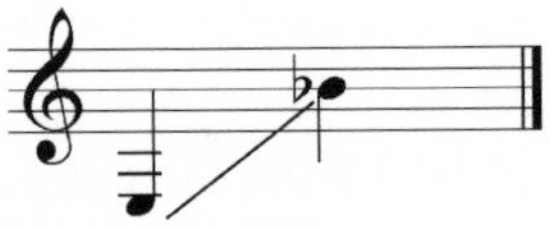

TESSITURA: Low staff

TIME: 3:50

PLOT: This play takes place before World War II in Berlin in the seedy Kit Kat Club, where the nineteen-year-old English cabaret performer Sally Bowles performs while in the midst of a relationship with American writer Cliff Bradshaw. The Kit Kat Club is a cabaret, a place of escape within a country facing growing Nazi terror. The songs and skits are a contrast to the real-world violence outside the club.

CHARACTER: Sally Bowles is a young English woman According to the script she is "rather pretty, rather sophisticated, rather child-like, exasperating and irresistible." She is worldly and shockingly independent and free in her views, and she has a strong personality—especially for a woman in the 1930s.

CONTEXT: The young American writer Cliff, visiting Berlin, intending to start a life as an expatriate writer, falls in love with Sally, who is performing at the cabaret. In act I, after living with Cliff for a few months, Sally tells him that she is pregnant. She lets him know that she will probably have an abortion. However, thinking that he could be the father, Cliff tries to talk Sally into keeping the child. Under the circumstances, Cliff would like her to leave at once and flee with him to the United States to raise their baby. She wants to stay in Berlin, because she loves her life there and does not see a reason to flee. Cliff tells her to wake up and see that the growing unrest in Germany is dangerous. Sally replies that the politics on the outside have nothing to do with them or the club. In act II, knowing that Cliff will leave Germany and that she does not want a family life (in fact, she tells Cliff in the next scene that she has had an abortion), she sings the title song of the show in the Kit Kat Club. Cliff has just been beaten up by Nazi sympathizers for his unwillingness to continue to smuggle for them, as he unwillingly did in Act I.

CONTENT: The song begins with the chorus, in a slow and easy delivery, as she invites the audience to "come to the cabaret." When she then sings that no one should yield to a "prophet of doom," and should instead "enjoy the holiday," it is meaningful within the circumstances of the show. In the middle of the song Sally goes off on a tangent with a little story about Elsie, a prostitute in Chelsea, quoting Elsie's words as Sally repeats the chorus, this time with a little more drive and momentum. She begins to sing the song with more and more abandon, threatening to drive the song out of control. In singing the song, the performer needs to have an understanding of the cabaret style, which was common in Germany and France in the first half of the twentieth century. Cabaret performance needs a direct contact with the audience, a presentational style. Front and center are the words of the song, which are sometimes cryptic. Most often the text sets an atmosphere for the song. The melody line follows the lyrics. There is rarely a sense that the melody can stand alone as a memorable melody that can stand alone, but the chorus of the song "Cabaret," with its combination of simple melody, harmony, driving rhythm, and text, can be haunting in its delivery. Great cabaret performers included Edith Piaf in France, Lotte Lenya in Germany, and Georgia Brown in England. While the presentational style is important, the singer needs also to digest all that is going on around her. Even though she has an independent spirit and does not seem to care about what is going on around her in Berlin, Sally is affected by her relationship with Cliff. His idealism and his fear of what will happen to Germany under Nazi control are what results in him getting beaten up before Sally sings "Cabaret." Sally is not aware of this at the time, but the audience sees the juxtaposition of the violence onstage and her denial of what is upon Germany. The song needs a take-charge drive in the chorus with momentum that portrays Sally's desire to escape reality combined with a realization of the momentous circumstances.

VOICE: The song begins slowly, deliberately, in the low chest voice of the singer, in the ledger-lined notes of low E and F-sharp below middle C. There is a deliberate punch to the notes and text, but the song does not begin with a strident tone. The melody is doubled in the accompaniment. As Sally sings "Life is a cabaret, old chum," higher in her range, in the middle of the staff, she loses herself in the moment. The verses are sung/spoken syllabically, in the cabaret style. In the last repeat of the refrain, the song accelerates as Sally tries to escape the reality of the situation in Berlin and in her life. The cabaret style of singing is not to oversing the vocal line, and also involves speech-like declamation that does not sustain pitch, except when marked (whole note, or whole tied over the bar), and of course the final pitch (B-flat), extended over the final nine (accelerated) measures, underscored by an accompaniment punctuated by accents.

BEHIND THE SCENES WITH THE ARTISTS: JOHN KANDER, COMPOSER

Mr. Kander told me that the intention of the song from the beginning was for Sally to sing the title song "Cabaret" at the Kit Kat Club, angry after the argument with Cliff. In the middle of the song she makes up her mind to get an abortion, and then "all of the tension buildup of leaving Cliff and the denial of the fact that the Nazis were a threat to Berlin and the world, all accumulates to the point where the song accelerates and almost loses control."

Applause

Applause

"[What is] unusual here is that the singer of the song earmarked for this purpose [showstopping title song] is not performed by one of the lead role performers."
— Charles Strouse, composer

CHARACTER: Bonnie

MUSIC: Charles Strouse

LYRICS: Lee Adams

BOOK: Betty Comden and Adolph Green, based on the screenplay from the 1950 film *All about Eve,* which was based on the original story "The Wisdom of Eve" by Mary Orr

SETTING: New York City, 1970

BROADWAY PREMIERE: 1970

CLASSIFICATION: Alto-belt showstopper

RANGE: 

TESSITURA: Low-middle staff

TIME: 3:24 (with cuts)

PLOT: As the overture ends, Margo Channing is presenting a Tony award to Eve, who credits her winning the award to Margo. What follows is a flashback sequence as we hear Margo reminiscing about meeting Eve. They go to a discotheque in Greenwich Village and experience other party scenes. Margo feels alive. Four months later, Eve has become Margo's girl Friday and impresses Margo's friends, including her producer, Howard. Howard takes Eve to a "gypsy" hangout—"gypsy" is the name that dancers give themselves when they are between performing shows. At the hangout, the gypsies celebrate the "sound that says love" (applause). The song "Applause" is introduced by Bonnie, the outspoken leader of the performers.

CHARACTER: Bonnie is the leader of the dancer/singer gypsies. She is feisty and courageous and is not shy about speaking up in Howard and Eve's presence in the bar-restaurant: "Do you know we make a hundred and sixty-four dollars and fifty cents a week?" She continues: "So, minus acting classes, singing and dancing lessons, equity dues, social security tax, and cat food... [that] leaves about twelve dollars and fifteen cents take-home pay." Bonnie continues her sarcastic rant, saying that a dancer only has to "study for ten years," and if that performer is lucky the career is going to "last another ten," unless an injury occurs. "But then you can always make eccentric jewelry at home and sell it to your friends." The stage directions describe what follows: "She does a warm up and has an idea, and goes over to Howard and Eve's table, where she whips off the tablecloth without disturbing a thing. Eve spontaneously applauds."

CONTEXT: The song is sung in the middle of act I (scene 6). Joe Allen's, a bar and restaurant in New York, is located on West 46th Street. The gypsies (dancers and singers who are patrons of Joe Allen's) carry in tables covered with bright red-checkered tablecloths for the scene shift. There are three large window arches and a door arch. The décor is of simulated red brick. Waiters in shirt sleeves are dashing between the kitchen door and the bar.

The second scene that Bonnie appears in (act II, scene 3) is also set in Joe Allen's, the hangout of the gypsies. Duane, a dancer friend of Bonnie's, satirically interviews the fictional "Miss Starshine" (Bonnie), mimicking the grand manner of Eve, making fun of her in her presence. Duane is posing as a reporter from *Screw Magazine* during the mock interview: "Our readers want to know if success will change you." Bonnie responds that "I plan to be as obnoxious as I ever was!"

CONTENT: Bonnie begins to sing the song "Applause," asking the question: "What is it that we're living for?" sung a cappella. The tempo and quarter beat pulse is indicated to be counted in an easy four. The catchy melodic phrase is first sung in an understated, simple delivery. The the melody continues a cappella, the accompaniment only coming in when the voice line rests in between phrases, punctuating them with "sassy" staccato chords in syncopated rhythm. "You're thinking you're through," the song continues, as the melody unfolds and the accompaniment joins in, doubling the voice. When Bonnie "hears it [the applause] starting" and her friends applaud on cue, she swings into the next verse of the song, "and somehow you're in charge again," as the song begins to build in energy. Then there is an amusing section of spoken rhythmic narrative describing Bonnie's first recollection experience of applause at her school play. This is followed by a repeated chorus with a counterpoint describing the addictive thrill of applause, which can be sung in the sung-alone solo version with piano playing the melody, or the melody (chorus) alone can be sung. The following section is another rhythmically spoken declaration, "There's wondrous applause, there's thunderous applause." In the extended chorus (and dance) version, there are modulations building to the climactic chorus. Some of these sections can be cut (the section marked "Rock!" for instance), going directly to the final chorus (in the solo "sing alone" version). The modulation in this version is rather abrupt, but still is effective in a solo performance. Within the context of the staged performance, the entire song extends over twelve pages in the piano/vocal score and anticipates a positive audience reaction by adding a written encore of "Applause" immediately following the number.

VOICE: Strong and confident vocal delivery is important in the delivery of this song, building to the end. Although the beginning of the song is very low (G and A below middle C), the climactic ending needs a secure, high-belted E-flat (top space of the staff). Punching the text and selling the song are musts, especially given that Bonnie is singing this song for an important producer, Howard. A sense of conviction, especially in the spoken, rhythmically delivered narrative section, is also needed. This number is usually highly choreographed, and the character is a dancer, so an energized body is important. The song needs to project an inner joy and a sense that the performer cannot live or breathe without applause.

BEHIND THE SCENES WITH THE ARTISTS: CHARLES STROUSE, COMPOSER

The composer observed that this show, based on the film *All about Eve*, is a 1970s show that features conventions of all the hit shows of the time, including a semi-nude homage to *Oh! Calcutta!*, a Broadway hit then. Of course, it had to have a title song, a showstopper, but what is unusual here is that the song earmarked for this purpose is not performed by one of the lead-role singers. The logical principal performer to be given this song to perform was Lauren Bacall, but Betty (as Charles Strouse told me she preferred to be called by her friends) allowed a newcomer to sing it, which was a mark of her generosity. It was performed by a very young Bonnie Franklin, and designed to be a highly choreographed dance number. The song starts in an understated, low key style, a cappella, and then develops and unfolds to become a large dance number, a showstopper that closes act I.

Time Heals Everything

Mack and Mabel

Finally, the song came together—built from the inspiration of the passages of time in his mind.
—Jerry Herman, composer and lyricist

CHARACTER: Mabel Normand

MUSIC AND LYRICS: Jerry Herman

BOOK: Michael Stewart

SETTING: Hollywood flashback, 1911, Keystone Movie Studio

BROADWAY PREMIERE: 1974

CLASSIFICATION: Alto lyric torch song

RANGE: 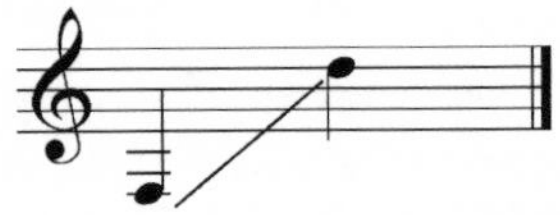

TESSITURA: Lower middle in staff

TIME: 3:26

PLOT: The show is based on the true story of the rise of Mabel Normand, discovered as a young delicatessen worker and quickly becoming a popular movie star, making an interesting plot for a musical. It also centers on the tumultuous romantic relationship between Normand and the man who discovered her, the Hollywood director and producer Mack Sennett. The musical unfolds through a series of flashbacks.

CHARACTER: Mabel Normand, the movie star (later to own her own studio), is discovered by moviemaker Mack Sennett in 1911, when she is a teenager. She comes onto the movie set with deli sandwiches and refuses to leave without being paid in full. Mack discovers that she has a flair for comedy and casts her in his early pictures. The established movie mogul and young woman have a contentious relationship, which is exacerbated by her workaholic life and eventual dependence on drugs. She would like Mack's help to appear in more serious films, with or without him, and eventually they go their separate ways.

CONTEXT: Later in the show (act II, scene 3, the 1920s), Mabel runs into Mack at 11:30 p.m. on Pier 88 in New York at a sailing party. Mabel is very successful in the entertainment business at this point and is traveling with a companion, Bill Taylor, and a secretary, while Mack Sennett's career has waned. She is on her way to Europe to see the sights. Mack and Mabel haven't seen each other for a long time. They make conversation, and they begin to reminisce about their relationship years ago (as "I Won't Send Roses" plays softly in the background). Mack tries to make small talk, then leaves her on the deck as her companion returns. Taylor tries to distract her from the shock of seeing him by insisting that she indulge in "a whiff of angel dust," which she does, "to drive away any sad thoughts from that dizzy little brain," he says. She knows that she will not see Mack again, but, she sings, "Time heals everything."

CONTENT: The music is marked "freely" at the top. The song begins with a bluesy alto sax for four measures, and the sax weaves throughout the piece in a countermelody. The accompaniment is written in a four-beat repeated rhythm pattern that contrasts nicely with the dotted values in the melody. If one looks at the chart, that is, the chords played by the keyboard/guitar, you will see many chords with jazz inflections, such as added sixths, sevenths, and ninths—extended harmonies added to the tonic root of the chord. The song has two verses; the second strophe has melodic variations. The melody unfolds by expanding the intervals before the listed elements of time. The first section talks about the healing of past wounds that occurs in the past, and then the singer addresses dealing with the pain in the future, next year. This haunting song has the magical quality of an intimate, personal feel at the opening, then opening up to a more expansive and "bigger" ending at its conclusion. There is a nine-measure instrumental break before the last verse.

VOICE: The song is written mostly in the low, chest-voice range, but there are cadential phrases where Mabel needs to sing up in the high belt range of C-sharp and D, sustained. At the climactic phrase at the end of the song, she needs to sing the sustained last D on a *u* vowel ("*you*"). At the beginning of the song, the vocal line is low in the singer's range and sung slowly, in a contemplative and introspective manner. Even though the melody is soft, low, and reflective, the performer still needs to enunciate the wonderful text distinctively and clearly and find the vocal core for presence of tone, avoiding breathiness. The vocal line has many accidentals and wide intervallic leaps and thus needs to be tuned carefully. And when repeating the time elements of the song, it is best to carefully sing each unit of time, giving weight to the words separately, rather than thoughtlessly stringing them together.

BEHIND THE SCENES WITH THE ARTISTS: JERRY HERMAN, COMPOSER

This song came to Jerry Herman without much struggle. He had in his mind the passing of time, "Tuesday, Thursday, months, etc." and he knew he wanted to do something with that. Finally, the song came together, built from the inspiration of the passage of time in his mind. That is the root of the song—each element of time that has ticked by, and is now in the past.

Crossword Puzzle

Starting Here, Starting Now

"It is important not to 'underline' comedy for the audience."
—Loni Ackerman, who originated the role

CHARACTER: Girl

MUSIC: David Shire

LYRICS: Richard Maltby Jr.

SETTING: Chicago, 2000–

NYC PREMIERE: 1977

CLASSIFICATION: Patter song for alto

RANGE: 

TESSITURA: Middle of staff

TIME: 4:40

PLOT: *Starting Here, Starting Now* is a revue that thematically explores romantic relationships. This song is a clever piece that is sung by the lead while working through the Sunday *New York Times* crossword puzzle, weaving personal interjections into the puzzle. She is constantly distracted because of her failed relationship with Hecky. She remembers that they used to do the *Times* crossword together.

CHARACTER: Even without a book that we can refer to for character development, we know a lot about this character just from the song. As lyricist Richard Maltby observes, she is a "motormouth," which she shows by the way she delivers the song. She is insufferable; a smug know-it-all who is overconfidently sure of herself (until she has a revelation at the end of the song); she has irritating traits (for example, the way that she goes about working the puzzle) that drive Hecky away.

CONTEXT: The song is placed after an ensemble number ("Just Across the River") toward the beginning of the show. However, as Mr. Maltby explains, "Crossword Puzzle" is a "stand-alone" song that is "self-contained" and character-driven in its concept and function.

CONTENT: The song begins slowly as she works on the puzzle. The tempo picks up as the piano plays an incessant eighth-note rhythm pattern, off the beat, pushing the tempo. She is so distracted about Hecky that the song takes a hard turn, veering off into the story about doing the crossword puzzles with him, which led to frustration and arguing. She begins to understand why he left her. Going back to the puzzle, the piano goes to an accompanying pattern which sounds like quiz-show countdown music, before the song goes back to repeat the opening lines and music. Maybe she should have "played dumb," she says, as she recounts their arguments about the puzzle. She starts the puzzle again, only to be distracted again by the memories of the puzzle with Hecky. Why is it a crime that she is intelligent? Why should she be punished?

VOICE: Singing this song will require the ability to deliver text rapidly (patter) and develop a character from the performer's imagination from the text and the situation. The singer also needs to take command of every twist and turn of the song. At the beginning, the setup of the song, a steady rhythmic pattern is heard, which is repeated a number of times. There is the actual recounting of the puzzle itself in a different musical pattern, as well as a recitative-like section in which the actor must control the pace of delivery. There is also building frustration, and of course the occurring distracting thoughts that cause the singer to change the course of the song midstream a number of times.

BEHIND THE SCENES WITH THE ARTISTS: LONI ACKERMAN, WHO ORIGINATED THE ROLE

Ms. Ackerman has made this song a signature piece of hers. She has opportunities to coach young singers on this song and many other experienced singer-actors, as she now engaged in teaching and leading workshops. When she coaches this song for a young singer, she obviously emphasizes the text and, as in all "list songs," memorization. She will make sense of the words, finding the story and where the words are going, and she is a believer in learning by writing the lyrics down and going through them, line by line. This is a comic song, and it is very funny. Loni says that it is important not to play the song for laughs and not to go "over the top." She advises respecting the audience's ability to understand the comedy in the song. It is important not to underline comedy for the audience. Just tell the story with truth, and "find the love" in the story, which is a bit of advice she often uses for comic situations onstage.

Richard Maltby, the lyricist, observes that there is a "formula" in self-contained songs like this. Learning to sing this song well, processing through it, is an acting exercise. First of all, there is a perception. Something is odd, something wrong—*why* am I feeling that there is something wrong? Ah yes! I know what it is! There is a discovery, a revelation that is revealed by the end of the song. "Crossword Puzzle" is a humorous song, and it "could be a one-joke song, or just silly and funny as is," Richard explains. However, it is definitely character-driven, and is a complex, important "discovery song," a theatre song. "In a nutshell she is saying that she is brilliant, a Phi Beta Kappa, a 'world beater.' Why is she alone? 'Ah! That's why!' she discovers. 'I am an idiot!' she says, and she is finally sad and angry as a result." Finally, in tribute to the lyricist, composer David Shire has dubbed Richard "King of the Crosswords." In fact, Mr. Maltby is the architect of "cryptic crossword puzzles," in which by definition each clue is a puzzle unto itself. He has contributed puzzles to *Harper's* and *New York Magazine*.

You Can Always Count On Me

City of Angels

" 'You Can Always Count On Me' is a good song for a young singer to work on, for the exercise of singing one song that is shared by two characters played by the same actress."

—Randy Graff, the original Oolie/Donna

CHARACTERS: Oolie/Donna

MUSIC: Cy Coleman

LYRICS: David Zippel

BOOK: Larry Gelbart

SETTING: Hollywood, late 1940s

BROADWAY PREMIERE: 1980

CLASSIFICATION: Up-tempo belt

RANGE: 

TESSITURA: Lower staff, sustained low A below middle C

TIME: 3:06

PLOT: The concept here is from the film noir Hollywood detective story in the late 1940s, but here the creators of the book the story is based on appear onstage along with their creation on film. The "real-life" scenes are in color, while the movie scenes are in black and white. The movie is based on a novel by Stine. The plot becomes very complicated because the author Stine keeps changing the script, which in turn changes the course of the film.

CHARACTER: Although both roles (Donna/Oolie) are performed by one person (in the novel and the film), the two characters are not alike. Donna is the secretary of movie producer/director Buddy Fidler in the "Hollywood cast" of Stine's novel, while Oolie is the black-and-white "movie character"; she is brassier, the more straightforward and streetwise of the two, the stereotypical film noir gal Friday.

CONTEXT: "You Can Always Count On Me" is placed in act II and is the twenty-third of the thirty-six numbers in the show. Stone (of the film) is in jail. He has been framed for a murder, and his only visitor is his secretary, Oolie. Oolie, like her counterpart Donna, is becoming fed up with men. "Good girl, Oolie," she remarks to herself, sarcastically. She then launches into the song "You Can Always Count On Me."

CONTENT: Oolie sings first, entering immediately. The line "You can always count on me," when it is sung, is the underlined "truth" of the song in each of the two verses sung by Oolie before the set change, after which the song continues with Donna. The most recognizable musical difference in Donna's rendition of the song is the walking bass line, which gives the song a different feel. After Donna sings two verses, there is some dialogue with Stine over the instrumental accompaniment as the music continues, and then she sings two more verses, which conclude with a tag at the big finish of the show-stopping song. The text is set through a variety of rhythmic pattern combinations, including syncopated rhythms, consecutive eighth notes, and many triplet rhythms. The accompaniment does not double the melody; the accompaniment is punctuated by chords, and sometimes offers a countermelody. The harmony is light-jazz inflected to reflect the setting of the 1940s. Even if the song is excerpted, the lyrics of the entire song(s) give insight to the characters. The tone is clever, confidential, sarcastic, and humorous.

VOICE: Both parts of the song are written in the same low range and tessitura, so delineation comes from character and articulating the text in clearly different ways. Words must be enunciated clearly, because the delivery of the song is largely text driven. If the belt is too heavy and driving, the singer will need to keep in mind that the song builds to the end, and that is the place in the song where the singer should project the most, in the tag of the final cadence, which ascends to the D-flat on the word "count," then resolves to B-flat in the middle of the staff, with Donna finishing with the word "me," giving the tone enough space so that the *i* vowel is not too bright and constricted.

BEHIND THE SCENES WITH THE ARTISTS: RANDY GRAFF, THE ORIGINAL OOLIE/DONNA

The song was written very late in the creation process. Lyricist David Zippel told her one month before rehearsals were to start that he and composer Cy Coleman had just written a show stopper, "You Can Always Count On Me," for Oolie/Donna. The verse was written during technical rehearsal. Cy Coleman coached Randy Graff in making the song swing musically, which affects phrasing. He told her to "think Sophie Tucker." The two characters (performed by the same person) are delineated by their language, the words given them, which affects their delivery. In Ms. Graff's words, Oolie, the black-and-white movie character, is more straightforward and streetwise, whereas Donna, who is Stine's secretary, is more sophisticated and urbane. "It all comes from character, from the acting of the lyric," explained Ms. Graff. She also explained that at first in the staging process the song was heavily choreographed, but this did not feel right to Ms. Graff, and after a discussion with director Michael Blakemore, she worked through the songs in a more natural and organic manner. The song became a showstopper, and Randy Graff won a Tony Award for her performance. She comments that "You Can Always Count On Me" . . . "is a good song for a young singer to work on, for the exercise of singing one song that is shared by two characters played by the same actress.

Trina's Song

March of the Falsettos

"The music and lyrics capture Trina's state of mind at the particular time of the play."
—Alison Fraser, the original Trina

CHARACTER: Trina

MUSIC, BOOK AND LYRICS: William Finn

SETTING: New York

BROADWAY PREMIERE: 1981

CLASSIFICATION: Alto lyric art song

RANGE: 

TESSITURA: Lower middle of the staff

TIME: 2:40

PLOT: This musical follows the life journey of Marvin and his search for inner peace. He has left his wife for his gay lover, Whizzer. His ten-year-old son and his psychiatrist also feature prominently in the story.

CHARACTER: Trina was raised to think that marriage and family are the most important priorities a woman should have. As a little girl she probably envisioned living happily ever after with a perfect husband and perfect children. Because of this hope, she marries Marvin, has a son, and stays with her husband for twelve years, even though she suspects that he has not been faithful to her. Trina has very little confidence or self-respect, and she ends up contracting diseases passed on to her by her husband. She is clearly shocked and devastated when he confesses that he is gay and leaves her for another man. Trina is lost and knows nothing about the world outside when her home becomes broken. She now has difficulty getting through the day.

CONTEXT: At the beginning of the show, Marvin has already left Trina for Whizzer, his lover. Acting on a referral from Marvin, Trina pays a visit to his psychiatrist, who is attracted to her. Later, the psychiatrist will question Marvin about intimate details regarding Trina. As Whizzer spends more time with Marvin and Trina's son, she grows concerned that their son will distance himself from her. Mendel, the psychiatrist, visits the family, and he and Trina become closer. Although Mendel is clumsy and neurotic, and in some ways she is repulsed by him, Trina accepts him, and Marvin loses a therapist. In "Trina's Song," she reflects on her situation. She observes that Mendel is just as broken as Marvin, but Mendel belongs to her. Most important, he loves her.

CONTENT: This song is a revealing glimpse into Trina's psyche, featuring a warm melody and attractive accompaniment along with words that reveal complex, negative emotions, including layers of hurt and anger that needs to be released. The form of the song is two verses followed by a bridge, and then a final verse (with tag) to finish.

She sings that she is "tired of all the happy men who rule the world," as the A natural in the melody lowers the fifth degree of the scale, which gives the shape of the melody a blues color that changes the meaning of the word "happy" that she sings, at least in Trina's present state of mind. Lines like "They grow, but don't mature," and "I'd like the chance to hide in their world" are tinged with sarcasm but are not so blatantly or bitterly presented as to be harsh. The second verse continues to talk about men in the same vein, which is again a warm melody with attractive chords contrasted with text which is both witty and biting: she is observing "these men who aren't quite men (but aren't boys)." They "throw their knives. Their toys . . . are people's lives," she says. It is very clever how William Finn connects these phrases, these fragments of text-thought, in ways that attract our attention as specific words seem to leap out of the phrase-fabric. During the B section, or bridge ("It's crazy how they're acting"), the tempo is marked "sprightly," as the accompaniment and melody become more active rhythmically and more animated. The text "stupid, childish, and charming" are words that she chooses, referring to men, slowing somewhat to draw the text out more. In the final verse, it is clear that she is "tired"—tired of all the "happy men, the jerks, who rule the world." That being said, she makes a decision about her relationship with Mendel at the end of the song to marry him, as she sings: "I'll be his wife—I'll wed and change my life" to force a "happy" conclusion—for the moment. And most likely she will "act" happy, but true joy will elude her.

VOICE: The song is driven by the text, and it is important for the words to come through with commitment and deliberate clarity. Except for a few pitches below middle C, the singing range is narrow, in the middle of the staff. Even though the sentiment behind the words is one of hurt and disillusionment, there are phrases which the singer can sing lyrically when desired, and it certainly has an attractive melody and accompaniment. The most important task for the performer is taking charge of the song's momentum of phrasing, which is connected to the singer's commitment and courage. This song should never be sung metronomically, and it needs to be driven by the actor's emotional choices, since the tempo and tone are marked "freely."

BEHIND THE SCENES WITH THE ARTISTS: ALISON FRASER, THE ORIGINAL TRINA

"Trina's Song" is extremely well written, with melody, words, and accompaniment that are extremely well crafted. The music and lyrics capture Trina's state of mind at the particular time of the play.

The Story Goes On

Baby

"This is the moment when she realizes that she has a new life inside her, and Lizzie matures and grows up with the realization."
—David Shire, composer

CHARACTER: Lizzie

MUSIC: David Shire

LYRICS: Richard Maltby Jr.

BOOK: Sybille Pearson

SETTING: New York City

BROADWAY PREMIERE: 1984

CLASSIFICATION: Mezzo lyric/belt anthem

RANGE: 

TESSITURA: Lower and upper staff

TIME: 4:38

PLOT: Three couples at three different times in their lives are expecting a baby. Liz and Danny are juniors in college just moving in together. "What Could Be Better" is a duet they sing at the top of the show, and they reprise the song midway through act I. Pam and Nick, who sing "Romance" and "With You," are having trouble conceiving. "The Story Goes On" is sung by Lizzie at the end of act I. The song builds through to the end, with a strong ending that closes act I. The song has a big message—that life and the instinct to continue the "chain of life" are what makes the story go on.

CHARACTER: Lizzie, who has a close relationship to her mother, has always been able to handle anything that life hands her. She is pregnant, but it hasn't fully registered with her how her life is changed.

CONTEXT: The song is sung in Lizzie's bedroom at the end of act I, as she looks at her pregnant self in the mirror. The singing of the song is precipitated by her noticing a movement in her body, feeling her stomach, and exclaiming, "It moved!" She first tries to call someone, anyone, to tell them this news. She calls her mother, but instead gets her answering machine. Lizzie really wants to tell her mother. She recalls that when she was a little girl her mother told her stories that didn't hold her attention. All Lizzie wanted out of life was getting a kick out of it, and now the biggest kick is the one in her body, telling her that, beginning with the stories her mother told her, "the story goes on."

CONTENT: This song is a "discovery" song, which provides an important numbers of realizations that drive the song forward. It builds from an almost spoken delivery, in the very low range, to the top of Lizzie's high-belt voice. Although the first section of the song is repeated, the song subsequently unfolds from section to section with a through-composed form that is linked by the words "on and on" as it builds to the climactic last section. The performer will need to carefully plan the execution of the building of the song through dynamics, range, and vocal color. But the singer will also need to project the sense of spontaneity that comes from an awareness in the moment. It is important that the singer understand why correct rhythmic values should be observed. For example, the sixteenth-note-rhythm pick-ups (text: "that tale *that was* much too dull"), as those specific rhythms are needed to spark the momentum of the vocal line and capture the urgency and excitement of the moment.

VOICE: First of all, the performer will need to read the text of the song and observe the intended phrasing and inflections that give the song meaning. Carefully observe the places where the singer should take full breaths and "lifts" indicated by punctuation that give the phrases clarity. At the beginning of the song (in the low range), the singer does not need to put pressure on the vocal production; pushing is not necessary, nor is it desirable. Although there are low Gs written in the score, these are not full-belt projected tones; the tone is more intimate and conversational in intent (e.g.: "The tale my mother told me . . . was much too dull to hold me"). It is important to stress the important syllables in this section. Many of them land on the dotted-quarter-note rhythmic patterns, and the inflected syllables can be slightly lengthened (which is called *tenuto*). With the text "And this is the surge and the rush she said would show," the dynamic is marked "crescendo." Although the line is still set low here, Lizzie has a dotted-quarter-rhythm A in the middle of the staff on the word "rush" that the singer needs to underline and inflect to shape the phrase. As the words "Our story goes on" are sung, the sections of the story are connected by the repeated phrase. There are other crescendos that shape lines as the song unfolds ("And now, like a joke, something moves to let me know our story goes on") with the dotted-half rhythm notated at the word "moves" this time. The song now builds with the words "A chain of life begun upon the shore," as the vocal line is a little higher and each note is longer in note value. The singer cannot belt in the chest resonance too strongly or heavily, because there are some higher passing tones she also must negotiate (C and D) that need to match the chest resonance and sound as even as possible as the song is building. "And thus it is our story" calls for a vocal line that stretches from the upper C down to low G below middle C, and is marked "diminuendo" as the line descends. The final, climactic section begins with full orchestra and a countermelody in the strings, is marked "forte," and has a range that stretches between middle C and the upper E (an octave and a third). Although the song is picking up in momentum and is a constant ebb and flow of tension and release, it also has a "broad sweep" feeling that gives the song stability and cosmic importance. Lizzie is aware that the story began even before her mother, and these realizations of common experiences shared by all expectant mothers about to give birth are what drives the song forward ("I can see the chain extending," she sings).

The song still continues to build and sustain excitement, as Lizzie goes higher in her range to sing the words "on and on," and extends with an arched line that includes sustained higher belt tones in Lizzie's range. The orchestra also becomes more rhythmically active and swells to support her voice at the top of her range for an effective climactic finish.

BEHIND THE SCENES WITH THE ARTISTS: DAVID SHIRE, COMPOSER

Lizzie, who always seems to be in control of every situation, feels a kick in her stomach. "This baby is real," she thinks. This is "new news" for her. This is the realization when it hits her that she has a new life inside her, and Lizzie is responsibility for that life. She also has a revelation that this is a "bigger moment," one that connects her to a meaning and greater purpose in life.

Children of the Wind

Rags

"It is a very personal song, which has a universal message for [Rebecca] and many who follow her."
—Charles Strouse, composer

CHARACTER: Rebecca Hershkowitz

MUSIC: Charles Strouse

LYRICS: Stephen Schwartz

BOOK: Joseph Stein

SETTING: Ellis Island

PREMIERE: 1986

CLASSIFICATION: Alto anthem

RANGE: 

TESSITURA: Middle of staff; modulates and builds higher on the staff

TIME: 2:43

PLOT: Rebecca Hershkowitz, a Jewish mother, is emigrating from Russia to America on a ship with other hopeful immigrants. She is traveling with her young son, hoping to meet up with her husband, Nathan (already in the United States), who has not communicated with her for a long time. Their passage and documentation processing prove to be difficult, but Rebecca finds a job in a factory and eventually becomes a union leader. She finally finds Nathan, but he is not pleased with her union activities. Having grown close to Saul, another union activist, who has taught Rebecca and her son to speak English and introduces them to cultural enrichment in New York, Rebecca finally follows her heart and starts a new life with Saul in the new world.

CHARACTER: Rebecca Hershkowitz is a strong-willed woman of courage and hope. Fleeing Russia alone with her son would be a frightening endeavor, but she is a survivor and proves it by starting a new life while also searching for her husband, Nathan, a man with Old World ways who had come to America earlier on his own. Rebecca's story is the journey of a woman adjusting to a new environment and discovering new things about herself, while caring deeply for her family.

CONTEXT: Arriving on Ellis Island at the beginning of the show, the passengers are herded onto land like cattle. With no male there to vouch for them on land, they are in danger of deportation until one of the passengers they have befriended stands up for them and they are able to enter America. Rebecca feels lonely but still hopes that she can provide a home for her son. She sings "Children of the Wind," reflecting this hope.

CONTENT: The song begins with Rebecca remembering "hiding in the wheat fields," and her descriptive memories bring alive escaping the "screams, flames, and blood in the streams" that she remembers. Echoing in her mind is the question she asked her son, which continues to haunt her: "David, did they hurt you, darling?" The verse continues to describe running through the snow forty miles to escape, when she sings, "all the world [was] burning." The verse is syllabically sung, and the feeling created by the combination of a vivid narrative of their flight with syncopated rhythms and the anxiety-inducing device of incessant eighth-note repetition of high B-natural (marked "staccato") is effective in the song. Another device that creates an unstable atmosphere is the change of meter from common meter (4/4) to 5/4 to 3/4 back to 4/4, and so forth. The refrain is much more lyrically written and poetic in text, suggesting that the "children of the wind" are blown with their "pieces of the heart" away from the ones that they love. The B section of the song takes Rebecca back to her syllabic delivery (with forward momentum) to describe the dreams she has of "noisy children" joyfully running through her kitchen again, though this "will never be." The next chorus has an extension that builds climactically toward a strong, hopeful conclusion. Rebecca sings, "We will make a way," as the large transport ships bring people safely to shore so that they are no longer the "children of the wind," as the music modulates upward from the key of E minor/G major to B major. The accompaniment includes a momentum-building device in the bass line of a dotted-quarter rhythm on the downbeat followed by an eighth-note rhythm in a pattern that continues to the end of the song. The treble accompaniment includes accented chords strongly played.

VOICE: Most importantly, the singer needs a wide range that can climactically ascend to the soprano range with power. The verse, beginning in the middle range, at times descending below middle C, needs to be powerfully sung in the chest voice, with emotion. However, the singer cannot sing these passages too heavily or forcefully, because there are also upward intervals within the verse line that are higher in range, ascending to C and D at the top of the staff. In the climactic section toward the end of the song, the singer will need to sustain a high E and F-sharp natural. The words and circumstances call for a singer who can portray the hope at the moment of arriving at the "new world" while also reflecting the harrowing experiences of familial and communal tragedy at the same time. It is not necessarily a prerequisite of age or maturity as it is a haunted look that can be seen even in a youngster's eyes in similar circumstances.

BEHIND THE SCENES WITH THE ARTISTS: CHARLES STROUSE, COMPOSER

Mr. Strouse composed the music for *Rags*, with Stephen Schwartz writing the lyrics. Mr. Strouse explained that although the placement of the song was changed early in the creative process, the idea was for the song to establish the tone of the show's theme. Rebecca's husband has immigrated earlier, and at this point, as she comes to America and sums up her emotions, she speaks for many people who have been expelled from Russia and are "blown about Earth" as a "child of the wind." "It is a very personal song, which has a universal message for [Rebecca] and many who follow her."

Opera singer Teresa Stratas, who showed a full commitment to the role, was the original Rebecca. Mr. Strouse knew that Ms. Stratas was an operatic soprano, and he told her that he was willing to transpose it higher. However, Ms. Stratas said that since the key of the song as written, starting on an F-sharp, was the tessitura that Mr. Strouse had in mind, she wanted to keep that color, and, Ms. Stratas revealed, she was acquainted and experienced in singing the cabaret style.

Since You Stayed Here

Brownstone

"I've always felt that the song should be sung without self-pity."
—Peter Larson, composer

CHARACTER: Claudia

MUSIC: Peter Larson

LYRICS: Josh Rubins

BOOK: Josh Rubins and Andrew Cadiff

SETTING: Present day, New York City

OFF-BROADWAY PREMIERE: 1986

CLASSIFICATION: Mezzo lyric

RANGE: 

TESSITURA: Middle of the staff

TIME: 2:46

PLOT: *Brownstone* is about a small apartment building in New York City and five of its inhabitants. Set in the present day, the show explores the interwoven lives of urban apartment living, with the thirtysomething married couple Mary (English teacher) and Howard (blocked novelist); two single women: Claudia and Joan, who is involved in a long-distance relationship; and Stuart Reed, newly arrived from Wisconsin, who moves across the hall from Claudia. The musical is nearly all through-sung, that is, with very little dialogue.

CHARACTER: Liz Callaway, who originated the role of Claudia, observes that she is a "free-spirited" single woman. She has just come out of a long-term relationship. She hears that her ex has changed, but she is skeptical, suspicious, and angry: "You always lie," she says, adding: "Why should I believe you this time?" in the first scene of the show, speaking with him on the telephone. At the opening of the show, someone new is moving into the brownstone apartment building, and the introduction of new characters results in the entrance and response of the characters that already reside in the brownstone. This theatrical device introduces all characters in the show.

CONTEXT: The song is placed in act II. Composer Peter Larson remarks that "Claudia is in her own world and trying to get on with finding a joyful life. In the moments preceding 'Since You Stayed Here,' Howard has just walked out on Mary, with much angst on both their parts—more fear than anger. Then Stuart uses all the charm he can muster [singing 'See That Lady There'] to win some affection from Joan. She's slow to give in, but eventually does, and they walk offstage smiling at each other. Claudia has by now finished putting her newly arranged apartment back in order, and finishes by hanging a reframed painting. She looks around, feeling comfortable in her solitude for the first time. And she sings . . ."

CONTENT: The song has three verses. At the opening, the lovely piano introduction is simply a two-measure repeated motive, setting up Claudia's musings at the beginning of the song. The meter changes subtly in each verse from 4/4 to 2/4 to accommodate the line structure of the text. At the end of each of the three verses is the all-important line "Yes, there have been changes made . . . Since you've stayed here," repeating the title of the song, as the text is underlined each time by the melodic line. At the end of the first verse, Claudia leaves the apartment and walks downstairs during the brief instrumental interlude. During the next verse, she talks about the changes on the street as it relates to the changing of the seasons, changes in store fronts coming and going. After the second verse, there is a short bridge, more a four-measure transition, with some accidentals and enharmonic tones, but without a key change. Each of the three verses begins with the same text: "You'd never recognize . . ." After the final third verse, the song ends with the line "You'd never recognize the room," wistfully sung two times, the same phrase that begins the song.

VOICE: Each verse is reflective and personal, but also calls for vocal projection in the upper-middle voice belt when Claudia sings, "I've thrown out every souvenir," with full breath-support connection as she sings the D and E-flat that are not composed as sustained tones but should be sung with powerful conviction. The ascending intervals can be tricky to sing in tune, so the performer should take care especially in these places in the verses, and in the bridge. It is interesting how the composer has placed this line at the end of each verse: "Yes, there've been changes made since you stayed here," a phrase that ties the song together (as does the first phrase in the opening line) and is filled with emotions which are revealed in part through the manner of extending rhythmic values with text. For example, the changes are described in the opening of the phrase in a semiconversational tone, but when Claudia comes to ".since you stayed here," the note values are greater (half notes), which allows the performer to capture a layer of wistfulness and regret at the end of each verse.

BEHIND THE SCENES WITH THE ARTISTS: PETER LARSON, COMPOSER

While much can be done by the performer to take the words and notes on the page and understand the emotional power that comes from performance interpretation, it is also important to realize that emoting is not necessary. Composer Peter Larson, writing to Liz Callaway, the original interpreter of the role of Claudia, writes: "What has always struck me as the song at its best, is when you (and a very few others) sing it without self-pity. You know it's for the audience to read in the sorrow from themselves, not for the singer to underline it. You've always understood that so very well."

I'm Not Alone

Carrie

"Her innocence was the key to my interpretation."
—Linzi Hateley, the original Carrie on Broadway

CHARACTER: Carrie

MUSIC: Michael Gore

LYRICS: Dean Pitchford

BOOK: Lawrence Cohen

BASED ON: The 1974 novel *Carrie* by Stephen King and the movie of the same name

SETTING: A high school gym

BROADWAY PREMIERE: 1988

CLASSIFICATION: Lyric/low register

RANGE: 

TESSITURA: Low to middle of staff

TIME: 3:39

PLOT: See "It Hurts to Be Strong."

CHARACTER: Carrie is a young high school girl. She has been sheltered most of her life by her mother. Carrie is introverted and has grown up in a judgmental environment. She is naïve and has very little confidence and few friends except Sue, who feels sympathy for her. Carrie possesses a temper when she is pushed too far, and has access to superpowers, especially during episodes of anger. She has fantasies, and dreams that she may be liked—and perhaps even loved someday. Eventually, she uses her power in anger for the purpose of revenge.

CONTEXT: Carrie's powers anger the girls at the school. They retaliate by setting up a "date" for the prom wherein a popular boy, Tommy, will pretend to be attracted to Carrie and ask her to the dance, and then the girls will have their revenge. Carrie thinks that she loves Tommy (who is actually Sue's boyfriend), who asks her to the prom. Her mother forbids her to go, but relents when Carrie forces the issue and threatens her with her supernatural powers in order to get her way. In the second act Carrie is getting ready for her night out, as she sings "I'm Not Alone." She believes that Tommy really wants to take her out (Sue actually arranged it), and she is happy and excited to be going out with him.

CONTENT: The song can be characterized as a lyric piece with syncopated rhythms that are often not strictly observed. The song begins unaccompanied, in clipped phrases reflecting Carrie's insecurities. But as she thinks about her "love," her confidence grows, and she begins to believe her "lovely balloon doesn't have to burst." She thinks that maybe the demons that she has are "all in my mind," and then she begins to talk about Tommy specifically with his qualities that attract her, and how wonderful that makes her feel. He's "prob'ly a prince," she says. The melody moves into a faster tempo and a higher key, and the accompaniment has more rhythmic excitement (a constant eighth-note rhythmic pulse) in the bass line. The song moves into more of a popular groove, as the accompaniment plays an incessant eighth-note broken-chord rhythm pattern, beginning when she sings, "Somebody's freed me from this lonely tower," and the song continues to build momentum as she gains courage and hope.

The words "I'm not alone" in the attractive refrain, rhythmically syncopated to increase excitement, are repeated over and over, as if, if she says them enough times, mantra-like, she will believe they are true. The rests that are indicated between phrases are provided for the singer's purpose of reflection, allowing for dramatic beats. During the B section bridge, the song continues with the same tempo and rhythms. At the end of the B section, the song modulates upward, the quicker tempo increases the momentum as the singer embellishes the melody slightly in gospel style to increase excitement and power, and to suggest even more self-confidence.

VOICE: The singer needs to build this song from the initial, fragmented phrase of the opening (sung a cappella), showing insecurity and lack of confidence. The beginning is freely sung, and the performer must be in control of the delivery. The notes are set low in the singer's range, touching low Fs and Gs below middle C, but none of the tones are sustained, and the opening is half spoken in understated delivery. The singer must use the text and situation and the power of the music to inspire the confidence of the character that, in turn, drives the song forward. It is a terrific song to show an actor moving from cautious delivery to discovery leading to total abandon by the last chorus. The singer needs a solid sustained B-flat in the middle of the staff, as well as a free (without constriction) C and D above that, although the pitches are not sustained.

BEHIND THE SCENES WITH THE ARTISTS: LINZI HATELEY, WHO CREATED THE ROLE OF CARRIE

Linzi was only seventeen years old when she first performed the role of Carrie on Broadway, so it wasn't much of a stretch for her to take on the persona of a high school girl on stage. "I brought a lot of myself to the part," she said. She both saw the film *Carrie* and read the Stephen King novel before performing the role. The novel was helpful to her, as she was able to feel through reading the book the struggle Carrie experienced in trying to fit in at high school, and, she said, "how cruel life can be. Her innocence was the key to my interpretation." She feels that the strength and power needed in singing this song comes from feeling "love for the first time. And she naively thinks Tommy really likes her. Through all her sadness she has hope." Linzi observed that this emotion was not lasting: "It's a brief moment of happiness for her." She then notes a key aspect of how her powers worked: "Carrie's telekinetic powers only work when she is emotionally charged," she said. While singing "I'm Not Alone" her powers are used in a positive way, as she is getting ready for the prom, and she brings her prom dress and hairbrush to life through theatre magic.

Heaven Help My Heart

Chess

"It's a plaintive understanding of their passionate love affair and the doom to come"
—Elaine Paige, the original Florence in *Chess*

CHARACTER: Florence Vassy

MUSIC: Benny Andersson and Bjorn Ulvaeus

LYRICS: Tim Rice

SETTING: 1979 World Chess Championship, Merano, Italy

BROADWAY PREMIERE: 1988

CLASSIFICATION: Belt/lyric mezzo/alto

RANGE: 

TESSITURA: Middle of the staff

TIME: 3:44

PLOT: This is the story about a Russian chess master (Anatoly Sergievsky) who defects to England during a world championship in Italy; his American challenger (Freddy Trumper) who resigns the tournament, and an English woman who changes her affections from the American to the Russian. The play is not based on a true story, but was inspired by the matches between American and Russian chess champions Bobby Fischer and Boris Spassky in 1972.

CHARACTER: Florence is a bright, self-possessed, Hungarian-born Englishwoman with a complicated past who is outspoken and has a temper. She is twenty-seven years old and is concerned and opinionated about how Freddy's remarks and attitude are perceived by the press. She is also aware of his own temper.

CONTEXT: Although the match is on neutral ground (Italy in 1979), there is much political posturing and jockeying for power. The American challenger is accompanied by his partner, Florence Vassy. After later discovering that Freddie's outburst at a match was engineered to bring him profits, Florence is increasingly angry with him, even after arranging a meeting between Freddie and Anatoly for them to iron out their differences. The difficult Freddie does not show up at the meeting, causing an awkward moment as Florence and Anatoly are left alone together. We realize that they are attracted to each other, and end up in each other's arms. Florence leaves Freddie, and she and Anatoly become lovers, even though he is married.

CONTENT: During the song Florence speculates about her future. She knows she has fallen in love with Anatoly, though she never planned to. She also knows that he worries that the Soviets won't allow his wife out of Russia after he defects, that he is torn between his life with Svetlana and his passion for playing chess. In her heart, she knows that these factors will be the undoing of her relationship with Anatoly, and that their love will not survive. Although the song begins with a string background, the introduction reduces to the instrumentation of a sole keyboard, almost as if Florence is suddenly alone with her thoughts. The rhythm of the accompaniment signals that the singer is about to sing a pop song with a hook, which is to be expected in a major song from a show composed by musical theatre lyricist Tim Rice with the songwriting team who happen to be former members of the band named ABBA (who composed so many Top 40 hits) . However, when the singer looks into the situation and character, there is more of an intensity and emotional reality of a melody that is unfolding, not just propping up a predictable popular song form. She is struggling and honestly working through the conflicting emotions of her character in this song. When she gets to the title line, "Heaven help my heart," a real cry for help, it contrasts beautifully with the next reflective phrase, "I love him too much." The second verse starts hopefully. But it continues: "Time is not my friend. I'll fight it to the end," and Florence struggles to hold on. The song builds as the orchestra swells with more variety of articulation and fullness of texture, but by the end the song again becomes more reflective, with tentative pauses signaled by fermatas and caesura before the final, poignant "my heart."

VOICE: The singer needs to resist falling into a pop-music groove. This character is in distress and is looking for answers. The performer should emphasize a contrast between a cry for help and a reflective emotional and musical dynamic, rather than just getting into the melody/rhythm and settling for a monochromatic emotion. The singer needs to look at Florence's character and situation in depth, preparing herself for delivering the song with vulnerability and honesty. Florence is an outspoken character, and she wears her emotions on her sleeve in this song. These characteristics rationalize the complex rhythmic choices in the song—which are as complex as her character. As far as vocal demands are concerned, the song is not challenging in range, never straying at the top beyond B in the middle of the staff, and only rarely descending below D above middle C. The challenge here is to sing what is essentially a lyric song with many rhythmic variants in the vocal line, and many words to enunciate and project clearly, in addition to Florence's need to find answers.

BEHIND THE SCENES WITH THE ARTISTS: ELAINE PAIGE, THE ORIGINAL FLORENCE

Ms. Paige has a strong grasp on Florence's character and sums up her background and personal traits with understanding and thoughtful consideration. Her analysis of Florence is based on her knowledge of the original writing and character of Florence Vassy as she explains her history: "Born in Hungary, she left the country when she was only two years old with her mother in 1956, during the uprising, and became a naturalized British citizen. Her father 'disappeared' when the uprising was over, but she has never found out what happened to him. This personal history makes Florence distrusting and cynical." Other traits include an intelligence and determination that mask vulnerability. "She says it like it is, and embraces the truth." Furthermore, "she realizes that in life you have to go it alone." Regarding her relationship with American chess master Freddy Trumper, she says, "She meets him at a chess championship and is immediately attracted to him. He is eccentric, 'wild' and a challenge. She admires his talent; he's someone to pit her wits against. They become good friends then eventually lovers, and she becomes his 'minder' too. He is not easy to be around with his temperamental moods, and after seven turbulent years together she eventually quits."

Hold On

The Secret Garden

"[What is important is] the enunciation and especially inflection that the singer discovers from reading the text a number of times, finding the important words and syllables to inflect."
—Alison Fraser, the original Martha

CHARACTER: Martha

MUSIC: Lucy Simon

BOOK AND LYRICS: Marsha Norman

BASED ON: The 1911 novel *The Secret Garden* by Frances Hodgson Burnett

SETTING: Yorkshire, England, early twentieth century

BROADWAY PREMIERE: 1991

CLASSIFICATION: Anthem/belt

RANGE: 

TESSITURA: Lower range; the end has extended, sustained tones of B natural

TIME: 2:40

PLOT: Mary Lennox, born and raised in British East India in the early 1900s, is orphaned by a cholera outbreak and is sent to Yorkshire, England, at age eleven to live with relatives she has never met. It is considered a miracle that she has not contracted the disease, since she was drinking the same water as her parents in India. The story is about the family members Mary interacts with in the old English house and the ghosts who continue to haunt her.

Characters referred to as the Dreamers are family and friends from Mary's life in India who are deceased and are used in the show as a Greek (ghost) chorus who narrates the action. Among the departed are her mother, Rose, and her aunt, Lily. These ghosts haunt her until she finds her new life in the course of the story. They appear to comment and are seen and disappear at will. The original production's set resembled a Victorian toy theatre, with pop-out figures, large paper dolls, and surrealistic experimental collage. One of the relatives she meets in Yorkshire is her uncle Archibald Craven, who is a hunchback. He is the widower of Lily, and continues to mourn her death. His young son, Colin, is Mary's cousin. Archibald is sure that Colin will also become a hunchback, and thus he confines his son to bed. Dr. Neville Craven, Archibald's brother, makes the household decisions and manages the manor house. Upon Mary's arrival in England, the housekeeper, Mrs. Medlock, says about her: "I've never seen a child sit so still or look so old." The house is on the moor, where "nothing is heard but the 'awful, howling sound of the wind.'"

CHARACTER: Martha is first described in the script as a sturdy, curious Yorkshire servant girl, "humming to herself as she enters the room." She enters carrying a breakfast tray and a skipping rope as she begins "Martha's Ditty," which resembles a nursery rhyme. A couple of days later, Mary is "better at skipping rope." Martha is a no-nonsense, straightforward character, who at first disturbs Mary with her direct honesty, which can reduce Mary to tears. In time, however, Mary grows closer to Martha, who encourages Mary to get out into the fresh air and look around. Martha sings her the song "If I Had a Fine White Horse," leading Mary, while singing, to the garden, where Martha's brother, Dickon, works as a gardener. Mary is growing stronger emotionally in the house, especially now that she is closer to Martha. There is a visit from the headmistress of a boarding school, but Mary doesn't want to go. Mary prefers to stay in the house with Martha.

CONTEXT: The intense scene that precedes Martha's singing "Hold On" in scene 6 is between Dr. Craven and Mary, as he insists that she go away to school. In response, Mary has a tantrum and Craven grabs her, telling her that Archibald, who has always been kind to Mary, wants her to leave, because Mary reminds him of his deceased wife. Dr. Craven tells her angrily, "You drove him away," and he almost strikes her in anger. Craven furthermore tells her that she is hurting Colin, not helping him. "You don't want Colin to get well at all. You want him to die so that you can have this house!" Craven "almost raises his arm, as though to hit Mary." Then he screams:

"You will leave Saturday week!" Later, Martha is packing Mary's clothes before she leaves. Martha tells Mary that she has been an important presence in the house, and her kind words are comforting. Mary has helped Colin come out of himself, Martha suggests. Mary says that she feels like a ghost, like she is gone already. As she begins to sing, Martha tells her that she has to finish what she has begun. She doesn't know exactly how, just that Mary needs to finish it somehow.

CONTENT: The form of the song is verse-chorus, verse-chorus, and it modulates to a strong finishing cadence. There is heavy orchestration, with strings, and very little doubling of the vocal line, and the accompaniment is rhythmically busy. Instead of doubling the melody in the chorus, the orchestra is sounding quarter-note chords against the more complex rhythms of the voice. The manner in which the text and vocal line is rhythmically set brings out the confidence of the message, which Martha conveys with commitment and love.

VOICE: Alison Fraser, the first Martha, has told me that since the song begins so low and there are so many words, enunciation and inflection become very important. The singer discovers from reading the text a number of times how to find the most natural words and syllables to inflect. The line "It's the storm, not you, that's bound to blow away" leads Martha to the chorus, as she implores Mary to "hold on." The chorus requires a solid belt sustained tone, along with a legato line as the voice also displays warmth. The singer must be careful not to sing the chorus too stridently, because although Martha is offering inspiration and strength, the tone also needs to be warm and lyric.

The song requires a strong attention to text, especially in the verse. The singer needs to know what the accompaniment is doing, even if it is a solo vocal performance with piano. During the verse the accompaniment will play the melody, freeing up the singer to approach the verse with more of a speech-like attention to text. As the song unfolds, there is a countermelody heard in the orchestra the second time through, which will support the melody, giving the song an anthem-like inspirational frame. The chorus begins with a solidly sung middle A-flat belt, and then the phrase is sung higher, at the B-flat level, which will require some light/high voice mixed in for flexibility and agility as the melody ascends into that area. The song modulates from its original key of D-flat up to E-flat and finally one-half step up to E major, finishing on a sustained, bright B natural, the fifth of the chord in the final ending tag.

BEHIND THE SCENES WITH THE ARTISTS: ALISON FRASER, THE ORIGINAL MARTHA

Alison told me, "As she begins to sing, Martha tells Mary that she has to finish what she has begun, and at the beginning of the song does not know yet how—but just that Mary needs to do it somehow."

It Might As Well Be Spring

State Fair

"This is Margy's 'I want' song."
—Randy Skinner, the choreographer-director of the 1996 Broadway production

CHARACTER: Margy Frake

MUSIC: Richard Rodgers

BOOK AND LYRICS: Oscar Hammerstein II

BOOK: Tom Briggs, Louis Mattioli

BASED ON: The 1945 movie musical *State Fair* and Phil Stong's book *State Fair*

SETTING: The Iowa State Fair in Des Moines, 1946

BROADWAY PREMIERE: 1996

CLASSIFICATION: Lyric alto-mezzo

RANGE: 

TESSITURA: Low in the staff

TIME: 3:03

PLOT: Rodgers and Hammerstein songs taken from different musicals, a 1945 movie musical, and the book *State Fair* are the three ingredients that are combined in this 1996 Broadway incarnation. In the late summer of 1946, the Frake family of Iowa plans to visit the Iowa State Fair. While the parents would like to win some blue ribbons at the fair for their prized boar and their mincemeat pie, their children, Margy and Wayne, are more interested in finding romance. The songs extracted from different Rodgers and Hammerstein musical stage productions include a song cut from the original production of *Oklahoma!* Other Rodgers and Hammerstein songs in the show are from *Allegro, Me and Juliet, Cinderella,* and *Pipe Dream.*

CHARACTER: Margy has a beau, Harry, in her hometown, but she is not happy with him. He has already planned out their life together, while she is looking for something more exciting. As the song indicates, Margy "wants more." She doesn't know why, but she is restless and jumpy. She would attribute her mood to spring fever, "but it isn't even spring."

CONTEXT: The song is placed at the beginning of the show, before the family leaves for the state fair. Margy has just met with hometown beau Harry, and she is clearly eager for something new and unexpected in her predictable life. The song, while attractive enough to be placed in a more prominent place in the show, establishes Margy's need to stretch her wings and fly beyond the confines of their Iowa farm.

CONTENT: The four-measure orchestral introduction is marked "grazioso." Before the opening of the song, the setup before the well-known melody, there is a repetition of scale-like passages (marked "andante moderato") that shows a weariness with the repetition of her life—she is going through the motions. Margy yearns for other things that she doesn't have, and she is prone to sitting around and moping, as her mother observes. She confesses, "I am wonderful and know I'm a dope!" There is a four-measure introduction before the well-known refrain begins, which is marked "meno mosso" and "con languore" (sung languidly). The chorus is repeated two times, then there is a bridge," marked "con moto" (with motion). The B section, which talks about her continuing to wish she was somewhere else, even though on this "strange new street" she would hear words that she has never heard from a man she has yet to meet (poco rallentando). The music moves into the final chorus, marked "a tempo," which continues to be a languid expression of wonder and longing. The accompaniment has a marked legato in the bass, and is largely of slower, more sustained rhythmic values. However, at the ending of the song, the orchestra is more active and playful rhythmically.

VOICE: There is an ease to the opening melody, a dreamy quality, and the attractive melody belies the fact that the pitches are not all that simple to tune with the many intervals and accidentals. In the opening melody and the repetitions of it, it's important to keep the first eighth-note rhythms even and not dot them. "I'm as jumpy as a puppet" *is* dotted, however, and the two phrases should not be sung the same. Although this song is an expression of longing, it is important to think of it as wistful longing and dreaming, without a dramatic or pushed delivery in vocal production. The range demands are also not great, so that the languid quality may remain. The bridge, with its A-flat and B-flat, is the most demanding as far as range is concerned, but it is not a sustained challenge, as the vocal line quickly returns to the same lower pitch level as before, finishing at an E-flat on the bottom line of the staff. One word of warning about singing the melody throughout with a languid quality: remember that "languid" can mean a low-energy quality that can result in pitches being sung with a flat intonation, but the restless quality can and should inject some needed energy into the expression, especially when singing the sixth and seventh ascending intervals in the final phrases.

BEHIND THE SCENES WITH THE ARTISTS: RANDY SKINNER, CO-DIRECTOR AND CHOREOGRAPHER

Randy recalls the setup of the song: "In the song *It Might As Well Be Spring,* Margy is expressing her longing for something to happen to her, outside of her life on the Iowa farm. It's all in those wonderful Hammerstein lyrics—the emotions one feels when you want something new to happen but can't quite put your finger on it. This is Margy's 'I want' song—and then she goes to the Iowa state fair and experiences a love that changes her life."

I Will Be Loved Tonight

I Love You, You're Perfect, Now Change

"It's about the *tactile*, about touch."
—Joel Bishoff, the original director

CHARACTER: Diane

MUSIC: Jimmy Roberts

BOOK AND LYRICS: Joe DiPietro

SETTING: Contemporary suburbia

OFF-BROADWAY PREMIERE: 1996

CLASSIFICATION: Lyric song—alto

RANGE: 

TESSITURA: Mostly low centering on middle C

TIME: 2:45

PLOT: *I Love You, You're Perfect, Now Change* was written in the form of a series of vignettes connected by the central idea of love and relationships. Key to the show is this tagline: "Everything you have ever secretly thought about dating, romance, marriage, lovers, husbands, wives, and in-laws, but were afraid to admit." Most scenes stand independent of the others but progress in a fashion designed to suggest an impression of overall stages of relationships in one's life. The stages include dating, marriage, and child rearing. Even though the show has a large number of characters, the actual number of people interpreting all of these characters totals four. "I Will Be Loved Tonight" is sung by Diane.

CHARACTER: According to Jennifer Simard, who created the role, Diane is "funny, quirky, sweet, insecure, genuine, vulnerable, and brave." The closest model, Jennifer told me, is the character Elaine Benes from the popular TV show *Seinfeld.*

CONTEXT: Jennifer, summarizing the show, says: "Act I reflects the earlier parts of dating/relationships culminating in a wedding to end act I. Act II reflects the latter stages from having children, trying to maintain passion in the relationship while juggling responsibilities, the journey through divorce, death, and perhaps finding love again. So, even though the show is organized by divisions into vignettes/sketches, there is a thru line." Scene 6, titled "The Lasagna Incident," leads into "I Will Be Loved Tonight." Ms. Simard says: "Rob [Robert Roznowski] and I used to comment we both knew what it felt like to always feel like you're saying the wrong thing, the feeling of putting your foot in your mouth and the feeling of hopeful vulnerability. It is so sweet and funny to see these two characters trip all over themselves, both feeling the same way toward one another and risking their hearts by letting their walls down. At any moment, either one of them could face rejection. Instead, they fumble their way through to taking the next step in their relationship." Jennifer goes on to say that the song could also be sung from the male point of view. "It's a reflection of them both, of any lonely soul taking a chance on love and intimacy."

CONTENT: The song begins with shorter, almost breathless phrases that indicate Diane's palpable excitement, which leads to her confident phrase: "I will be loved tonight." The accompaniment is marked "gently, not too fast," and the vocal line is first marked "freely." The song is lyric, but also has a syncopated feel, which gives the song momentum. There are no declamatory lines of powerful delivery. The first A section's syncopated melody is doubled in the treble of the accompaniment. It is marked "gently, not too fast." It should be sung freely—the performer should not sing the melody metronomically, or mechanically. At the line "A man is in sight," there is a fermata rest, which is dramatic in its silence, and creates expectation, before she sings, "And I will be loved [another brief rest] . . . tonight." This short phrase acts as a chorus and glues the song together. The second section, "To fondle his skin," has the same melody as section A, but the accompaniment here is more independent of the melody and more rhythmically active. The rests before and in the chorus are the same. In the following section, the bridge, as she sings, "You can go from week to week," the vocal line moves a little faster, with greater momentum, and the accompaniment responds with appropriate energy and activity. The meter alternates between 6/4 and 4/4 to reflect the text inflections, which cannot be placed symmetrically in 4/4 meter, and gives the section forward momentum. As she arrives at the transition, "It's just the nights—that always hurt," the music is marked "slowly, freely," and there is a fermata rest, giving Diane time to reflect, before she begins the final recapitulation of the verse-chorus. There is another poignant moment in the last verse as Diane sings the plea "But please, hold me tight," which is also sung freely and controlled by the performer. At the end, the final chorus, there is an extended tag of whole notes, with an accompaniment which remains gentle, rocking, comforting, and reassuring.

VOICE: The singer needs to capture Diane's combination of quiet confidence and excitement as she looks forward to love. The song wants to be a pop song because of its rhythmic lilt and accompaniment, as its rhythmic chords capture a popular song feel. But the singer needs to be in control of the moment and not follow the accompaniment, or it will wind up in a pop groove. During each chorus, "I will be loved," the singer will sing a low A below middle C on the word "loved" that is extended and deep, but the tone should be warm and not belted. During the bridge and at other times in the song, the melody will extend up to a B and C in the middle of the staff, but these notes should also be sung lyrically, not belted. During the bridge, there are a number of written accidentals that flirt with the possibility of changing key, but Diane finds her way back to the tonic for the recapitulation of the verse-chorus to the end of the song.

BEHIND THE SCENES WITH THE ARTISTS: JOEL BISHOFF, THE ORIGINAL DIRECTOR

Joel has directed multiple productions of the show throughout the world; he recently returned from the latest production in Japan. When he meets the cast for the first time, he has them read through the entire script, both musical lyrics and dialogue. Instead of a sing-through of the songs, they speak the lyrics as if they are in a play. His blocking for all of the productions is nearly identical. He feels it is imperative that all of the actors who go through the movements know that behind each blocking move is an important reason to move, a motivation. He doesn't like the ballad to be too busy, but he also says that in musicals there are times in which the actor who is about to sing a song "stops" to sing the pop song, and he works against this tendency. In speaking about the song, Joel says it is about the tactile, about touch ("To fondle his skin . . .").

A New Life

Jekyll and Hyde

"The story of Lucy Harris is the seemingly hopeless situation of a woman who knows that her tragic character will never know the love of Dr. Jekyll because she is not of his class and will never be."

—Linda Eder, the original Lucy

CHARACTER: Lucy Harris

MUSIC: Frank Wildhorn

LYRICS: Leslie Bricusse

BASED ON: The novella by Robert Louis Stevenson *The Strange Case of Dr. Jekyll And Mr. Hyde*

ORIGINAL STAGE CONCEPTION: Steve Cuden and Frank Wildhorn

SETTING: London, the nineteenth century

BROADWAY PREMIERE: 1997

CLASSIFICATION: Alto-mezzo belt-anthem

RANGE: 

TESSITURA: Beginning of the song is quite low in tessitura, but the last section is pitched toward the top of the staff

TIME: 3:58

PLOT: At the beginning of the show, Dr. Henry Jekyll is seen in an insane asylum with his comatose father ("Lost in the Darkness"). He addresses the audience in song ("I Need To Know"). Jekyll believes that the cause of his father's serious illness is the inherent evil in his father's soul. Jekyll is passionate in his belief that man is both good and evil, and he speaks of his attempt to scientifically separate the two forces.

Jekyll is engaged to Emma Danvers of high London society. She is the daughter of Sir Danvers, the chairman of the board of St. Jude's Hospital. Jekyll presents his research proposal to the pompous hospital board to general derision. He decides to take his research into his own hands, experimenting on himself, which creates the alter ego that is Mr. Hyde.

CHARACTER: Lucy Harris is a prostitute who hangs out at the Red Rat tavern, where Jekyll's bachelor party is held. She is the main attraction in the tavern. Lucy arrives late and immediately is in trouble with the boss, who often abuses her physically and is known by the sinister name "Spider." Jekyll observes her boss's behavior and tries to help Lucy. Despite her situation in life, she appears to be kind-hearted and well-liked. Jekyll offers his business card and suggests she contact him if she needs help.

CONTEXT: After their first meeting, Lucy arrives at Dr. Jekyll's residence to be treated for a nasty bruise on her back, which she says was caused by a man named Hyde. Not aware of his alter ego's behavior, Jekyll hides his horror. Clearly in love with Jekyll, Lucy kisses him. Later, again at the Red Rat tavern, Lucy is visited by Hyde, who tells her that he is leaving for a while. He then warns Lucy to never leave him, which terrifies her. However, she appears to be held under his sinister spell.

Meanwhile, stress is taking its toll on Dr. Jekyll as he tries to control his alter ego. Jekyll's lawyer and good friend, John Utterson, visits Jekyll's laboratory and learns of his terrible secret. Utterson takes a letter from Jekyll with money to deliver to Lucy at the Red Rat. The letter instructs her to leave town and start "a new life" somewhere else. Lucy thinks about the possibilities.

The song is placed toward the end of act II (there are forty musical numbers in the show. "A New Life" is thirty-sixth); Lucy is in her bare room at the tavern, a bed and a dressing table the only furniture in the room.

CONTENT: It is important to observe how this song builds through its verses to a high-belt climactic ending. The brief opening melodic motive, repeated throughout the song (with variations), is the building block of the piece. The song begins with eight measures of introduction played by solo flute. The first vocal phrase, beginning immediately with the refrain motive, is sung a cappella, while Lucy contemplates the possibility of starting a "new life." The phrases at first are sung without a great deal of vocal lyricism, but are intoned in almost a speech-like manner. When the orchestra enters, it supports the melody with a very simple chordal accompaniment. When the singer is accompanied on piano, the accompanist (and singer) needs to recognize that the voice part is doubled in the score. Also, there are many moving lines in the accompaniment that need to coordinate with the vocal line. The first choruses (with slight variations of melodic line) are not intended to be strictly sung rhythmically, and the voice is free to find its own phrasing, including rubato. When Lucy sings: "A New Hope" at the third refrain, marked "rubato con moto," the motive is pitched up one step. As she sings the words "A new dream," the rhythm becomes more strict and defined, as the orchestra enters with more support. There are little woodwind flourishes (also replicated in the piano accompaniment) that connect the ends of melody lines to the next vocal phrase, which propels the momentum of the song. After the text "A new chance" is sung, the song slows a little, as the singer will observe a fermata as Lucy sings "a touch of romance." At this point, there is a marked accelerando. Also observe the specific musical instructions of pianissimo as the meter changes for one measure to 3/4, then notice the markings ritardando, another fermata before "the chance for me," as the song is restored to a tempo, then moving forward toward "A new dream," as the melodic motive is restored down a step. At this point, a transition refrain with more active rhythm is inserted, which builds (after a ritard), to "A new world," modulating from E major (four sharps) to the key of G major (one sharp), continuing with an active variety of rhythms combining triplets, sixteenth notes, and dotted values. The song culminates with a slowing and broadening toward a dynamic building to sustained, high belt pitches.

VOICE: The song deserves a singer with the ability to build a song to a climactic high belt and requires maintaining a strong tone and emotion through a long phrase to build the song. Recognizing all of the dynamic variety in the markings is helpful for the performer in pacing the song while maintaining emotional intensity. Lucy is hoping that she will have "a new life," while at the same time, with her background and history, fighting what she knows is an uphill battle. This conflict provides layers of conflicting emotions. A variety of vocal colors results from her emotional roller coaster, including a breath-supported lyric-soprano clear tone, and a full belt in the middle and upper ranges of the voice, between B and D toward the top of the staff.

BEHIND THE SCENES WITH THE ARTISTS: LINDA EDER, THE ORIGINAL LUCY

Ms. Eder told me that the story of Lucy Harris is the seemingly hopeless situation of a woman who knows that her tragic character will never know the love of Dr. Jekyll because she is not of his class and will never be. She is a prostitute, and she will always be a "fallen" woman. On the other hand, she dreams of "a new life" and sings about this hope. The conflict is between her dream and the reality of her situation. Linda observes that the bed (which is onstage and which she ends up on at the end, gripping the bedpost), is a symbol of her situation. It is the place where she works, and it also serves as a symbolic cage. And it is true that by the end of the song she appears to be a caged animal, struggling to be free. In this environment and situation she conveys a restless energy.

Raise the Roof

The Wild Party

"There are [voices] that belong to peers of mine that simply knock me out in terms of their dexterity with tone and power—but I do know that I like to tell a story."
—Julia Murney, the original Queenie

CHARACTER: Queenie

MUSIC, LYRICS, BOOK: Andrew Lippa

BASED ON: Joseph Moncure March's 1928 narrative poem of the same name

SETTING: New York, the 1920s

OFF-BROADWAY PREMIERE: 2000

CLASSIFICATION: Belt with high extension

RANGE: 

TESSITURA: All over the place

TIME: 3:11

PLOT: The show is about vaudeville life in the 1920s, set in a Manhattan apartment. The central character is Queenie, and the plot's major focus is on the a wild party with its invited guests, eccentrically diverse characters, including a hooker, a mute dancer, and a prizefighter. The party eventually becomes the tragic scene of the result of jealousy and passion, as Queenie's boyfriend, Burrs, is shot at the end of the play in the style of verismo opera.

CHARACTER: Queenie is a free spirit. She is a vaudeville showgirl performer in the 1920s, residing in Manhattan. She lives with Burrs, a clown in the same show she is performing in. Queenie is looking for passion and adventure in her life, especially after her relationship with Burrs has gone stale over a few years. She has a large number of friends, all looking for fun and excitement, but they are not particularly close to her. Queenie is starving for a jolt of adrenaline and likes to live on the edge.

CONTEXT: With Queenie and Burrs, distrust has replaced passion in their relationship. Wanting to escape Burrs, Queenie plans to throw a party where she can embarrass him. The guest list is a mixed group of eccentrics. Fashionably late to the party is Kate, a semireformed prostitute and Queenie's rival as party diva, accompanied by a young gentleman named Mr. Black. Queenie is instantly attracted to him, and thus sees an opportunity to make Burrs jealous. A neighbor is annoyed by the party noise, and Queenie responds to the neighbor's complaints by yelling and rallying the party with "Raise the Roof" in response.

CONTENT: The song begins with Queenie and the crowd engaged in a high-energy call-and-response exchange as the Latin-tinged four-measure introduction starts. Queenie exhorts the crowd to "gather round and listen well," telling them, "We're not here to eat! We're here for the heat!" going into the first chorus of "Let's raise the roof!" The second verse begins with a guttural sound in her throat as she prepares to sing the first words of the verse, "Cruuuush the ice and shake forever," in a sensual and anticipatory kick-start of the line. There is another chorus followed by a bridge that ascends to D at the top, building the excitement. At the third verse, Queenie is directed to sing a vocal slide (not pitches) from low A below middle C up two octaves to the high A. At the end of the song there is a tag which culminates in an ending of commanding flair. This song creates a lot of heat, with its Latin rhythms and exotic percussive instruments, as well as its clever use of one-syllable words. Queenie exhorts and takes charge in the song. It is a very high-energy song, and gives the singer the opportunity to dive in without caution or self-editing.

VOICE: The song keeps the singer at high energy because of the active rhythms of each phrase. The song begins quite low (sustaining the low F-sharp below middle C), so initial consonants as the rhythm is defined are very important. The vocal lines ascend to a high belt (D toward the top of the staff), before the second verse. The bridge of the song (beginning with "Let the neighbors scream and shout—who cares if they do?") is vocally exposed, as Queenie sings the *u* vowel (of "do") on the high D pitch, extended and without accompaniment on that measure, before the final verse begins ("Cut the strings and set the table"). When she sings (at the end of the song) the phrase "Let's call the shots" and sustains the C in a crescendo with "so put away that smoking gun," Queenie provides a foreshadowing of the tragic ending to the show. The words she sings are almost sensual to linger on, especially with the one-syllable words such as "shots" and "dice," as well as "grab," "bribe," and "shake."

There is very little time for the singer to rest in the performance of the song. Even though the range is in the singer's upper belting area, the diction and inflection are important. The momentum of each line must also continue to push forward in a breathless rush of action.

BEHIND THE SCENES WITH THE ARTISTS: ANDREW LIPPA, COMPOSER, AND JULIA MURNEY, THE ORIGINAL QUEENIE

Andrew Lippa says that he had an "instinct thing" when he first heard Julia Murney sing: he was convinced that she was the right person to cast in the leading role of Queenie. "It was her essential quality as a person, the way she interpreted lyrics," he said. Julia Murney said that she appreciates the way that the composer works, and likes it that "he tends to compose 'right in the pocket'" of where she sings. She continues: "He lets me find my way and put my spin on stuff, and then as time goes on, character choices are made by me and suggested by him, and then you end up with somewhat of a final product." She says she makes initial character choices that are basically "instinctive," and then goes from there. As for how she delivers a song, Julia says she "likes to tell a story." She needs to get "inside the story" to learn the song. Otherwise, she has a difficult time learning it. In regard to finding the way to properly phrase the song, she needs to know why she is saying these particular words and, she says, "understand why I'm saying them at those particular pitches or at that particular speed." Julia has one more important piece of advice for young singers: "The more different styles you get to (or make yourself) sing, the more layered your vocal encyclopedia."

Through the Mountain

Floyd Collins

"It is about her certainty that she is a savior, a mother, a messenger."
—Theresa McCarthy, the original Nellie

CHARACTER: Nellie Collins

MUSICAND LYRICS: Adam Guettel

BOOK: Tina Landau

BASED ON: The historical event of the death of Floyd Collins

SETTING: Kentucky, January 1925

PREMIERE: Chicago, 2001

CLASSIFICATION: Alto/mezzo anthem–folk flavor

RANGE: 

TESSITURA: Below staff, middle

TIME: 2:55

PLOT: Based on a true story; Floyd Collins (a legendary cave explorer), becomes trapped down a deep passageway fifty-five feet below the earth's surface while exploring a cave in central Kentucky. Food could be sent down to him for a number of days, but after a more serious collapse, the cave was completely closed. During the seventeen days he was trapped in the cave, there was a media circus above ground surrounding the rescue efforts. By the time Floyd was finally reached, he was dead.

CHARACTER: Nellie is Floyd Collin's younger sister, aged twenty-five (thirteen years younger than her brother). She is a strong-willed young woman with a mind of her own, unusual qualities in rural Kentucky. When she is introduced at the beginning of the play, it is revealed that she has just come from a long stay at a mental hospital. Because of her medical history, she lives in her head in order to cope with the obstacles in her life. In act II, she "hears" Floyd and sings to him. She is thought to be crazy. In the show, Nellie has a psychic ability to connect with Floyd in a way that is mystical. During their final communication she helps him transcend the physical world to travel from his underground tomb to heaven to escape his pain and suffering.. The irony in the musical is that Nellie is thought to be crazy and no one believes that she can help in any way, yet she "saves" him in the end.

CONTEXT: The height of the media frenzy occurs in act II. Countless reporters are asking repetitive questions of family members. It is eight days after the initial cave-in, and now another cave-in is imminent, possibly because of the frantic rescue effort. No one knows what to do, but Nellie does. She knows that the time is soon approaching when they will lose communication with Floyd. She is told that she "can't go there," because the cave is closed off to everyone (especially women) for safety reasons. However, Nellie is stubborn. She wants to go underground to be with her brother, until she realizes that she can "talk" to him above ground.

CONTENT: The wind (heard in the music) is a signal to Nellie that Floyd's spirit is available, that she can connect with him now. In the opening of the song (a nineteen-measure setup) she is angry and frustrated that she has been prevented from communicating with him (marked "flexible tempo"). "It's not fair," she sings, "you men going under," and this section is faster and marked "playful attack," and the meter changes between 4/4 and 3/4; the notated rhythms are not predictable. Nellie is "achin' to set him free"; "What's wrong with me?" she asks. She can get him out, she sings in the chorus. She can transport him "to the other side," to a place that sounds like a heavenly release from his physical state. It is a descriptive passage that includes colors, smells, touch, and the warmth of a "goodnight hug," as she weaves through a melodic line with many accidentals and rhythmically syncopated figures. "To a land of babies dancing with a banjo in the air" is a good example of the imaginative text. She repeats the chorus verbatim. The music in the song is composed in the styles of bluegrass and folk, combined with repeated motives and themes.

VOICE: In the opening of the song, the singer needs to follow the specific articulation markings to bring the text alive, including accents, staccato, legato, and two markings that indicate bending the note upward and downward. The opening is enormously varied in range (from low F below middle C to high F at the top of the staff) and articulation markings. There are wide intervallic leaps notated, and the negotiation of these pitches means quick switching of vocal registers to the lighter (soprano) head resonance, a timbre of a lighter weight. Diction is also important, as it is sometimes difficult to enunciate in the higher pitches. Also important is vocal flexibility and legato passages that simulate the sound of the wind, symbolic of Nellie's intent to communicate with Floyd psychically. In the verses that describe what heaven will be like, the voice is placed in the lower (below the staff) chest-resonance range (low F). To project the text clearly in such a low register, the singer should observe the rhythmic inflections and define them clearly, including syncopated rhythms.

BEHIND THE SCENES WITH THE ARTISTS: THERESA MCCARTHY, THE ORIGINAL NELLIE

Ms. McCarthy says that the first time she heard the song "Through the Mountain" was during a workshop for the original project in Philadelphia in the early 1990s. Her first thought was that the song was the perfect choice for that moment in the play. "It's late at night and people are going home after another unsuccessful day attempting to save Floyd. The intro-song proper structure fits the classic mold for music theatre standards." The song is also the only love song in the piece. "It is not a romantic song, but a song of love that Nellie has for her brother, and her fierce determination to connect with him."

The singing of the song poses some challenges for the singer. "The approach for this intro has to be legit—rhythmic and melodic challenges dictate a placement that is epic compared to the more relaxed country feel of the song.... Hearing that intro with its rare tonalities and intervals, I knew that the composer was going for a statement that was coming from a higher place than just the standard emotional response actors bring to work." She also talks about the dramatic importance of the introduction: "So the intro is bigger than Nellie—wiser than she is—though it...contains the frustration of being a woman thwarted from helping, it also has the quality of a godlike creature on a mission. It's tough to say how to act that! But anger is not enough—it is too small a choice."

She also recognized the difficulty in playing the character "crazy" during this song, though Nellie had been in a mental institution before the accident. "There's a stigma surrounding Nellie that is never explained." The song should not be "about Nellie's emotional journey. It is about her certainty that she is a savior, a mother, a messenger."

It is important for the actor to realize what it means to Nellie in the family when Floyd is gone. Still, she remains strong during this song, and almost heroic in her efforts to save him. "Nellie must appear supernaturally strong and determined to get to him; she must know that she will get down there and she must not know on any level that she won't."

Another challenge of the piece is the staging of a song in which the sister is trying to communicate with her brother fifty-five feet below the earth: "Several times . . . she sings to the ground—she believes that she is communicating with him, and there are also instances when Floyd says that he can hear her. Of course we know that he can't, but we played with the idea that there was a true bond between them, that they had survived a lot at the hands of their raging father during their lives and that she could almost get inside his mind." Theresa also describes how the staging of the song could appear to comfort him: "The staging was a journey around the stage to where Floyd lay. When Nellie says 'I'm a- take you by the hand and with a gentle tug we'll be gone,' I reached my hand to just next to Chris Invar's, and he reached up to me and I pulled very easily and subtly—as if I was leading him out of the cave. I was standing right next to the platform on which he lay—not in the tunnel that the rest of the cast used to reach him. I walked through rock walls—I felt I was a spirit."

A Part of That

The Last Five Years

"It became important to play this character not totally likeable, which is against my nature in general. Sometimes Cathy is a little needy, selfish, petty, and ambitious. In other words, Cathy is flawed."
—Lauren Kennedy, the original Cathy Wyatt

CHARACTER: Cathy Wyatt

MUSIC, LYRICS, AND BOOK: Jason Robert Brown

SETTING: Chicago, 2000–

PREMIERE: 2001, Chicago

CLASSIFICATION: Mezzo/alto up-tempo

RANGE: 

TESSITURA: Middle of staff

TIME: 3:58

PLOT: *The Last Five Years* is a one-act, two-character musical by Jason Robert Brown. The story is about the five-year relationship between Catherine Wyatt, a young actress trying to establish a career, and Jamie Wellerstein, a novelist who achieves surprisingly early success. The show tells the story in reverse order for Cathy's character, beginning at the end of their relationship, with Cathy singing "Still Hurting" after their breakup, while Jamie's story unfolds chronologically. The stories of the characters intersect only in the middle as Jamie proposes and they sing "The Next Ten Minutes" to each other (scene 8). Otherwise the characters do not interact onstage.

CHARACTER: Cathy is Jamie's "Shiksa goddess," which, as Jamie reveals early in the show, does not please his parents at all. His dating history involved a string of girls by the names of Greenblatt, Mincus, Pincus, Katz, Kaplan, and Rosen. As far as Jamie's Jewish relatives are concerned, she has "broken the circle." Cathy is a struggling actress, but to Jamie, writing comes easy, and success has come fast (he is not yet twenty-four), as he says in the song "Moving Too Fast," which precedes "A Part of That." She might have thought that life as an actress would be glamorous, but then she spends "a summer in Ohio" alone in summer stock. Cathy sees Jamie's acclaimed book in a bookstore window in Kentucky while she has to suffer the humbling experience of auditions. Cathy has flaws, she confesses to Jamie. She is not always on time. And she is a dreamer, a romantic. The lyrics that she sings show her to have an edge and a caustic wit. She is in "Jamie land," as she describes where they are in their marriage.

Other Cathy characteristics: She has grown up in a small town and doesn't want to end up like a friend of hers from high school ("I Can Do Better Than That"). She is the one who asks Jamie to move in with her. She feels that she is "climbing uphill" in life. Wanting to fix problems in their relationship is her goal while they are together. He says that he believes in her, and says, "We'll be fine," but later he betrays their marriage with a relationship with another woman. Cathy feels victimized by Jamie's success, and claims that he has sacrificed their relationship for the sake of his career. However, she says that she still loves him.

CONTEXT: The song occurs in scene 5 (of a total of fourteen scenes). Cathy is at a book-signing party for Jamie. This song is sung during a celebration of his success, and she feels lost, as if she is merely along for the ride. Cathy has lost direction in her career and in her marriage. Now she follows, walking in his footsteps.

CONTENT: The form of the song is a verse/refrain construction. The verse is up-tempo (the four-measure piano introduction is marked "bouncy in 6" in 6/4 meter, which alternates with 4/4). The voice line is rhythmically syncopated, and the vocal entrances are seldom on the beat, while the piano accompaniment remains four- or six-beat steady in the opening, quick-paced phrases. The accompaniment has a playful jauntiness and is busily energized, with added riffs in the treble, never doubling the vocal line. The singer should observe the staccato and other articulation markings in the accompaniment. Also, notice that at the end of the song, there are a number of fermatas in the vocal line, and indications of a tempo, poco ritardando, throughout the final iterations of "I'm a part of that." The rhythm patterns in the vocal line must be clearly defined by the singer and coupled with the lyrics so that the enunciation of text is underlined. In the lyric section (refrain), which has a half-time feel, as Cathy sings: "And then he smiles," the vocal line is more legato and smooth, though syncopated rhythmic patterns remain. The repeated lyrical refrain ("And then he smiles") shows that Cathy, singing warmly, still is very much in love with Jamie, and can easily recall why she is attracted to him, even through her feelings of hurt and anger. Cathy also feels more in control during these lyric passages, and the composer has given her a number of fermatas in this section so that she can linger in these moments of affection for him. She repeats "I'm a part of that" at the end of the refrain each time, and when repeating these words the singer can think of different emotional colors while delivering the repeated phrase, determined by actor choice. This is how the song ends, with the repetition of "I'm a part of that," which can be reflective, inwardly directed echoes at the song's moving conclusion.

VOICE: The song sits in the middle belt area of the voice, but the singer has to reach the higher-octave C with strength as well, so too much vocal weight in the lower vocalizations at the beginning is not recommended. This singing in the opening section contrasts with the lyric "And then he smiles" section that follows, which requires a legato lyric line in the middle of the range and a warmth in the lower B-flat and middle C tones, sung with steady breath support. These sections are marked "piano" in the accompaniment, so it is not necessary to belt for a powerful delivery. During the bridge, as she sings: "There's no question, there's no doubt," the singer needs to sing decisively an E-flat (the top space of the staff), which will require a high-belting, mixing the light (soprano) mechanism with the belt of the chest-voice resonance.

BEHIND THE SCENES WITH THE ARTISTS: LAUREN KENNEDY, THE ORIGINAL CATHY

Ms. Kennedy talked about the challenges of performing a role in reverse. The opening scene occurs at the end of the love affair, with her singing "Still Hurting" in emotional pain. She was able to make it work for her because going to a dark place, the place where Cathy starts in the show, is generally more difficult for her. She is usually sunnier in disposition, and playing dark is not as easy. However, in the show, moving the story for her character toward the beginning of the journey allowed her to go "toward the light," and this idea worked for her. This song that Cathy sings has her repeat the same words over and over, "I'm a part of that." The repetition of this phrase becomes "like a mantra" to her. Perhaps if she repeats it enough times, it will be true. "And there is also a part of her that does believe it, too."

Still Hurting

The Last Five Years

"'Still Hurting' is cathartic. It still pains her to sing his name, Jamie. But she does."
—Jason Robert Brown, composer

CHARACTER: Cathy Wyatt

MUSIC, LYRICS AND BOOK: Jason Robert Brown

SETTING: A small town in Ohio

PREMIERE: Chicago, 2001

CLASSIFICATION: Mezzo lyric

RANGE: 

TESSITURA: Lower-middle staff, then middle staff

TIME: 4:35

PLOT AND CHARACTER: See "A Part of That."

CONTEXT: "Still Hurting" is placed at the beginning of the play for Cathy, but she has already accumulated the relationship history that contributes to the breakup of the marriage. While she is at the end of their story, Jamie has just begun.

CONTENT: The song is written in 9/8 meter and begins with a four-measure introduction, featuring a simple two-measure repeated chord progression. It is rather melancholy in tone, with both lines written in the bass clef for a darker color. The marking is "spare and thoughtful, mezzo piano," and the metronome marking is—the dotted quarter = 60 (sixty beats per second). There are two verses, which end each time with "and I'm still hurting." The chord progression from the introduction is repeated at every two-measure phrase, as is the rhythm of the vocal line/text patterns. The relationship has residual resentment, frustration, and anger. There are two different sections that follow. The B section, which asks: "What about lies, Jamie?" is higher and more active, and more confrontational. There is another verse: "Jamie is sure something wonderful died," which is essentially the same as the first two verses, but there is a little more active movement in the accompaniment. The following section, labeled C, resembles B in its expressive drama and range: "Go and hide and run away!" This text is pitched higher, and is marked "forte." There is more of a working through key progressions in the music, with many accidentals. "Go and ride the sun away!" Cathy says. The next section is an instrumental break of nine measures of imitative polyphony, stylistically baroque in its flavor, which builds to Cathy's pleading with a musical repetition of B: "Give me a day, Jamie! Bring back the lies; hang them back on the wall." Finally, the song finishes with one last verse, followed by an extended cadence: "And I'm [dotted-quarter rest] still hurting." The chorus which connects the sections together is simply "And . . . I'm still hurting," which is motivically small, but is the mantra-like repeated thought that the song has sprouted from.

VOICE: The verses linger between the middle C and the fifth above it (G). The B sections are more projected and emotionally expressive, and leap up to C and D toward the top of the staff. Deep breaths and supported initial consonants are very important. These "crying out" sections also require freeing the jaw and opening the throat to make space, so that throat constriction does not occur.

BEHIND THE SCENES WITH THE ARTISTS: JASON ROBERT BROWN, COMPOSER

I asked composer Jason Robert Brown about what he looked for when he was auditioning singer-actors for the role of Cathy. He told me, "Holding a stage, creating a character, singing their asses off." He told me that the creative process of writing a song like "Still Hurting," included singing while he was composing. He felt that it was crucial that he sing *words* while he composes the song. He never collaborates with a lyricist, as he feels that words are inseparable from the music. He is also conscious of working toward an emotional build while writing a song. He likes to "act" the song. He started with the title, "Still Hurting," and he found a chord progression that made him happy. Then he sang the title over and over until he came up with the next line—it "unfolded" from the title. These lines surrounded the title, and finally he had a structure. Jason adds, "'Still Hurting' is cathartic. It still pains her to sing his name, Jamie. But she does."

I'm Not That Girl

Wicked

"Something passes between them, but she needs to stop her feelings, before she gets hurt."
—Stephen Schwartz, composer

CHARACTER: Elphaba

MUSIC AND LYRICS: Stephen Schwartz

BOOK BY: Winnie Holzman

BASED ON: The Gregory Maguire novel *Wicked: The Life and Times of the Wicked Witch of the West* (1995), the film *The Wizard of Oz* (1939), and the L. Frank Baum story *The Wonderful Wizard of Oz* (1900)

SETTING: The mythical country of Winkie in the land of Oz

BROADWAY PREMIERE: 2003

CLASSIFICATION: Lyric, intimate song for alto

RANGE: 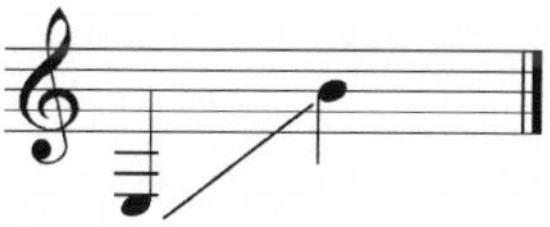

TESSITURA: Very low, bottom of staff

TIME: 3:03

PLOT: The country of Winkie is a province of the fictional Land of Oz. It is distinguished by the color yellow, worn by all locals. The land was ruled by the Wicked Witch of the West before she was melted by a bucket of water. Since then the land has been ruled by the Tin Woodman as its emperor. The other important characters are the witches Elphaba and Galinda, both protagonists in this story. At Shiz University, the Winkie prince Fiyero arrives. He is initially attracted to the lovely Galinda.

CHARACTER: Elphaba, known as the new Wicked Witch of the West, is a sympathetic, victimized character whose behavior is a reaction to the villainous Wizard's corruption. She is a misunderstood girl with the green skin, repulsive to everyone since birth. The show is also about her relationship with Galinda Upland, who eventually becomes Glinda the Good Witch of the North. The name Elphaba was creatively fashioned from the phonetic sounds of *L*yman *F*rank *Ba*um, the author of the original 1900 novel, on which the show is based.

CONTEXT: As Elphaba and Galinda get to be closer friends, Elphaba feels comfortable enough to tell her about the origin of her green skin and the tragic story of how Elphaba's mother, hoping to prevent her second child from being born with green skin, ingested milk-flowers, causing the next child to be born crippled and killing the mother in childbirth. Feeling sympathy, Galinda offers to give Elphaba a personality makeover to help her popularity. The next day, in their history class, the new teacher brings a caged lion cub to class for an experiment. The cage takes away the animal's speech, the teacher declares. An enraged Elphaba and her classmate Fiyero steal the cub and set it free. As Elphaba begins to realize romantic feelings for Fiyero, she admits that she does not feel that she was born to be loved, as she sings the song "I'm Not That Girl" to Galinda.

CONTENT: The form of the song is simple: two verses, bridge, two verses, with a slowing last phrase marked by a caesura before the final words. The song begins gently, with an attractive chord progression, repeated over eight measures, before the voice enters. The first words sung are on the same note, emphasizing the words by separating each phrase into two expressions, before the brief chorus: "He could be that boy, but I'm not that girl," with an turned phrase of varied intervals that attracts the listener's attention with an interesting twist of text that is not expected in a love song. The next verse ("Blithe smile, lithe limb") repeats the same chords, but instead of repeating the same one-note phrases, the singer adapts her melody to a more expressive melodic shape, before repeating the same hook. "She is winsome. She wins him" is one of several original and clever lines within the verses. The bridge ("Every so often we long to steal . . .") is eight measures of syllabically set eighth-note rhythms, for the most part. One of the most attractive qualities of the song is the chord progressions with an accompaniment figure that begins the piece and is heard in the intervals of the song. There is also is the hook of the repeated short chorus.

And not to be forgotten are the emotional colors that the choice of words conjures. It is a magic spell that is created with words, turns of the melody, and accompaniment. "Don't wish, don't start" adds a final verse. The final phrases slow and linger on the concluding, chord, as she sings, "I'm not [pause] that girl."

VOICE: The range is not challenging, nor are the dynamic demands. The song's tessitura is very low, ending on a low, extended E below middle C. The song only ascends to a middle B-natural. The bridge is the most challenging section to sing, because many accidentals are notated, and these need to be negotiated with tuning resulting in good intonation. The performer needs to sing this song as honestly as possible, without artifice or the "plastic" approach that sometime accompanies pop songs or songs that are heard often and are familiar. The singer should prepare to sing this song with the character, text, and context of the song in mind.

BEHIND THE SCENES WITH THE ARTISTS: STEPHEN SCHWARTZ, COMPOSER

Mr. Schwartz told me that the song (and the role) was not written with any particular singer in mind, as Idina Menzel was not yet cast in the production. This particular song was written for this highly charged situation, in which something romantic passes between Fiyero and Elphaba, and she worries that what she thinks has happened may have been misconstrued, and she needs to stop these feelings before she is hurt. In other words, during the song she is persuading herself not to get her hopes up—it would be dangerous to go down that path. I asked Mr. Schwartz to tell me, since he is front and center for all auditions for prospective Elphabas in touring productions of *Wicked*, what he is looks for at the auditions. He told me that the finalists for the role all have to sing "I'm Not That Girl." He said that he is not looking for any one special thing, except for someone who sings a lyric song well, knows how to manage "acting beats," and can handle the range of the song. However, he told me that if the performer has difficulty with the final (low) pitch of the song, an extended low E below middle C, it is not a deal breaker if the singer needs to sing the final pitch an octave higher than written.

Astonishing

Little Women

Ms. Schulman observes that "the song's lyrics have a lot of clues in them when choosing how to shape and play it [the song]."
—Susan Schulman, original director of *Little Women*

CHARACTER: Jo

MUSIC: Jason Howland

LYRICS: Mindi Dickstein

BOOK: Allan Knee

BASED ON: The novel by Louisa May Alcott

SETTING: Concord, Massachusetts, 1869

PREMIERE: 2005

CLASSIFICATION: Mezzo/alto up-tempo

RANGE: 

TESSITURA: Middle of staff

TIME: 4:31

PLOT: See "Some Things Are Meant to Be."

CHARACTER: Jo is a headstrong tomboy who knows what she wants. She loves her home and family, and it is difficult for her to find the courage to go out on her own when she is of age, but she is also trying to be brave. She hopes of becoming a professional writer, a lofty goal for a woman in 1869. Jo is a dreamer, and throughout her childhood she shares a fantasy life with her sisters, which she will draw upon in her future profession as a writer. Jo has flashes of rebelliousness and anger, but, although flawed, she is an appealing character.

CONTEXT: The song "Astonishing" takes place at the end of act I, following a major crisis in Jo's life, which is the hinge point of the show. During her youth, she had enjoyed (with her sisters and the neighbor boy Laurie) acting out stories in the attic, which is her place of refuge, her safe place. When Laurie asks her to marry him, it is a great shock to her. It is a betrayal, after many years of youthful play and friendship. In the show's dialogue with Laurie preceding the song, Laurie boldly presents a ring before popping the question. At first Jo thinks he is joking, because as children in the attic they all had shared a silly, fun fantasy life. When she realizes that he is serious, Jo thinks he has gone mad, and tells him to go find "an accomplished girl." "I don't want an accomplished girl," he says. "I want you!" In anger and agitation she tells him to go, and moves further into the attic (her safe place, as director Susan Schulman calls it) as he exits and she sings the showstopper that ends act I.

CONTENT: Jo has much to process after Laurie shocks her with his proposal; she must sift through important questions, including the most important one: Does she have what it takes to go out into the world, away from her safe place, and make her way alone? As the song begins, she has to honestly analyze and question herself. She needs to know if she can be astonishing. She thinks about her relationship with Laurie. "Who is he? I thought I knew him, thought that he knew me." The song moves through key changes during these first expressions of emotional instability, with the strings playing nervously after the downbeat in an agitated manner. Everything is coming apart, because she thought they would always be great friends and he would support her and her ambitions in the world, and now it is clear that that is over. The line "I thought that home is all I'd ever want" begins a slower, more lyric section. Out of all of her doubts comes the discovery of the word she wants, "astonishing," as the orchestra swells and becomes more active, reflecting her discovery. There are further aha moments and decisions for Jo through the remainder of the song. Once she makes the decision to be courageous and fearless, the song takes on a new hopeful direction that leads the music and text toward the climactic phrases, "Here I go," and "There's no turning back" (projected in a high belt in the octave above middle C). Holding her book in hand as she lifts it skyward, she sings, "I'll shout and start a riot. I'll be anything but quiet! Christopher Columbus!" (she exclaims). "I'll be astonishing... astonishing [up to high D], at last!!" The variety of rhythmic patterns in the accompaniment reflects emotional shifts and decisions made in this complex song.

VOICE: The song needs to gradually build musically and vocally toward its climactic finish, while projecting a sense that it is unfolding spontaneously, without preplanned structure in the performer's mind. The song begins in a very low register, as the accompaniment plays eighth-note rhythms, accented off the beat. While Jo is singing very low in her range, and very quickly, in a rhythmic pattern of sixteenth notes and eighth notes, she must articulate the syllabic text clearly, without tension in the throat. Consonants are important here. As she moves on to "I thought I knew him," the vocal range moves a little higher, coming to a declamatory "How could I be so wrong?" projected in quarter-note rhythms that descend from B-flat. Her thoughts then move to her sisters. If she was wrong about Laurie and misread him, what else about her life needs to be questioned? This section is sung more lyrically and is more reflective, as she thinks about her home. She always thought that home and family were all that she needed. Her intervals here become wider. She needs to connect her lower register to her higher, lighter voice in this section. There is a change of key here, as she sings with determination: "I've got to know if I can be astonishing," sung on a sustained middle G. As she feels life pulling her from within, a life, as she says, that she "is aching to begin," the vocal line moves faster and is more expressive. Jo finds courage: "I'll find my way!" she sings. The orchestra plays strongly accented quarter-note rhythms here, which leads to another emphatic declaration as she sings, "Here I go!" (another key change), and then announces: "I may be small, but I've got giant plans," sung in a high belt. She will make waves in life. "I'll shout and start a riot!" she sings. Finally, she ascends up to a sustained D for the final, sustained "Astonishing, at last!" to close act I.

BEHIND THE SCENES WITH THE ARTISTS: SUSAN SCHULMAN, DIRECTOR OF THE ORIGINAL PRODUCTION

Ms. Schulman observes that the song's lyrics have a lot of clues in them as to how to shape and play it. The opening of the song has the words "I thought" and "How could I?" It is filled with doubt and confusion, until the words "I don't know how to proceed. I only know that I'm meant for something more. I've got to know if I can be *astonishing*." She says the word for the first time in the song. After that, the language Jo chooses changes to "I've got to . . . there must be . . . I'll find my way . . . I will not . . ." Her words are filled with action, not what-ifs.

Don’t Ever Stop Saying I Love You

A Catered Affair

“Don’t fall into the ‘ballad trap’ of slowing these songs down, especially at the cadences.”
—John Bucchino, composer

CHARACTER: Jane Hurley

MUSIC AND LYRICS: John Bucchino

BOOK: Harvey Fierstein

BASED ON: The 1956 film *A Catered Affair* written by Gore Vidal (original teleplay by Paddy Chayefsky)

SETTING: The Bronx, 1953

BROADWAY PREMIERE: 2008

CLASSIFICATION: Lyric, intimate anthem for mezzo

RANGE: 

TESSITURA: Low staff

TIME: 3:10

PLOT: As described by composer John Bucchino, this is a character-driven show set in the 1950s. Young Jane Hurley would like to get married to Ralph, but her father, a taxi driver, is planning to buy out a third partner’s share and cannot afford an expensive wedding. Also, Jane’s brother has just been killed in the Korean War, and it does not seem like a good time for a wedding. Jane’s mother, Aggie, helps them plan a very small City Hall ceremony, but neighborhood opinion plus dinner with Ralph’s well-off parents cause Jane’s mother to want to help plan the “white wedding” that she never had, which is complicated by many factors. At first Jane is pleased with the attention and the preparation as she picks out a white dress, but soon relationships are affected by the costs of the wedding. Jane is not so sure that the big wedding is so important. She begins to think that about her parent's strained relationship, especially since her father is so unemotional and quiet.

CHARACTER: Jane Hurley is a self-sufficient young woman engaged to a teacher. She is from a hard-working lower-middle-class family. The older brother received all of the attention, but was killed in the Korean War. The mother was never able to deal with the trauma from the loss of the favorite child.

CONTEXT: The song is placed toward the end of the show. The young couple has a plan. They want to elope, against the wishes of the mother, and there is a small window of time when they can ran off and get married, quickly followed by a cross-country drive for the honeymoon. In other words, the mother's wishes are ignored. Aggie Hurley (the mother) wants to use the family's life savings for a wedding ceremony the couple will remember forever, while Tom (the father) wants to pay off his taxi. Mother is strong-willed, and there is tension in the family. She has already made plans to invite 180 people to the wedding and doesn't want to disappoint them. On the other hand, the father argues against using their life savings for one event. Before the song is sung, the daughter realizes that she has only ever seen her parents bicker as she is growing up. The situation strengthens her resolve to see that this does not occur in her marriage. In an uncharacteristic moment, Jane opens her heart and is vulnerable, and she needs reassurance.

CONTENT: There is an introduction of twelve measures in 4/4 meter before the voice enters. In the opening melodic line, the shape of the phrase clearly underlines the words "guess" and "less," and "They won't go *near* the words," with the rhymes "fear" and "hear." Jane continues, singing a lovely lyric refrain, now in 3/4 meter, beginning with the word "please," that moves with momentum and urgency toward the end of the phrase, revealing the key line: "Don't ever stop saying I love you." The moving lyrics lead to three words described in the song as a "three syllable bouquet" : "I love you." The refrain of ten measures is repeated in the melody. The B section is less lyric, more text-driven, and includes many accidentals in the vocal line. Another refrain is followed by an eight-measure transition between choruses. The composer/lyricist (at *poco più lento*) underlines the words "I want you so, that I don't mind needing you," as a fermata rest, creating a dramatic space, or beat, is observed. The song continues with a ten-measure refrain, then an interlude of eight measures, followed by an interesting variation of the B section in which the text is again clearly served by the music. Again, there are many accidentals, but these enharmonic tones do not lead us to a different key, with the song remaining in F major to the end with a final chorus, marked "piano," "lento," and "rallentando," slowing further (ritardando) to its conclusion.

VOICE: To sing this song well requires attention to text and underlining important words and phrases. Before singing the song, one should go through the words, speaking them as if they were written dialogue. The singer needs to also recognize that the central melody is composed lyrically and needs to be sung with sincerity, warmth, honesty, and directness. It is not a stereotypical pop melody as such. The vocal line unfolds from the text and does not need simple repetition to be an effective, compelling song. The vocal line requires a good deal of breath support, and the melody should be sung evenly, though the range is certainly not challenging. Although the line includes B-flat and B-natural in the middle of the staff, many of the pitches are composed low, near middle C and below, and they should be sung with warmth and care. Observe the rhythmic values, which have variety and meaning, and include dotted triplets and even quadruplet patterns. All of these different values can lend the song momentum, energy, and rhythmic variety, and should be sung exactly as written for that purpose. Other important markings to follow are the dynamics. Ballads are often sung at one dynamic level, but John Bucchino has clearly specified various dynamics and tempi. For instance, the tempo and dynamic level for the very last chorus is marked "più lento" (slower) and "piano." This ending, sung in this manner, creates an emotional effect that is moving. The refrain melody itself is ten measures long and repeated twice each time. The rest of the material in the refrain is melodically transitional and contains many interesting chromatic twists and turns.

BEHIND THE SCENES WITH THE ARTISTS: JOHN BUCCHINO, COMPOSER

John described to me with great detail and care Jane Hurley's character and the circumstances which culminate in the singing of this beautiful and moving song. He also recommended the song that Jane sings earlier in the show as Jane tries on a wedding dress for the first time, "Visions," for young singers as a piece worthy of study and performance. John cautions singers not to fall into the "ballad trap" when singing "Don't ever stop saying I love you," which is to slow down all cadences at the end of every vocal line, oversentimentalizing the text/music. The song does not need it. "Just follow the directions" is a good rule for everyone wanting to sing this song.

John Doyle, who directed the original production, recalls that "the song was staged on the fire escape of her house, somewhat Romeo and Juliet, but also a means of escape—which she just might do if he isn't able to say what she needs him to say."

In order to obtain the solo version of the song, you must go directly to the composer's website: http://www.johnbucchino.com.

I Miss the Mountains

Next to Normal

"Keep the emotions simple.... Let it build, then as the song rises in energy and emotion open it up, and allow yourself to go for it."
—Tom Kitt, composer

CHARACTER: Diana Goodman

MUSIC: Tom Kitt

BOOK AND LYRICS: Brian Yorkey

SETTING: Contemporary suburbia

BROADWAY PREMIERE: 2009

CLASSIFICATION: Up-tempo folk-rock—alto

RANGE: 

TESSITURA: Low in staff

TIME: 3:50

PLOT: Diana Goodman is a suburban mother. At the beginning of the show, she oversleeps and wakes up to find herself facing a number of domestic problems not unlike the problems of other mothers: she has an anxious daughter, a curfew-ignoring son, and a cynical husband. As she makes sandwiches in the kitchen for her family this particular day, she becomes agitated and her behavior grows erratic, with the sandwiches ending up on the floor. The family realizes that she needs help. Over the next weeks she repeatedly visits her doctor. Her husband, Dan, deals with his own depression. We find out that their young son died earlier of health complications before their daughter was born. Diana is diagnosed with bipolar disorder, and she suffers from hallucinations, seeing and talking with her deceased son. The doctors continually adjust her medications until she cannot feel anything, at which time she is declared stable.

CHARACTER: Diana believes that her best years are memories. She misses the emotional feelings of highs and lows, a metaphor for the mountains. However, taking her prescribed medicine dulls both emotional spectrums. With the ghost of her (deceased) son's encouragement, she throws away her meds as she sings this song. She loves her family but is overcome by grief at the loss of her son sixteen years ago, as well as the figurative loss of her daughter to adolescence and through mutual neglect.

CONTEXT: The song occurs in act I, after a number of weeks of visits to her doctor. He has increased her medications until she feels nothing, at which point he feels that she is "normal." Diana sees that her daughter is infatuated with a classmate, Henry. The mother witnesses an innocent profession of love and a first kiss by the youngsters, which causes her to realize that perhaps these emotions are just distant memories to her.

CONTENT: The song begins with her recounting memories of the past, after four softly played chords, marked "piano." Each chord has a fermata marked above it. When Diana enters, she sings in a folk-like country style, with pure tone and simple accompaniment. She looks at herself in the past as if she is now detached from that person. The opening (verse) is marked "freely, wistful." More instruments join in as she sings the text "All those blank and tranquil years seem to dry up all my tears," and she continues to observe herself in a detached manner. There is a fermata at the end of the verse ("...seems my wild days are past"), with an unaccompanied pickup eighth note ("But...") before the refrain begins. As she moves into the chorus, which adds an acoustic guitar (marked "country/folk-pop" in the score), the melody continues with a simple, pure tone with longing: "Those days are gone." She talks about missing the highs, and also about "the dark, depressing nights," as you hear the descending cello line in the accompaniment, a strongly enriched musical/dramatic color. The piano is added, and the accompaniment grows more filled-out and rhythmically active. After the first chorus of the song, there is a key change to a second section, from C major to A-flat. The accompaniment and key area become less stable and more agitated, as she sings, "The mountains make you crazy," and after only four measures there is a transition toward another key change to D major, as she makes an important decision to stop taking her meds, whatever the cost, because she misses the feelings, the highs and lows of life. The hard-driving rhythm in the accompaniment is more of an even, repeated pattern here, pushing the song forward to its conclusion. The variety of rests and spaces are so important dramatically at the end of the song, and should be observed and practiced, suggesting emotional subtexts and ideas with each repetition of "I miss the mountains" and the fermata rests and the caesura.

After singing one last time "I miss the mountains," there is a final fermata rest in the accompaniment, marked "piano," as the G chord is sustained. She sings: "I miss my ...," which is followed by one last caesura and the word "life," and she finally sings the words "I miss my life" slowly, with held notes on the words "my" and "life," descending down to A below middle C, resting on the fifth degree of the D major chord.

VOICE: This is a very interesting song to perform, and the challenges are many—to verbalize and vocalize Diana's inner emotions and struggles in order to virtually turn her vocal delivery inside out during the song. The range of the first, "detached" section is very low, moving around the middle C, and only moving up to G in the middle, and to the G below. Although she doesn't have any sustained high notes, Diana needs a higher belt position to be able to reach some higher pitches, including D above in the staff.

BEHIND THE SCENES WITH THE ARTISTS: TOM KITT, COMPOSER

Tom Kitt chose to set Diana's song "I Miss the Mountains" in a folk-like country style for a number of reasons. First of all, the country sound evokes the references to mountains metaphorically. Also, the folk sound has a plaintive quality to it, a stylistic detachment in its delivery suggesting the detachment that Diana is feeling at the time. By the same token, it is a "decision" song, one during which she is emptying out the vials of prescription drugs so that she can feel emotions again. Tom advises young singer-actors singing this song, "trust the song and do not overdo or over dramatize it. Keep the emotions simple." He suggests, "Let it build, then as the song rises in energy and emotion open it up, and allow yourself to go for it."

Fly, Fly Away

Catch Me If You Can

"This is one of my very favorite songs to sing."
—Kerri Butler, the original Brenda Strong

CHARACTER: Brenda Strong

MUSIC: Marc Shaiman and Scott Wittman

BOOK AND LYRICS: Terrence McNally

BASED ON: A 2002 film of the same title and the 1980 autobiography of con artist Frank Abagnale Jr.

SETTING: The 1960s

BROADWAY PREMIERE: 2011

CLASSIFICATION: Lyric/belt alto

RANGE: 

TESSITURA: Middle staff

TIME: 4:51

PLOT: The musical is based on the true story and movie rendition of the life of con artist Frank Abagnale. Abagnale would masterfully take on professional identities such as that of a copilot and pediatrician and also posed as a lawyer in New Orleans. He is pursued by police lieutenant Carl Hanratty.

CHARACTER: Brenda Strong is very smart, a little innocent, and trusting. She confronts Frank when she learns the truth about him, and doesn't let him get away without knowing how she feels. Although Brenda is basically sweet and innocent, and also loyal, she is not afraid to dig deep inside herself to discover what her true feelings are and then express them.

CONTEXT: The show begins in the Miami airport, where Frank, a young man, is arrested. As Frank explains his story to Hanratty, the show rewinds in flashback to recount his personal history. The main points are that in his youth he began a pattern of daringly taking on professional identities, as he has the intelligence and brashness to teach a French class (for example) when the teacher is absent. He has a troubled youth and runs away. He survives by writing fake checks, eventually for millions of dollars. He does not plan to fall in love with a nurse, Brenda, but it happens in the show. He cares for her enough to confess his crimes to her, yet she still loves him enough to vow never to betray his secrets to the authorities. Right before the engagement party, when Brenda is the happiest, she is questioned by Hanratty about Frank. Left alone, Brenda lets him go in the song "Fly, Fly Away," hoping that he is not apprehended. She loves him and will never turn him in, but she is later tricked into doing so by Hanratty.

CONTENT: There is no musical introduction. The voice begins immediately in a recitative-like opening, with changing chords (marked "colla voce") as she sings freely. In the beginning of the song, Brenda explains that she was saved by Frank, who brought her hope and healing "with his song." People have just seen his fraudulent person as smoke and mirror," but, she sings, "he was just a lonely little boy to me." As the song swings into the chorus, with a more fixed tempo, she says that she wants to see him "fly away," using the sustained tone on the word "fly" to express her desire that he be set free, but also the longing and pain that comes from being parted from him. She does have hope that he might come back some day. The second verse has a brilliant irony, as she sings that "men who they call real were really fakes who left me nothing," meaning that Frank, for all of his cons and phony occupations, was genuine with her and always true to his word. She recognizes what he gave to her, what she became because of him. The song builds through its choruses with added background singers and the addition of instruments (the sound of the organ and brass on underlying chords). Finally, the song builds to modulation into a higher key. The song ends with the hope that he will come back to her (after a short eighth-note rest) "one day." Although the original key is written in six flats (the key of G-flat), the accompaniment is not that difficult to play, with its repeated patterns and block chords.

VOICE: The beginning of the song is very low, and should be understated in its delivery. It is marked "moderately slow" and the sustained chords in the accompaniment allow the performer to take control of the tempo of the vocal line. Although it is sung rather slowly, the faster note values of eighth-note/sixteenth-note combinations allow a gentle swing to keep the song moving forward with energy, propelling it toward the chorus, which requires sustaining a high belt tessitura (beginning on C-flat) without closing the throat. This is especially challenging since it is an emotional expression and continues to build with feeling. All of the many decorative, embellished notes are still part of the song's rhythms and should be sung as such, but they should also be sung from the heart, from the emotional core of the song, and not sung too carefully or mechanically. The embellishments should have a spontaneous, improvisatory feel to them. The composer and lyricist have chosen the word "fly," which has a very good vowel for the singer to sustain. It is important to sustain this vowel center, and not be tempted to go toward the second part of the diphthong (*i* vowel) in sustaining the word. In the chorus-refrain, Brenda is pleading with Hanratty, but it is wise for the singer to try in the verses to be rational in talking to the lieutenant, not too emotionally, so that the total song expression has range and builds in dynamic power.

BEHIND THE SCENES WITH THE ARTISTS: KERRI BUTLER, THE ORIGINAL BRENDA STRONG

Ms. Butler observes that she went through the audition process to get the role, and therefore the role was not written for her. She was able to build the song line by line, and the process was well worth it, as this song is one of her favorites to perform. Kerri told me, "Brenda is in shock when the song begins. She has just found out who Frank really is." She goes through a number of emotions in processing her feelings, and these range from disbelief to anger to mystification, from doubt to love, as the song builds, piece by piece.

PART THREE

Tenor/High Baritone

Come with Me

The Boys from Syracuse

"[I remember the Sergeant] as a simple fellow, good natured, who was dutiful and anxious to do a good job."
—Fred Inkley, the Sergeant in the 2002 Broadway revival

CHARACTER: Sergeant

MUSIC: Richard Rodgers

LYRICS: Lorenz Hart, as adapted by librettist George Abbott

BASED ON: William Shakespeare's play *The Comedy of Errors,* which was loosely based on a roman play, *The Twin Brothers,* by Plautus

SETTING: Ephesus, in Ancient Greece

BROADWAY PREMIERE: 1938

CLASSIFICATION: Upbeat tenor/baritone

RANGE: 

TESSITURA: Beginning section is low on the staff, then high

TIME: 2:54

PLOT: See "Falling in Love with Love."

CHARACTER: The character of the Sergeant is not fully dimensional in the play. He is agreeable and committed to doing his duty, but conflicted because he is respectful of Antipholus and his place in society. Antipholus (of Ephesus) is described in the script as a womanizing roguish man who makes many demands of his wife (when he is home). He is a man of status in the city and is always addressed with respect. He uses his status and finances to have a good time with the ladies.

CONTEXT: The song (is sung in act II. Antipholus of Syracuse has ordered a piece of jewelry from a merchant, who of course mistakes his twin, Antipholus of Ephesus, for him. He demands that Antipholus of Ephesus pay for the bracelet, but of course the twin doesn't know what the man is talking about, and the merchant thus demands that the Sergeant arrest him. The Sergeant, confusing the twins with each other, therefore believes that the man has stolen a bracelet and is committed to do his duty, arresting the man and taking him to jail, while respecting that the gentleman (Antipholus of Ephesus) is a very important man.

CONTENT: When sung as a solo, all of the other character lines (sung by the Policemen) can be sung by the Sergeant. The accompaniment does not double the voice line and plays its functional chords in off-the-beat rhythms, in order to keep the momentum going forward, and also gives the song an upbeat, comic feel. After two eight-measure phrases of the opening melody, there is a sixteen-measure transition-like bridge to a repeat of the opening melody, then a tag extended ending to the conclusion of the first section.

The second part of the song, performed onstage by the Sergeant and the Policemen trading solo lines, is much more relaxed in its delivery (marked "much slower—in 2"), and shows some of Lorenz Hart's acerbic wit ("You needn't take the annual trip to the Oracle at Delphi"). It is almost recitative-like in its freely sung lines. The vocal line twists and turns through many accidentals, and the accompaniment is doubled. The piano accompaniment is marked "staccato" throughout the section. Finally, there is a recapitulation of the opening section (music and text), once again to be delivered with punch and vigor, to its final energized ending as the song concludes with sustained notes at the top of the staff.

VOICE: The Sergeant paints a rosy view of going to jail, where "the food is free" and you have "your own little room." It is not vocally demanding, except for the *u* vowel at the top, perhaps. The song is sort of punched in its delivery, very much in character for a police sergeant. The singer needs to sing this up-tempo song with personality, strength of character, and declamatory style. The Sergeant is a good natured, well-meaning character, singing a simple melody as befits the character. The drama in the song comes from the Sergeant arresting a man who resists and tries to claim innocence, while the Sergeant mistakes Antipholus of Ephesus's attempt at clarification, attributing it to him not wanting to go to jail.

BEHIND THE SCENES WITH THE ARTISTS: FRED INKLEY, WHO PERFORMED THE ROLE OF THE SERGEANT IN THE 2002 BROADWAY REVIVAL OF *THE BOYS FROM SYRACUSE*

Fred remembers the character of the Sergeant as a simple fellow, good natured, who was dutiful and anxious to do a good job. While he arrests Antipholus of Ephesus, he tries to portray jail as a great place to stay, since the policeman is respectful of the man he is arresting, and that bright spirit as he sings gives the song a comical feel. Fred remembers that the number always garnered a terrific ovation from the audience. As to why the number was so popular on Broadway, Fred thinks that it was because the audience appreciates the fact that at this point of the show (toward the end, where traditionally the "charm" song is placed), an energized song that is good natured and fun is relief from the contrived plot. We both recognized that this character—and situation—is a remarkable parallel to the end of act I in *Die Fledermaus,* when Warden Frank is arresting a person he thinks is Rosalinda's husband (Eisenstein) but instead is her lover, Alfred. Frank characterizes jail as "my lovely, lively pigeon house."

Fred enjoyed performing the song, and it is clear that his tenor-placed voice was able to negotiate the high notes at the end of the song (optional high A) with freedom and confidence.

Kansas City

Oklahoma!

"I think Will Parker was always something that was in me from the very beginning . . . . I was well aware of how hard it was to earn a living as a cattle rancher or farmer."

—Justin Bohon, Will Parker in the 2003 Broadway *Oklahoma!* revival

CHARACTER: Will Parker

MUSIC: Richard Rodgers

LYRICS: Oscar Hammerstein II

BASED ON: Lynn Riggs's 1931 play *Green Grow the Lilacs*

SETTING: Oklahoma Territory outside the town of Claremore, 1906

BROADWAY PREMIERE: 1943

CLASSIFICATION: Character song for tenor

RANGE: 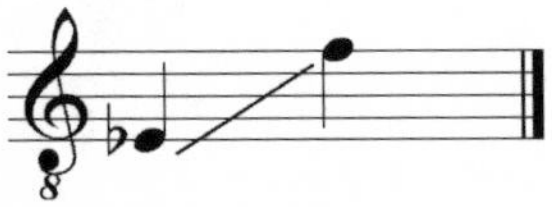

TESSITURA: Upper middle of staff

TIME: 5:06 with dance/dialogue

PLOT: The plot revolves around the major characters Curly and the girl he is wooing, Laurie, in rural Oklahoma in the early twentieth century. Will Parker enters in the first scene after the exit of Curly ("Surrey with the Fringe on Top"), providing comic relief (along with his girl, Ado Annie) in the show. His is a dancing role, and Will Parker will learn how to handle a lasso as well. While Will was away, Ado spent a lot of time with the local peddler, Ali Hakim.

CHARACTER: Will Parker is a lanky cowboy, a young man of simple values. His is a naïve and youthful character, and he returns from the big, sinful city of Kansas City wide-eyed and suddenly "worldly." He is a little goofy, and really knows how to "spin a rope," as Curly says. He can move with abandon. His girlfriend is Ado Annie, and she is the other half of a singing and dancing comic-relief team in the show.

CONTEXT: The song gives us insight into the character of Will Parker. He has just been dazzled by his trip to ultramodern Kansas City. He is excited because he won fifty dollars at the fair there, which, according to his girlfriend's father, is the amount of money he needs to claim Ado Annie's hand in marriage.

CONTENT: The song doesn't begin with an instrumental introduction; Will jumps right in. He is eager to describe what he saw in Kansas City, beginning with a setup, which is simple and slower paced in delivery. He got there on a Friday, and by Saturday he had "learned a thing or two." The vocal line is not doubled in the accompaniment. In fact, almost all of the measures only have an eighth-note chord value written on the downbeat of each measure for rhythmic punctuation. He is happy to roll into the chorus, with boundless enthusiasm and energy, singing "They've gone about as far as they can go." There are basically two choruses of sixteen measures each, which are then repeated, so there are a total of four choruses of the same music, but with different texts, as he tells his story. As his friends respond to his story, Will's narration grows more sensational. The first refrain simply talks about how large the town is, with its skyscrapers in the "modren world." By the second chorus, he is telling them about a burlesque show, shocking them in the process. In between choruses there are interludes for dialogue and dance.

VOICE: Will is a song-and-dance role, and the song should not be oversung but delivered with wide-eyed simplicity. A real, honest character should be portrayed, not a caricature or cartoon-like figure. He needs to move well, and he clearly has skills—he is a ranch hand who has learned at a very young age how to handle a rope, which is by now almost an extension of his body. The orchestra for this song is heavy in brass and winds, in eighth-note chord values, so a strong text delivery is important. The performer will need a good, projected E-flat and F at the top of the staff, and will need to sing the text with clarity—it is important for comedic effect—without tightening the throat and rendering the lyrics incomprehensible.

BEHIND THE SCENES WITH THE ARTISTS: JUSTIN BOHON, WHO PORTRAYED WILL PARKER IN THE *OKLAHOMA!* REVIVAL

"Where *Oklahoma!* is concerned, I think Will Parker was always something that was in me from the very beginning. I grew up in Missouri riding horses on my grandpa's farm, and while I never 'worked the land' per se, I was well aware of how hard it was to earn a living as a cattle rancher or farmer." Justin had a very good initial audition for Trevor Nunn for the role of Will, and the production team was impressed enough to call him back for a dancing audition for choreographer Susan Stroman. Justin tells the story: "It was several months before the dance audition was to take place, and in the interim I began experimenting with rope twirling, as I understood that it was a vital necessity for the role. After the audition for Ms. Stroman, I was told that they thought that I looked too young for the part." The entire process that led to finally landing the role was an enormous challenge for Justin and a lesson in perseverance. "I auditioned, I estimate, six times for the part. After I was told that I was too young, I tried growing a beard, and wrote a number of times to Trevor Nunn and Susan Stroman, having realized that they were still auditioning Will Parkers, since the role was not yet filled. I pestered those already in the cast, and called my agent daily—who had pretty much given up." Finally, Justin said, "Perseverance, tenacity, talent, and fate aligned," and a grateful Justin Bohon was cast in the *Oklahoma!* revival on Broadway.

Younger Than Springtime

South Pacific

"It is a song about awakenings."
—Matthew Morrison, Lt. Cable in the Broadway revival

CHARACTER: Lt. Joseph Cable, USMC

MUSIC: Richard Rodgers

LYRICS: Oscar Hammerstein II

BOOK: Oscar Hammerstein II and Joshua Logan

BASED ON: James A. Michener's 1947 book *Tales of the South Pacific*

SETTING: A South Pacific island during World War II

BROADWAY PREMIERE: 1949

CLASSIFICATION: Lyric song for tenor

RANGE: 

TESSITURA: Top of the staff

TIME: 2:45

PLOT: *South Pacific* is an iconic Rodgers and Hammerstein musical, one of their greatest successes. A common thread among the great American musicals is the juxtaposition of cultures, creating opportunities for interesting contrasts in characters and musical styles. We can see this in a number of great musicals, including *My Fair Lady, West Side Story, The King and I,* and *Miss Saigon,* to mention a few.

We meet Lt. Cable as he interrupts the sailors singing the song "There Is Nothin' Like a Dame" on the beach, as he and "Bloody Mary," the island character who sells trinkets to US sailors, share a scene together. Cable, in dialogue with Luther Billis and Mary, reveals that he has a Philadelphia girlfriend. Mary, a Tonkinese native, tries to give Cable a souvenir of a shrunken head, and then she sings of Bali Ha'i. This volcanic island, seen in the distance, appears to be a tropical paradise to the sailors, but it is off limits—except to the officers.

CHARACTER: Lt. Cable is an intelligent, serious, and charming young man we find is from Philadelphia, where he has a girlfriend. We learn of Lt. Cable at his introduction that he is no stranger to danger. He comes to the island having already been in the war, arriving from nearby Catalina, a little island he says is south of Marie Louise, where they used "real bullets." In the exchange between Nellie and him that follows, Cable reveals that he gets letters from his mother, and she thinks everything he does is perfect. He also reveals that his father served in World War I. We also learn, later in the show, that he has had a bout with malaria while on duty in the South Seas.

CONTEXT: In act I, scene 2, we see the interior of a native hut. The scene is lit beautifully. Mary enters, followed by Cable. Mary is presenting a native girl to Cable. Her name is Liat, and she is a French-speaking Tonkinese girl who does not speak English. They have an awkward, halting conversation, Cable struggling to speak in simple French phrases. After some time, he is shocked to find out that the beautiful young girl is Bloody Mary's daughter, and the mother has offered her to him. He instinctively pushes the girl away, but Liat throws herself into Cable's arms and tries to kiss him. He gently pushes her away again, holding her at arm's length, looking at her in amazement, shocked at both her natural beauty and the fact that her mother is Bloody Mary. The ship's bell, calling the sailors to the ship, interrupts him. "It's the boat all right," he remarks. "Aw, let them wait," he says, as he begins to sing "Younger Than Springtime" to the young girl.

CONTENT: The song is constructed in a simple, clear manner. After four measures of introduction, Cable sings the setup, or verse of the melody line, marked "with warm expression." This section of Hammerstein's poetic text of sixteen measures is a perfect prelude to the chorus melody, which is a classic, both melodically and in its poetic text. "And when your youth and joy" begins a bridge of only nine measures that seamlessly and naturally connects to a final chorus. The words "angel and lover" marked "with passion," lead to the final cadence as Cable sings whole-note rhythms on the text: "I with you!" on G and F (I- placed on G, while you [u] is set on F).

VOICE: Although the first chorus ("Younger than springtime...") is marked "slowly, with great warmth," the singer does not need to think of this directive too literally, for there is no need to slow this lyric melody down too much. On the next phrase ("Warmer than winds of June") it is wise for the singer to move the phrase with some urgency to the word "June," then to slow a little at the end of the phrase "lips you gave me" as the line descends by half steps, before moving to the next line. The singer will probably want to animate more the musical section that is the bridge, but the music is marked "stay in slow tempo" here. It is my feeling that since the signal that the boat is leaving has already sounded, there is some urgency, so indicated directions of "slow" are relative. Note: in the show, the ship's bells sound again at the end of the song. Words (vowels) that are challenging to sing at the top of this staff are "June," "with," and "you," especially in the climactic last phrase, with the sustained F on the *u* vowel of "you." The singer will need jaw space and support, and the *u* will require a high, forward placement, while the lips will round for the vowel without the jaw tightening.

BEHIND THE SCENES WITH THE ARTISTS: MATTHEW MORRISON, LT. CABLE IN THE BROADWAY REVIVAL

"'Younger Than Springtime' works for Cable on several different levels .... It is not just the usual 'I met the girl of my dreams and fell in love' song, although of course it is that as well. It is a song about awakenings:...for Cable, this is an awakening to the world outside of his formal, strict upbringing on Philadelphia's Main Line, a world Cable has never before been able to recognize and acknowledge. He is opening up to the beauty, exoticism, and even the exciting uncertainty of life and love—and he is discovering it as he sings .... The song is extemporaneous, spontaneous, and inspired—not thought out beforehand. I think it also works on yet another level, as a song about liberation...not only from convention and conformity, but also from prejudice, which is a very important theme in the entire show. Liat is not only Cable's love interest but also soul mate and savior."

No Other Love

Me and Juliet

"The composer, Richard Rodgers, who often visited the performances, told me that I should sing the song 'as written, no variations.'"
—Bill Hayes, the original Larry

CHARACTER: Larry

MUSIC: Richard Rodgers

BOOK AND LYRICS: Oscar Hammerstein II

SETTING: New York City

BROADWAY PREMIERE: 1953

CLASSIFICATION: Classic tenor ballad

RANGE: 

TESSITURA: Upper middle of the staff

TIME: 1:32

PLOT: A "show within a show," this musical is different because it is a view of backstage activities and the interesting characters and relationships found there. It is thought that this unique concept initially was an idea that was proposed by composer Richard Rodgers, and became a project that was evidently more important to him than it was to the lyricist (and book writer) Oscar Hammerstein. Since the project had come after the successes of *Oklahoma!* and *South Pacific*, it was not so difficult to sell a Rodgers and Hammerstein show. To prospective producers, the play was sure to have a light tone, mostly because famed director George Abbott was at the helm. Abbott was the successful director of such comic hits as *Pajama Game* and *On Your Toes*.

The story is about a backstage romance during a long-running musical. The assistant stage manager, Larry, woos Jeanie, a chorus girl, behind the back of her electrician boyfriend, Bob. At the opening of the show, we immediately observe the complexity of the relationships. We see that Larry is attracted to Jeanie, while we also see that Bob may not be the right man for her. It is also revealed that Bob does not plan to marry her.

CHARACTER: Originally, the assistant stage manager was not a very strong character, but before the official Broadway opening, Larry's role was strengthened in its dialogue, making him a more forceful character, and he woos Jeanie behind the back of her boyfriend, Bob. Larry is ambitious and has plans to someday direct, and so he is working his way up the ladder, the next step being stage manager. Mac, the stage manager, gives Larry advice, which gives us insight into the job of the stage manager: "The stage manager is like the mayor of a small town." Larry is coaching Jeanie to be the understudy for the main female role. Mac says that he is in danger of getting "stuck on her."

CONTEXT: The scene takes place on a rehearsal day in preparation for the show, and the dancers are practicing onstage. With Larry's urging and encouragement, Jeanie decides to audition for the part of second understudy to the lead. Jeannie practices for her audition backstage, singing "No Other Love" for Larry, and he tells her that the audience will love her if she's "real" and will reject her if she is a phony. Coaching her song, he listens to her sing it, then sings it for her the way he thinks she should deliver it for an audition. It is unusual that the hit song of the show is placed so early in the plot and set up in such a way that it is possible that the popular appeal of the number was not initially recognized.

CONTENT: The song is a classic romantic-melody lyric ballad that has subtle lilting syncopations that keep rhythmic interest and forward momentum. In fact, the tempo marking at the top of the song is "tempo di tango." There is only a two-measure introduction, and the dynamics are marked "piano, espressivo." The accompaniment to the song is very simply written, with some chromaticism in the bass line sustaining the energy and interest in the music while the singer is sustaining whole notes. The melody is doubled in the orchestra throughout. The form of the song is chorus—short bridge—chorus, and the song is brief, making it possible for the exact same song to be sung twice in succession first by Jeanie and then Larry.

VOICE: The song has a wide range for a mainstream song that became widely recorded by popular singers at the time. In the chorus, there are consistently low sustained tones of D and E at the bottom of the staff. On the other hand, the song also requires freely sung, sustained half-note rhythmic values at the top of the staff, with difficult-to-sustain words such as "home" on the F at the top of the staff (just at the tenor *passaggio*) that need to be clearly understood without high-note distortion. The other text that is placed on higher pitches (chosen by Oscar Hammerstein) are more singer-friendly, including "cry," "night," and "fly." At the end of the song is a high A-flat above the staff. Thankfully, it written to be sung on the word "love." Jeanie sings the song in the key of G major, while Larry sings it in the brighter, more confident key of A-flat, one half-step higher.

BEHIND THE SCENES WITH THE ARTISTS: BILL HAYES, WHO CREATED THE ROLE OF LARRY

Bill talks about singing the song, which became a Perry Como hit at the time. Bill says that the song was such a hit that he himself was attracted to the Como's phrasing, which was different from the way that the song was written to be sung in the show. The composer, Richard Rodgers, came frequently to performances, said Bill, and after one performance in particular, he remembers the composer telling him to sing the song "as written, no variations." That posed a number of challenges, Bill recalls, as there were no places for breaths in the song, even a catch breath. The song also has specific syncopations, which give it a momentum that a languid romantic ballad doesn't possess. Perhaps that is because the purpose of the song in the show is as an audition piece in the story, as well as providing romantic overtones.

What Kind of Fool Am I?

Stop the World—I Want to Get Off

"When it became time for Littlechap to sing that poem of forgiveness—'What Kind of Fool Am I'—the expression came from a place that Sammy Davis could identify."
—Mel Shapiro, director of the 1978 Broadway revival

CHARACTER: Littlechap

BOOK, MUSIC, AND LYRICS: Leslie Bricusse and Anthony Newley

SETTING: A circus

BROADWAY PREMIERE: 1961

CLASSIFICATION: Tenor/baritone lyric with drama

RANGE: 

TESSITURA: Generally low to high sustained at the end of the song

TIME: 2:30

PLOT: The musical has a circus for its backdrop. The character Littlechap, trying to better his existence, marries the boss's daughter. Growing more dissatisfied with family responsibilities, he has relationships with a number of women from Russia, Germany, Japan, and America, as he searches for happiness. In the twilight of his life he realizes that the love of his wife was more than enough to make him happy. He also comes to the realization that he has never loved anyone other than himself.

This show, which opened on Broadway in 1961, is often dismissed as being solely a vehicle for performer Anthony Newley, who wrote the music for this show (with Lesley Bricusse). "What Kind of Fool Am I?" reveals more power with an understanding of the character and situation in the show, which is seen as a cautionary tale in the early 1960s for those with blinding ambition. The song is one of two in the show that are standard classics in musical theatre repertoire, the other being "Once in a Lifetime." Surprisingly, the latter is placed in the show (with its reprise) only a few pages in the score before "What Kind of Fool Am I," which signals Littlechap's emotional and moral collapse in the play.

CHARACTER: Littlechap is the eternal opportunist, and with strong confidence that borders on arrogance, he turns less productive factories into successes. His wife's name is Evie, and they have three children. His social and financial success in England continues through the show so that he is Lord Littlechap by the end of the show, having been elevated to peerage. He has a seat in Parliament and becomes a member of Snobb's Club.

CONTEXT: Littlechap has everything anyone would want: he has achieved peerage in England and is wealthy. He also has a family, but because of his self-indulgence, he has taken them for granted, and now he realizes he has been a failure as a husband and father. During the introduction of the song, he speaks to his wife: "Well, Evie,—now you know everything.... I was only ever really in love with one person... and that was me."

CONTENT: The form of the song is basically ABA with a seven-measure instrumental introduction ("slow 4") over spoken dialogue. The song builds quickly to a climactic rise in pitch, dynamics, and emotion. After the A section returns, there are eight measures of interlude over dialogue before modulating to a higher key to repeat the ABA form with new text. At the final cadence the orchestra's texture becomes more full and dramatic. Emotionally, the song is ignited by using self-pity as its spark. With the opening three quarter-note rhythms in the lowest part of the voice (low A-flat pick-up), there is a weary heaviness which describes Littlechap's state of mind at this point of the show. The accompaniment will continue to play four beats (chords) per measure throughout the song. He continues to wallow in self-pity, describing himself as "an empty shell" and "a lonely cell in an empty heart," and the most important question he asks of himself is at the top of the climactic rise in emotion: "Why can't I fall in love?" singing an E-flat at the top of the staff. In the second verse, he castigates himself for being a "lover who has lied with every kiss" and modulates from the key of D-flat upward to the key of E-flat as he becomes more specific (and dramatic) about his faults. The final line, marked "grandioso," adds orchestra (after a caesura) in a repeated eighth-note chordal rhythm building to the singer's top F of his range, sustained (fermata), before he resolves to the final E-flat.

VOICE: The performer needs to be very conscious of building the song to the climactic phrases at the end of the verses, adding more breadth and momentum so that the piece doesn't become too ponderous or heavy. When Littlechap *really* wants to know the answers to his question, he will sing with more urgency, trying to find a lifeline and a way out of his self-pitying funk. "Why can't I fall in love?" is the question that, above all, needs an answer.

BEHIND THE SCENES WITH THE ARTISTS: MEL SHAPIRO, DIRECTOR OF THE 1978 BROADWAY REVIVAL

The legendary director was recruited to direct the Broadway revival of the show in 1978, which starred Sammy Davis Jr. At the time, Mr. Shapiro was not that familiar with the show, or Sammy Davis. He knew that the musical was an expression of the 1960s, a product of the time that introduced the world to a literary generation of "angry young men" from English society that were basically blue-collar in background and were anti-upper-class, especially the British Aristocracy. On the other hand, extravagance of lifestyle was a characteristic of this movement. The English playwright John Osborne (*Look Back in Anger*), an actor, screenwriter, and critic, was the main architect of this movement, and *Stop the World—I Want to Get Off*, written by English actor Anthony Newley and lyricist Leslie Bricusse, captured the imagination of audiences fascinated with both the wit and lifestyle of the iconoclasts. Mr. Shapiro, in directing the 1987 revival, was aware that both Newley and Bricusse came from this background and time, traveling the world and enjoying life's rewards. He also knew that as "wild guys" who were born on the other side of the tracks, they were also playboys, and Newley in particular had been married a number of times. (Note: Bricusse's wife is named Evie, the name given to Littlechap's wife.) There was no question in Mel Shapiro's mind that Newley, who reportedly had written the show in a thirty-day flurry of activity, knew Littlechap well from his own life's experiences. Sammy Davis, a member of the so-called Rat Pack, also knew Littlechap. Davis's extravagant playboy lifestyle was well documented, and "when it became time for Littlechap to sing that poem of forgiveness—'What Kind of Fool Am I'—the expression came from a place that Sammy Davis could identify." Mr. Shapiro remembers Sammy Davis in rehearsal as having "vocal cords of steel" and always rehearsed full voice. Mel finally asked him why he did not mark. Sammy Davis replied that this was how he placed his voice, that he needed to project it and keep it "forward, high above his face" in rehearsal as a kind of vocal gymnastic exercise, preparing for performance. It served as an example to Mel that he has subsequently passed on to his students, that rehearsal is the time when energy applied to practice must be realized in order for the singer to be fully prepared and ready to perform.

I Believe in You

How to Succeed in Business without Really Trying

"When Finch sings the song in the show, he is trying to 'psych himself up,' but at this point he is not so sure that he will succeed."
—Robert Morse, the original Finch

CHARACTER: J. Pierpont Finch

MUSIC AND LYRICS: Frank Loesser

BOOK: Abe Burrows, Jack Weinstock, and Willie Gilbert

BASED ON: Shepherd Mead's 1952 book of the same name

SETTING: New York City

BROADWAY PREMIERE: 1961

CLASSIFICATION: Tenor charm song with lyricism

RANGE: 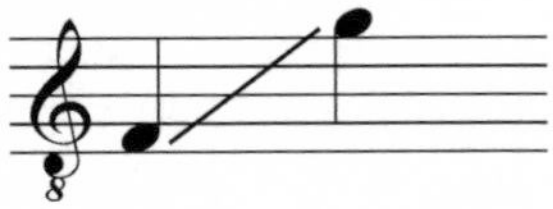

TESSITURA: Upper middle of the staff, sustained Es, top staff space

TIME: 3:32

PLOT: The satirical book the show is based on was a bestseller in 1952. The musical added romance to the story, as well as satire. J. Pierpont Finch is the lead character; he is a window cleaner in New York City, and he would like to rise to the top of the office ranks with the help of the book in his hand, *How to Succeed in Business without Really Trying.* Rosemary Pilkington is a secretary who Finch meets when he enters the offices of the World Wide Wicket Company looking for a job. She is impressed by his ambition and initially helps him to meet the boss. Rosemary daydreams about a life with Finch in the suburbs.

CHARACTER: Finch has a lot of boyish charm. He is young, eager, impressionable, and idealistic. He is eager to achieve his goals. At the beginning of the show, he is a window washer with little to no chance of succeeding in business without the requisite degrees and job experience, but he is naïve enough to think that with the assistance of a how-to booklet he can succeed in business without even trying, and that is the root of this classic comic musical.

CONTEXT: "I Believe in You" is sung in act II, by which time Finch has begun his ascent to the top of the company. He is now in the advertising department. The businessmen in the executive restroom are all out to get Finch, and they sing "Gotta stop that man," and this negative counterpoint introduces his song as he gazes at himself in the office bathroom mirror. "Good luck!" they say, with the implied subtext that he'll need it.

CONTENT: The song breaks with Broadway tradition, because Finch sings it to a reflection of himself in a mirror. The first lines (after a chord) are sung in the style of accompanied recitative and verse: "There it is, that face that somehow I trust." He goes on to say that even though it may be embarrassing, but "say it I must" (as he shyly looks away from the mirror, then back, with youthful charm). Finch is trying his hardest to psych himself up in a den of wolves trying to bring him down. He has his moments of strength, of doubt, and of charm. The song then goes into the melody, in a tempo that has a finger-snapping lilt and energy to it. The interesting phrasing of each important word ("cool," "clear," "eyes") is delineated each time by giving them half-note values of the same pitches, and two-beat rests in between the words in the opening melody, which repeats after the short chorus. The orchestral accompaniment is rhythmically active. The words "I believe in you" are the repeated chorus of only a couple of measures, but it is a memorable melody with chords that set off its appeal. This chordal progression is memorable because it is a plagal cadence meaning chords composed in a IV/I chord progression, which is also known as the "Amen cadence," familiar from the ending of hymns. Finch continues to psych himself up, swinging into the bridge of the song. He is inspired by Rosemary, his love interest in the show, to finish this section with the text: "I take heart". The final verse and chorus include the businessmen in the restroom singing "Gotta stop that man" repeatedly, but they also sing harmony to his chorus with chordal support.

Following Finch's singing of the song, Rosemary reprises it in a lower key (F major), this time slower, with warmth.

VOICE: Charm goes a long way in "I Believe in You." Projecting and underlining he important words in the chorus is more important than vocalizing them into the "mirror." The only warm-toned lyrical singing would be the short chorus of "I Believe in You." The song is not challenging as far as range is concerned, but the combination of youthful charm and emerging confidence, augmented by the composer's use of triplet rhythms, is an important quality to project. It is an interesting song to sing. We have all caught ourselves talking to the reflection in the mirror, so it connects with an experience that is real. And yet the scene also has a quality of fantasy in it because of the jealous competing businessmen in the washroom commenting negatively in counterpoint on his psyching himself up.

BEHIND THE SCENES WITH THE ARTISTS: ROBERT MORSE, THE ORIGINAL FINCH

I asked Robert Morse what it was like to be given the leading role at the tender young age of thirty, a role is which all of the story and action revolves around him. Robert told me that in 1961, at the time of the premiere of *How to Succeed,* he was not a newcomer to New York and Broadway. As early as 1957 he had appeared onstage with some well-known actors (Jackie Gleason, David Wayne) in shows such as *Take Me Along,* with David Wayne, and produced by Abe Burrows. This experience allowed Robert to showcase a number of his talents, including the stage style known as burlesque, which allowed him to play broad comedy. Still, to be handed a lead in a new Frank Loesser Broadway show was heady stuff, as Loesser was known as the brilliant composer who had already written *Guys and Dolls* and *The Most Happy Fella.* Without knowing the songs yet when he signed on to the role of Finch, Robert knew he was going to have some great songs to sing. Frank Loesser asked Robert to come to his office, telling him that he had a new song for him to sing and coach called "I Believe in You," which would be sung onstage into a mirror. Robert was given a tape of the song to prepare, a recording created by the production staff for the choreographer's use for rehearsal. As recorded, the song was upbeat and very rhythmic, unlike the version Robert would eventually sing. When he sang the song for Loesser the first time in his small studio, Robert would find that the phrase with the text "And I take heart" felt high to sing. Robert now laughs when he recalls the temerity with which he suggested that Mr. Loesser lower the key to make it more comfortable for him to sing. Frank Loesser taught Robert a lesson that day that he has never forgotten. In response to Robert's request that the key be lowered, the composer told him that he was singing the song at that point in his "small-room key," not the "big-theatre key." The "small-room key" was for his crooning "nightclub voice," the understated and nonenergized voice. He explained to Robert that once he sang the song in the theatre, eventually the "theatre key" would be too low for him! Frank Loesser then took Robert to the theatre to show him exactly what he meant. Taking the familiar song "Blue Skies," he had Robert sing the beginning; then he had Robert sing the song up a third in pitch, and so on. Robert soon observed that by singing the song in the theatre, utilizing his considerable energy and thinking about projection, the higher keys soon became more comfortable.

Robert told me how much he appreciated the words of the song. He admired that Loesser was such a marvelous wordsmith and could use text in a song like few others. Robert told me that when Finch sings the song in the show, he is trying to psych himself up, but at this point he is not so sure that he will succeed. He needed to find the joy in the song, and also find the pathos. There is subtext after each line that the singer needs to create and utilize. And after two years of playing Finch, Robert was able to realize all possibilities in the song. At one point in one performance, he told me, he looked up to God for divine assistance, and spontaneously crossed himself!

On the Street Where You Live

My Fair Lady

"[Cameron Macintosh] told me that all the qualities floating in my head about Freddy were completely accurate and that I should not be afraid to share them with the audience."

—Justin Bohon, Freddy in the Royal National Theatre revival of *My Fair Lady*

CHARACTER: Freddy Eynsford-Hill

MUSIC: Frederick Loewe

BOOK AND LYRICS: Alan J. Lerner

BASED ON: George Bernard Shaw's play *Pygmalion*

SETTING: London

BROADWAY PREMIERE: 1957

CLASSIFICATION: Tenor

RANGE: 

TESSITURA: Middle staff

TIME: 3:46

PLOT: This classic American musical is about a young, ill-mannered guttersnipe of a girl, Eliza Doolittle, who sells flowers in London. She becomes a pawn in a bet that a professor has with a colleague that he can train her to pass as a member of English high society. Their arrogance is later softened by her genuinely winning personality.

CHARACTER OF FREDDY: Freddy Eynsford-Hill is a well-to-do young man, the only son of Lady Eynsford-Hill. Freddy has most likely led a very sheltered existence and at first does not know what to make of Eliza.

A valuable description of Freddy can be drawn from the play *Pygmalion* by George Bernard Shaw: "Freddy is young, practically twenty years younger than Higgins; he is a gentleman (or, as Eliza would qualify him, a toff), and speaks like one; he is nicely dressed, is treated by the Colonel [Pickering] as an equal, loves Eliza unaffectedly, and is not her master, nor ever likely to dominate her in spite of his advantage of social standing. Eliza has no use for the foolish romantic tradition that all women love to be mastered." Eliza will eventually marry Freddy (in *Pygmalion*), but complications ensue, "but they [are] economic, not romantic. Freddy had no money and no occupation." A "lower position" was beneath Freddy's dignity. Finally, Eliza takes ownership of a flower shop. Freddy does not help very much. He can quote Milton and translate into Latin, but he is not helpful in the shop.

CONTEXT: This song is placed after the Ascot scene, which is the ensemble scene at the race track, Eliza's first appearance in English high society. It is clear that she is uncomfortable in the setting—she speaks her lines mechanically, like a trained animal. In trying to make conversation, however, her awkward syntax charms Freddy tremendously. And although she has been trained thoroughly, as she watches the final race (with all of the stuffy English sung by the chorus on stage), her enthusiasm makes her unable to stifle a yell of encouragement to the horse ("Come on, Dover! Move your bloomin' arse!"), as she forgets all of her proper etiquette training, stunning the ensemble. At the beginning of the next scene, a smitten Freddy is approaching Eliza's house. He buys a flower (from a flower girl on the street) before he knocks on the door, and is received by Mrs. Pearce, the maid. As he waits for Eliza on the street, he sings the song.

CONTENT: Freddy sings the verse to himself as he recalls the delight he felt when he saw her performance at the racetrack. Freddy is interrupted by Mrs. Pearce, answering the door. He asks if Miss Doolittle is at home. "Freddy Eynsford-Hill is calling, and if she doesn't remember me, tell her I'm the chap who was sniggering at her." Suddenly, Freddy has a sense of humor about life. He further tells her she doesn't need to rush. "I want to drink in this street where she lives," he says. The first chorus and bridge are marked "piano," with crescendos on the upper cadential phrases, but not above a poco crescendo. The top notes in the cadence are marked "tenuto," slightly held, but the singing still needs to be a little restrained. After all, Freddy is expecting Eliza to come to the door. The next dialogue is during the an instrumental interlude. Over the music, Mrs. Pierce tells Freddy that Eliza doesn't want to see anyone—"ever again." Freddy doesn't understand why. He says he wants to wait, that he is happier outside Eliza's door than any other place. And this is where Freddy wants to be, near her, on the street where she lives, where he can be himself and not have to pretend he is happy. Freddy digs in his heels, and as he sings the last chorus after this dialogue, his higher pitches are sustained with fermatas. The notes are clearly held longer, with a louder vocal dynamic that comes from a new, deliberate energetic enthusiasm that Freddy has not previously shown in the show.

VOICE: Although "On the Street Where You Live" is one of the great melodies of the stage, it is important while singing this song to pay attention to the text, and also to the tempo marking, allegro moderato, meaning that the tempo of the song is not slow or dragging. A challenge is the awkward range of the song for a tenor, which is most likely intended by the composer/lyricist. The chorus melody begins low, but it is marked "piano, con tenerezza" in the piano part, with a cello countermelody, and it is important not to push or force. When the line springs from low F, the bottom space of the line, to top-line E, the music is still marked "piano." It is important to add an extra chorus when singing the song out of the context of the show. The last chorus is more demonstrative, eager, happy, and hopeful, and Freddy sustains the high F, as well as broadening the final cadence, to prove it. Usually, the E-natural/F at the top is where the tenor will move into the higher vocal register through the *passaggio.* However, this modification will mean a change in the vowel, and it is possible for Freddy, in his eagerness and enthusiasm in the final chorus with the F held with a fermata, to sing the note more open, without the shift to the upper register. However, while singing the word "I" on the top note, the singer should be careful not spread the vowel, creating a high laryngeal position, causing tension and a tight tone. Think more of a vertical jaw space, and avoid the second syllable of the diphthong (i vowel).

BEHIND THE SCENES WITH THE ARTISTS: JUSTIN BOHON, FREDDY IN THE ROYAL NATIONAL THEATRE REVIVAL OF *MY FAIR LADY*

Seeing this role played so many times, I am used to an interpretation of Freddy that is conventionally portrayed. Freddy is a rich young man, perhaps spoiled and a mama's boy, who falls in love with Eliza; he is her romantic interest in the musical. However, the American actor Justin Bohon portrayed Freddy in the London revival as a sympathetically charming but painfully awkward character. He won over the audience immediately. Justin talks about his thought process and rationalization in creating this Freddy: "As far as Freddy goes; it was a combination of sources and consideration about the character that led to the interpretation of the role. In having been involved in several productions of *My Fair Lady*, I had always wondered why the character of Freddy was played by a dashing leading man, with such confidence, poise, and perfect breeding, when in fact, if *that* were the case, he would more than likely have found a wealthy wife and been married for some time. It seemed obvious to me that someone with such a strange infatuation with a girl who is clearly out of the ordinary, an unmarried man in a time period when someone his age would either be married or well on his way to doing so, living at home and unable to hold a job, would have many more quirks and unusual qualities than a typical leading man type." This led him to find a Freddy who was "loving, curious, passionate, awkward (at times), occasionally clumsy, hopelessly romantic, and swept up in a dream of a girl who didn't bow to the bores of upper-class society. In fact, while Eliza is completely shamed by her behavior at Ascot, it is her energy and vitality, even rule-breaking, that begins Freddy's infatuation with her." Fortunately, director Trevor Nunn and producer Cameron Macintosh agreed with Justin's assessment of the character, and encouraged him to follow his instincts: they "believed it would allow us to fall more in love with this hopeless, somewhat useless lost puppy dog if we saw his flaws and goofiness. Thus the floodgates were opened, and the Freddy Eynsford-Hill that I loved creating and portraying was fully realized."

The Only Home I Know

Shenandoah

"There is a longing in the lyrics and in tone that should not be oversentimentalized."
—Gary William Harger, the original Corporal

CHARACTER: Corporal

MUSIC: Gary Geld

LYRICS: Peter Udell

BOOK: Peter Udell, Philip Rose, and James Lee Barrett

BASED ON: Barrett's original screenplay for the 1965 film *Shenandoah*

SETTING: Virginia, during the Civil War

BROADWAY PREMIERE: 1975

CLASSIFICATION: Lyric, intimate anthem for tenor

RANGE: 

TESSITURA: top half of staff

TIME: 3:06

PLOT: A widower, Charlie, lives with his family in Virginia in the Shenandoah Valley during the Civil War. He doesn't want to be involved in the war but is forced to be when his youngest son, Robert, is taken prisoner by Union soldiers. He loses two of his sons to the war, and finally at the end is reunited with Robert.

CHARACTER: The role is that of a corporal, and that is all we know. He has very little time onstage, which means that we need to look at the text and imagine who this person is, creating the story of his life before the song and what happens to him afterward. At the singing of this song, the Corporal has been traveling for some time in a train car filled with prisoners. He is hungry and weak, not fully aware of what has happened to him and what will happen to him after the train is stopped.

CONTEXT: The song is sung midway through act II. Charlie stops a train by putting logs on the tracks. He has his sons burn and destroy the train so that it can never transport people to places "they don't want to go." Before the train is destroyed, the captured Confederate prisoners are freed. One of the prisoners is Sam, a confederate lieutenant. Sam tells the freed prisoners to go home to their women and children. The war is lost. The Corporal says, "Has it . . . has it all been for nothing, sir?" "Go home and live," says Sam.

CONTENT: There are three verses to the song, with a transition, or bridge (marked "quicker") of only four measures, before a last verse ("I can't remember why I left or what I hoped to find"). The opening is marked "andante rubato, freely throughout." The Corporal begins to sing a cappella the haunting melodic line, which is written entirely in eighth-notes. The melody is syllabically set with text, while inflecting the most important syllable/word of each phrase, which is notated in a longer value (quarter-note rhythms which sometimes are tied to another note sustained by fermata). The supporting chords in the accompaniment are softly "rolled" in the style of playing the harp. The song is joined by the chorus/ensemble in the show. There is a breaking of this pattern, indicated by a caesura marked in the music. The tempo indication is "a little quicker" here, and the accompaniment is composed in a block-chord pattern of half-note rhythms. At "I can't remember why," the indication "Freely, rubato" is again marked, and the rolled chord pattern returns, as well. Shenandoah is "the only home I know," the Corporal says in the final phrase, sustained on the word "know" by a fermata, and the phrase is repeated—again with a fermata on the word "home," followed by a caesura, and the song ends with two fermata-marked final words: "I know."

VOICE: The song requires the controlled singing of an exposed folk-like melody with a legato-lyric sense. The melody also projects a strong vocal line that is not overly emoted or artificially overacted. At the same time, the rhyming text, which is poignant and beautiful, needs to be articulated clearly, with a sense of which words (and syllables) are more important and need to be inflected for the purpose of phrasing and momentum. Much of the vocal line is written in diatonic (stepwise) motion, but at times there are wider intervals and accidentals. In other words, the phrases need to be negotiated carefully but cleanly with confidence. Most of the vocal phrases start at the top of the staff and descend, so the singer should not attack at each entrance with too much weight or force. Each entrance should be sung "on the breath," and without a glottal attack when the entrance word begins with a vowel. There are no pitches to sing above F at the top of the staff, but the vocal line should still be sung lightly, with ease of tone, and not pushed. Gary Harger, the original Corporal, chose the pitch to begin the song at the first rehearsal, since he was the first Corporal to sing "The Only Home I Know," and he was allowed to determine through this choice the key it was be performed in. However, he later thought that his choice of key was a little too low, due to vocal fatigue at the time, and as his voice developed during his three-year stint in the show, he surely could have set it higher.

BEHIND THE SCENES WITH THE ARTISTS: GARY WILLIAM HARGER, THE ORIGINAL CORPORAL

When cast in *Shenandoah* on Broadway, Gary had just graduated from college. He explained to me that at the time (1974) he was not able to major in musical theatre, since that program was not established at the time. He was, however, able to take voice lessons and theatre classes in New York while performing the show. When he auditioned for *Shenandoah* at the open call, his voice and appearance were very young, and even though he had advanced vocal training, his voice was not overly operatic. He remembers that he was very nervous at the first rehearsal, mostly because he came slightly late due to a previous vocal engagement. Although it was forty years ago, he remembers it well. The show originally opened in the Goodspeed Opera House in East Haddam, Connecticut, then moved to Boston for an out-of-town run before a three-year run on Broadway. He also remembers that since he has absolute pitch, it was arranged for him to come onto the stage in silence, and he began the song a cappella, before the orchestra entered. He remembers, too, that *Shenandoah* was a traditional Broadway show marking the end of an era in American musical theatre before more of a "rock" style became popular. His advice for young singers singing this song would be to take an approach that does not over sing or push. It is meant to be simply sung, folk-like. "There is a longing in the lyrics and the tone that should not be oversentimentalized."

Anthem

Chess

"The fact that he's defecting from his homeland and that he's taken interest, in a loving way, in Florence makes him extremely vulnerable."
—Tommy Körberg, the original Anatoly

CHARACTER: Anatoly Sergievsky

MUSIC: Benny Andersson and Bjorn Ulvaeus

LYRICS: Tim Rice

SETTING: 1979 World Chess Championship, Merano, Italy

BROADWAY PREMIERE: 1988

CLASSIFICATION: Anthem for tenor (or baritone with high notes)

RANGE: 

TESSITURA: Upper middle of staff

TIME: 3:27

PLOT: See "Heaven Help My Heart."

CHARACTER: Anatoly is a genius at the game of chess. However, like all of us, he's flawed. He's selfish, self-obsessed, vain, and naïve, all of which helps to lead to his decision to defect: his complex relationship with Florence is just the final straw. He also seems to be out of sync with the time and his country's ideology. He resents the control that the Soviet government has over how he lives, and more importantly their meddling in his way of playing chess and his personal affairs. He has no interest in politics and feels intellectually and personally trapped. Playing tournaments across the globe since childhood meant that he was constantly exposed to Western influences, and he became acquainted with what freedom meant outside the Soviet

Union; he wants more. In his other song in the show, "Where I Want to Be," he admits, "Once I had dreams, now they're obsessions," and he continues: "I feel I haven't won it all."

CONTEXT: Anatoly defects from the Soviet Union and seeks asylum in England through the English Embassy while in Italy. The story is leaked, and Anatoly is ambushed by a mob of reporters at a train station in Italy at the end of act I. Florence is now with him. When asked why he is deserting his country, he replies that his country's borders lie only around his heart. The original Anatoly, Tommy Körberg, cautions singers who sing this song to not oversing and "wail." There is more to it than that, Tommy says. "The fact that he's defecting from his homeland and that he's taken interest, in a loving way, in Florence makes him extremely vulnerable and conflicted. At the same time, as he sings, he's convincing himself that it's the right choice to leave the Soviet Union." Finally, after originating the role and singing the song out of the context of the show so many times, Tommy told me: "When you sing this material you have to make sure that you understand every word and every meaning between the lines as well."

CONTENT: The song lives up to its name as it ascends and speaks to everyone who has deep-seated feelings for their homeland. The short instrumental accompaniment that introduces the song features a solo English horn, conveying a mournful color. The song's form is basically in two verses, while the second verse expands to a climactic ending. The song builds after the first lyric lines and ascends through the top of the staff with chorus swelling underneath. The simple accompaniment does not double the vocal melody. It is important to build throughout and not give too much voice too early. Anatoly is a man who is in crisis and is conflicted. He has thought carefully about ramifications of defecting and what it means, and it is clear that he has love for his country, as his voice passionately sings above the staff, accompanied by chorus.

VOICE: Singing this song involves a tenor extension of voice above the staff, and requires sustained power and breath control. Long vocal lines need deep inhalations and smooth legato lines. The song begins low, at the lower end of the staff, and is sung softly before it begins to build. The first line, "No man, no madness," is an example of the tricky phrasing, as the final unstressed syllable "mad-*ness*" is at the ascendant D, and should not be emphasized, even though it is at the higher pitch. This same challenge occurs in the next line: "She is eter-*nal*," There are also small flourishes, called mordents, which are quick turns of triplet sixteenth notes, decorative pitches, which are more successfully sung when produced lightly and from the heart—in other words, not pedantically or carefully sung. The melody and text are so thrilling and inspiring that it is helpful that there is an interlude, where the accompaniment plays the major melody and allows the singer to gather his emotions, his energy, and his deep breath and anchoring support to crescendo and ascend to the climactic ending, sung at the very top of the register at F-sharp and G. It is difficult to sing at the top of the register while enunciating the very important text "Where would I start?" sung syllabically with chorus and full accompaniment underneath. It is important that the singer give all of these words strongly supported consonants, including final consonants, and also plenty of jaw space to discover the integrity (center) of the vowels—without diphthongs—and at the same time to find low breath inhalation and support to make sure there is power without tension and vocal constriction. The key line is at the climactic end of the song: "My land's only border lies around my heart," to close act I.

BEHIND THE SCENES WITH THE ARTISTS: DEREK METZGER, ANATOLY

Australian actor Derek Metzger shares his thoughts about the role that he has performed many times and the song "Anthem": "Of all the roles I've played in musical theatre over the years, I found Anatoly to be the most complex. The song 'Anthem' is a testament to his naïveté. He truly believes that they can't touch him, that the game and how he views his 'country' are somehow separated from the lives and influences of everything around him. The song is a passionate outpouring of his heart, and the fact the he uses the platform of the Western press to do so is yet another example of his vanity, naïveté, and hypocrisy. He's doing just what he accuses Molokov of—manipulation."

Marta

Kiss of the Spider Woman

"Have a 'bank of available emotions' to draw from, and keep your secrets."
—Anthony Crivello, the original Molina

CHARACTER: Valentin Arregui Paz

MUSIC: John Kander

LYRICS: Fred Ebb

BOOK BY: Terrence McNally

BASED ON: The Manuel Puig novel *El beso de la mujer araña*

SETTING: A prison in a Latin American country

BROADWAY PREMIERE: 1993

CLASSIFICATION: High tenor

RANGE: 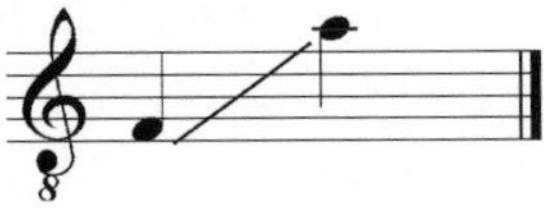

TESSITURA: Middle of staff, extended upward for climactic phrases

TIME: 2:16

PLOT: Molina is a prisoner in a Latin American country, sentenced to serve eight years for corrupting a minor. He lives in fantasy to escape the torture and fear of prison life. His fantasies mostly revolve around movie characters, which include the "spider woman," who kills with her kiss. Brought to share his cell is Valentin, a political prisoner, whose health is declining because of torture.

CHARACTER: Valentin Arregui Paz, a political prisoner, is described as a Marxist revolutionary and a political activist. He is brought into the cell, having been tortured, and is repulsed by having to share a cell with Luis Alberto Molina, a homosexual accused of sexual crimes. Molina describes to his cellmate in great detail the stories of films he has seen. Although Valentin soon tires of Molina's theatrical fantasies, he gradually becomes more interested and engaged in the stories. Valentin ends up sharing his own fantasies with his cellmate.

CONTEXT: Valentin risks his life for a political cause, while Molina is more interested in escapism and the culture he dreams of outside the prison. At first Valentin does not care for Molina and his fantasies—and in fact draws a line on the floor that he warns Molina not to cross. He continues, however, to talk about the "spider woman," and his fantastical meanderings continue, mostly to drown out the cries of tortured prisoners. At last, Valentin tells him about the girl that he loves, Marta.

CONTENT: The song is composed in three verses, preceded by whispered dialogue between Valentin and Molina. There are two measures of introduction, with a mournful oboe solo of two repeated sets of intervals that begin with quarter-note triplet patterns. Valentin begins to sing in a hushed, intense whisper the story of Marta. The memory of the girl keeps him alive in jail. The accompaniment is sparse, with the interesting color of a vibraphone playing chords; he lyrically and longingly sings, "Waiting there is Marta... over the wall," as the prisoner's chorus echoes the phrase. He thinks of himself together with Marta, and that memory helps him through each day. "But it's never her... it's just a dream of her," he realizes. Each melody line of the song ascends: the first line only to the D-flat, then the following line, which begins with the same rhythmic pattern, ascending higher, up to E-flat and F at the top of the staff. The intervals at the top of his range with sustained phrases are echoes of achingly painful memories. The second verse, beginning "So I close my eyes," has slightly different orchestration and arpeggiated spelling in the chords. The final verse, with the same text, "So I close my eyes," modulates to a higher key, up a major third to the key of F taking him to the climactic, sustained high A natural. The cello obbligato in the accompaniment is an important feature with its weaving, mournful line throughout the song. Each verse begins in a softer, more piano dynamic.

VOICE: This challenging song demands an ability to shape and build the song from a hushed whisper and a floated tone to a full-throated expression of longing. The performer will need to sing the high A-natural sustaining the *o* vowel in the word "hold." The singer is expressing intense passionate desires, but these emotions can be in opposition to freely sung vocalism at such a high range if the performer doesn't involve strong core-breath support.

BEHIND THE SCENES WITH THE ARTISTS: ANTHONY CRIVELLO, WHO CREATED THE ROLE OF VALENTIN ON BROADWAY

Tony said that it is important to look at the text, and from his experience in the Actors Studio, he is able to find honest feelings that he can tap. He has never been tortured as a political prisoner, but he can associate those feelings of helplessness and loss of power, and could compare them to the "torture" of suffering through laryngitis even as we conducted this interview, as it is feels helpless to suffer from that malady and have to call in sick for work on the stage. He further explained his work to prepare to sing a song like this as a process that requires relaxation/letting go while feeling intense, honest emotion, as well as exercising, practicing this expression without tension. He suggested that young actors observe people in life responding and reacting to different stimuli, by watching the news, for example. Reactions to disaster and adversity are not always "big" and demonstrative, for example. But they do resonate. Tony offers some important advice that he lives by: "Have a bank of available emotions to draw from, and keep your secrets." Another aspect of his performance of the song that is important is that while he sings he is in his fantasy mode, talking about Marta. That is his escape. He is not being tortured, he is in his escape mode. Finally, in speaking about his portrayal, Tony advises young actors to look between the lines, not just at the words themselves. What do the words mean? How do the music, the text, the environment, the novel, the character, and so on, inform the way that you sing the lines? "Keep asking yourself questions," advises Tony.

Your Eyes

Rent

"At the audition, the director told me to *open my eyes*. As a rock singer I was used to closing my eyes when showing/feeling emotion."

—Adam Pascal, who created the role of Roger on Broadway and in the film

CHARACTER: Roger

MUSIC AND LYRICS: Jonathan Larson

BASED ON: *La Bohème*, by Giacomo Puccini

SETTING: New York's Lower East Side

BROADWAY PREMIERE: 1996

CLASSIFICATION: Up-tempo folk/rock

RANGE: 

TESSITURA: Middle to upper staff

TIME: 2:35

PLOT: The opera *La Bohème* by Giacomo Puccini is the character/plot model for the show *Rent,* as the lead character in the opera dies of tuberculosis. Larson replaced Puccini's romantic Parisian setting with a contemporary New York Lower East Side setting and characters affected by AIDS, living together in an apartment. It was not just a show; it was a phenomenon. Jonathan Larson wrote the show in the early 1990s, after the years of AIDS epidemic in the 1980s, which was particularly focused on densely populated areas in New York because of drug use and widespread sexual activity.

CHARACTER: Roger is one of the starving, young free spirits living with AIDS. Formerly a successful musician, he is now struggling to make a living.

He hopes to write one last song of substance before it is too late. Although his friends know that he is dying, he is not at peace with it. April, his girlfriend, killed herself on discovering she had contracted AIDS. Roger (corresponding to the character Rodolfo in *La Bohème*) is roommates with Mark (Marcello in the opera). At the end of the show Roger watches his love Mimi die.

CONTEXT: The song is the last number in the show. It is a song that Roger sings to Mimi as she lies dying. He has been working on the song for a long time, and has not sung it to her before.

CONTENT: The song begins very quietly and slowly, with Roger accompanying himself in the staged show with an acoustic guitar playing broken chords, before setting it aside when the song builds and the strings enter, as the chords shift from the key of C abruptly to the B-flat-major chord ("How'd I let you slip away ..."). The song should not be sung too slowly, and the syncopations should be observed for rhythmic variety and energy in the slow-tempo piece. During the song, there are quotes and reminiscences from Puccini's opera. Musetta's waltz, first heard in the second act of the opera, is played as a solo melody by the electric guitar at the end of "Your Eyes" as Roger (Rodolfo) cries out Mimi's name as she slips away, similar to Rodolfo's expression at the end of the Puccini opera, crying out when he realizes that his love has died.

VOICE: The song should be sung tenderly in the opening page, but the tempo moves. In the next section ("How'd I let you slip away ...") the song goes up into the top of the staff for a more emotional and powerful delivery. He realizes that there is not very much time left to sing to Mimi, and he also thinks about his own impending death. On the repeat of the phrase "There's something I should have told you," the vocal line returns to a lyric delivery before moving toward the climactic phrase as Roger sings, "You were the song all along. And before the song dies ..." He dramatically sings a high G with full power (on the word "before"). He needs to tell her, "I have always loved you" because "you can see it in my eyes," he sings, as the electric-guitar solo quotes Musetta's waltz from the opera and Roger sings a high G, difficult to vocalize on the *i* vowel at that high range, as he cries out her name. Roger faces his own mortality as she slips away. The performer during this short, emotional song will forget vocal technique while singing, but it is wise for Roger to use full-body support and be aware of laryngeal tension that can limit vocal power.

BEHIND THE SCENES WITH THE ARTISTS: ADAM PASCAL, WHO CREATED THE ROLE OF ROGER ONSTAGE AND IN THE FILM

Adam was chosen to audition for the role of Roger by composer Jonathan Larson, who did not live to see the massive success of the show and its historic run on Broadway and great number of tours (and the film version). Adam had a rock-performance background, and he learned his first lesson about acting and singing onstage immediately from the show's director at the audition. During emotional, lyric songs, while singing in the rock band, he would commonly close his eyes to show greater emotion. However, at the audition, after Adam sang the first time for the production team, he recalls, "the director told me to keep my eyes open and to sing *to* the person onstage, Mimi." It took Adam a long time to feel confident and comfortable as an actor, but eventually Adam felt at home on the Broadway stage, and realized that was the place and performance style that best fit his personality. He never felt truly comfortable, he told me, "fronting a rock group and rallying the audience and whipping them into an emotional frenzy"; that never felt natural to him. Inhabiting a character satisfied his creative needs much more.

This Is the Moment

Jekyll and Hyde

"It is about inspiring and convincing myself that this is the time for action and I am the only one to do it."
—Robert Cuccioli, the original Dr. Jekyll

CHARACTER: Dr. Jekyll

MUSIC: Frank Wildhorn

LYRICS: Leslie Bricusse

BASED ON: The novella by Robert Louis Stevenson *The Strange Case of Dr. Jekyll And Mr. Hyde*

SETTING: London, the nineteenth century

BROADWAY PREMIERE: 1997

CLASSIFICATION: Baritone/tenor

RANGE: 

TESSITURA: Part 1 of the song (lyric) is low; climactic ending is at top of staff

TIME: 3:00

PLOT: See "A New Life."

CHARACTER: Dr. Jekyll is a scientist with core philosophical beliefs. The fact that his comatose father is in an asylum at the opening of the show reinforces elements of Jekyll's credo, especially since he reveals earlier his belief that his father is ill because of the inherent evil of the soul. It is important, too, that the play reveals the disdain that his hospital colleagues have for his beliefs and for his scientific study. We also are aware that, regardless of Jekyll's experiment (which results in his transformation into the monster

Hyde), Dr. Jekyll is equally comfortable moving in high-society circles with Emma as well as visiting low-life taverns, where he is attracted to the prostitute Lucy.

CONTEXT: Before Jekyll leaves Lucy at the tavern, she challenges him: "Here's romance to those unafraid of taking a chance," baiting him with her words. His response is to offer her his friendship. As he arrives at his residence in good spirits with his friend Utterson, Jekyll remarks that he has found a subject for his experiments. His friend wishes Jekyll would retire for the evening. This is the moment for him to prove himself to everyone—to show the world. He is about to inject himself with the drug HJ7, and he will then record the results of the experiment. Finally alone in his house, Jekyll goes quickly to his laboratory, anxious to begin his work. He tells himself in recitative style to put aside his fears. He feels like there is no place to hide. To make his scientific mark, to show them, he has only one chance, he sings, "when everything I've fought for is at stake."

CONTENT: Jekyll begins the song "This Is the Moment" in his lower range, in short phrases (marked "rubato"). The accompaniment is a steady, sustained whole-note support in the treble, with a rhythmic pattern of dotted-quarter-note and eighth-note rhythms. After two phrases of the melody at the lower pitch level, between low B and F-sharp at the low end of the staff in the key of E major, he leaps up an octave to repeat the melody's phrase at the top of the staff in the second verse. The accompaniment becomes more active as the song builds in power. In the B section, the bridge, Jekyll talks about "facing the world alone." He needs to prove, he says, "I made it on my own," as he leaps to the high G-sharp for an off-beat entrance to the next phrase that has him attacking the downbeat (before the beat) in anticipation of the orchestral entrance on the downbeat for an extraordinary dramatic/musical effect. The full force of the orchestra now enters with the addition of violins, horn, and trumpet. Here, at the height of the song, he uses the most inspiring language—"Destiny's beckoned, . . . I must not fall." The momentum slows a little ("ritardando" is marked), as more high strings enter—with rhythmic flourish—as one more verse fueled by more high-stakes declarations is sung: "This day or never I'll sit forever with the Gods," and the song powers toward its conclusion with a series of short phrases, or tags, which allow the performer to take deep breaths and gather all of his residual strength to finish powerfully. When Jekyll looks back, he will recall "the greatest moment of them all," as he concludes the inspiring lyrics, and a vocal line that sustains the high F at the top of the staff in the final cadence. There is much more singing in this scene for Jekyll to accomplish, continuing with his taking the potion, recording its effects, and suffering through the transformation. However, the sense (and illusion) at the end of the song "This Is the Moment" is that Jekyll has given his all in the performance of this anthem.

VOICE: The singer needs to pace himself in singing the song, keeping dramatic intensity without expending too much "vocal capital." Do not force the low tones, which if sung too strongly with weight early in the song can affect range and flexibility that will be needed later in the higher range. Jekyll is British, and the English accent will be helpful in keeping the tone free and open in the high range singing the syllable *-ment* of "moment." That being said, be careful that the syllable is not too opened up, or spread, because the syllable is uninflected and will sound unpleasant if strained. With all of the active rhythms, try to keep a vocal line connected with the breath support at the same time, so that the individual notes are not punched, creating vocal strain, which also can use up needed vocal resources. During the B section, if the singer gets too contentious and angry, that too will compromise the vocal freedom and power needed for the high-ranged climactic conclusion.

BEHIND THE SCENES WITH THE ARTISTS: ROBERT CUCCIOLI, THE ORIGINAL DR. JEKYLL

Mr. Cuccioli says his interpretation of the song "came out of the moment and the situation at that time in the show. It is about inspiring and convincing myself that this is the time for action and I am the only one to do it. Everything I have ever worked for has come down to this moment, so to speak." He told me that what is at stake for Jekll at that moment before singing the song is the important thing to think about.

I'd Rather Be Sailing

A New Brain

"It became everyone's favorite song of mine, for some reason."
—William Finn, composer

CHARACTER: Gordon Schwinn

MUSIC AND LYRICS: William Finn

SETTING: Contemporary suburbia

BROADWAY PREMIERE: 1998

CLASSIFICATION: Lyric with moving tempo for baritone-tenor

RANGE: 

TESSITURA: Upper middle of staff

TIME: 3:40

PLOT: Many of William Finn's works are indirectly autobiographical, and this work is directly taken from Finn's experiences and the lesson he learned of the healing power of art. The stand-in for Finn in the show is Gordon Michael Schwinn, a cynical composer of songs.

CHARACTER: Songwriter Gordon Schwinn collapses at a dinner with his agent, and through a medical crisis which involves brain surgery he worries that he will never compose again. His greatest fears are that his songs will die inside him, and through hallucinations in his hospital bed, in interactions with both real and imagined characters, these songs are brought to life.

CONTEXT: The composer William Finn speaks to the placement of the song in the show: "The first fifteen minutes of *A New Brain* are frenetic.

I wanted 'I'd Rather Be Sailing' to be the first time the audience relaxed. That is why it needs to be sung with great strength, control, and joy."

CONTENT: The song begins dreamily, with the accompaniment conjuring an image of sparkling reflections on the water. In the song the voice crescendos and builds in passionate delivery as the vocal line ascends through the bridge to the chorus, repeated at a higher key. The accompaniment bridges the modulation and with ascending octaves helps to prepare the singer's entrance with energy, as he begins to sing the chorus of "I'd rather be sailing." The images that are described, such as "The sun is on my neck, the wind is in my face," are sung at a high range on the staff. In-the-moment descriptions by the singer include "The waters are incredibly blue," a great image we can imagine and see in our minds. This becomes even more poignant imagining being in the hospital and facing a life-threatening problem that blocks those pleasurable memories, as the text of the chorus ends with "and come back home to you." The refrain is sung twice, followed by a B section. Then there is an antiphonal duet with Roger as the song modulates from F major to G-flat for final repeats of the refrain. "I'd Rather Be Sailing" is a pleasant song that moves with gently syncopated rhythms. The accompaniment is constructed beautifully, with countermelodies and woven-through polyphonic fragments, and with gently supporting chords. The song modulates up a half step. It begins pleasantly and ends more passionately, with a sustained high G-flat at the top of the staff in the baritone or tenor voice range.

VOICE: The singer should think about taking a whimsical, fantastical approach to a situation that is not necessarily humorous in context. The singer needs to have an easy vocal production (with some power). Also important is a good rhythmic sense that can vocalize a languid syncopation over the bar ("I'd rather be sailing, yes I would"), and sing a number of triplet rhythmic patterns that need to be articulated clearly, but so defined that they change the fantastical feel and dreamlike tone of the song. The singer needs to be aware of good vocal control at the D-flat (and above) without tension in the light, lyrical portions of this song. The singer will find the gospel-like style delivery that is called-for at the top of the range toward the end of the song challenging. The composer writes slight variations of the melody and the final notes that reach above the staff for a sustained high G-flat at the final cadence. The singer needs to capture the memory, the longing, the variety of emotions appropriate to the circumstances.

BEHIND THE SCENES WITH THE ARTISTS: WILLIAM FINN, COMPOSER

Mr. Finn says (in a self-effacing manner) that when he was writing this song, the verse wouldn't come—so he wrote a bridge, kept the chorus, and simply repeated it! "It became everyone's favorite song of mine, for some reason," he said.

The Old Red Hills of Home

Parade

"[The singer] should not concentrate too much on the 'message' of the song. The singer should think of the character and story."
—Jeff Edgerton, the original Soldier in *Parade*

CHARACTER: Young Confederate Soldier

MUSIC, LYRICS: Jason Robert Brown

BOOK: Alfred Uhry

SETTING: Georgia, 1860; Atlanta, 1913

BROADWAY PREMIERE: 1998

CLASSIFICATION: Tenor lyric

RANGE: 

TESSITURA: Upper staff

TIME: 6:34

PLOT: The musical dramatizes the events in Georgia in 1913 surrounding the trial and appeal of pencil factory owner Leo Frank, who is unjustly charged with the brutal rape and murder of a thirteen-year-old girl, Mary Phagan, who works in the factory. Frank is found guilty, but his death sentence is commuted to life in prison. However, a group of men kidnap Leo Frank from prison, take him to a rural area in Georgia, and hang him. The opening of the story takes place fifty years before these events, during the Civil War.

CHARACTER: The Confederate soldier is very young, and he has a young wife whose name is Lila. He looks back to the memory of her and home, and sings to her.

CONTEXT: The opening song, "The Old Red Hills of Home," is sung by a soldier as he says goodbye and goes off to war. He is singing about the wife and home that he is leaving in Marietta, Georgia. This is the place where Leo Frank will be taken in fifty years to be hanged.

CONTENT: The introduction is a theatrical flashback to the Civil War fifty years earlier. The soldier sings farewell to his wife, Lila; promises to write each day when he is gone; and tells her that he has carved their names together on a tree next to where he stands. The opening sequence, set in a place and time when racial intolerance was rampant, sets the tone for another intolerance the southerners feel for the character of Leo Frank, a Jewish man, many years later. Also resonating with the audience later in the show is the fact that Leo Frank, accused of raping and murdering a thirteen-year-old southern girl, is dragged from his cell by a lynch mob and taken to Marietta, Georgia, where he is strung up on an oak tree. The young soldier "fights for these old hills," he sings. It is ironic that he says that he is fighting to keep "a way of life that is pure," where "honor lives and breathes," when one takes into account what will happen fifty years later (and perhaps fifty years after that). It is a beautiful song that builds to a dramatic ending, where the tenor needs to sing up to a high, sustained pitch of A above the staff. The accompaniment (both lines written in the bass clef) plays a repeated rhythmic pattern, simulating the sound of a drum, as the soldier sings. When the song is performed onstage, the drum will play throughout the song. The melody is simple and straightforward, with a folk-song plaintive simplicity. As the melody unfolds and continues to evolve as a through composition (no section is musically repeated), there are an increasing number of embellished notes surrounding the melodic frame, which can be attributed to the character growing more emotional and agitated, thinking about the battles, as he hopes to return home after the war.

VOICE: The tenor needs to have an easy high range and must bring power to the song's delivery as the emotional fervor of the soldier increases. The first section of the song is in the middle range, but with "I go to fight," the melody ascends to the top of the staff. Some of the words to sing on the high pitches ("hills," "old," "spill") are not easy to sing without creating space in the jaw and keeping the tongue from being "swallowed" by allowing it to remain in more of a forward position. The singer should recognize an opportunity in the opening of the song to sing the dotted rhythms in a clearly defined manner, which gives the vocal line energy, purpose, and momentum. Also, attention to diction and sharp rhythmic definition will cut through a rather busy and energized accompaniment of a sixteenth-note repeated rhythmic pattern, masterfully conceived by composer-pianist (and lyricist) Jason Robert Brown. Although the song has a simple, folk-like style throughout, it also calls for high A naturals, and the ability to crescendo sustained tones in the high range, followed by a marked decrescendo, difficult to accomplish at the top of the staff without vocal tension. There are other clearly marked articulation directions, including accents, and there are some meter changes to observe. The last "farewell" high-octave skip up to an A can be sung in head resonance (mixed) voice. Note that some phrases, such as: "and there's peace in Marietta," are marked "piano," which provides contrast and a place where the singer can escape a constantly strong dynamic in the song which can result in a stridency, tension, and blustery, monochromatic dynamic.

BEHIND THE SCENES WITH THE ARTISTS: JEFF EDGERTON, WHO CREATED THE ROLE OF THE SOLDIER IN THE PREMIERE

In the original Broadway production, the role of Young Confederate Soldier was sung by Jeff Edgerton, who also performed the song on the original cast recording. Jeff suggests that the singer of "Old Red Hills of Home" should not concentrate too much on the message of the song and should think instead of the character and story only. Jeff told me, "This young soldier is going off to fight and he's angry, angry about the North. This is what happened. Let us never fight our brothers again."

Jeff continues: "The young singer should make the song your own. Don't just listen to the recording and imitate it. Look at the text and see how you relate to it. Think that it is *your* story to tell. Yes, the story is ironic, but the audience needs to connect the dots; it is not for you to connect them for the audience. Also, the accompaniment is busy and challenging, so make sure that the pianist can play this piece, and can follow *you*."

Jeff learned an important lesson when director Harold Prince participated in the process of building the show toward the premiere. Mr. Prince was very concerned with the visual aspects of the production, but he trusted Jeff to deliver the text and music with his own take on the character and situation. Jeff was singing this song and creating this character for the first time, but the director trusted Jeff's instincts as a professional to perform. Mr. Prince would tell him what was working and what wasn't, but in the professional theatre the director will trust the actor to have thought the song through and to bring ideas to the first rehearsal. Jeff is now active with presenting singing/acting workshops. He says that it is clear that there are a lot of pretty voices, but few young singers bring ideas to the table when they audition.

The title of the song comes from the inscription on Mary Phagan's tombstone: "She died for the glory of the old red hills of home."

Tell My Father

The Civil War

"The singer shouldn't act, but instead should tell the truth."
—Frank Wildhorn, composer

CHARACTER: Private Sam Taylor

MUSIC: Frank Wildhorn

LYRICS: Jack Murphy

BOOK: Gregory Boyd and Frank Wildhorn

SETTING: A Civil War battlefield

BROADWAY PREMIERE: 1999

CLASSIFICATION: Lyric anthem for tenor/baritone

RANGE: 

TESSITURA: Middle of staff

TIME: 3:18

PLOT: *The Civil War* is often produced in concert version. The show is not a traditional, plot-driven musical; instead it integrates thematically consistent songs that do not drive or narrate a plot and could be classified as a song cycle. The production utilizes projected photos and letters from the time to evoke the period setting. The musical numbers are from the viewpoints of the soldiers of both sides, as well as that of the slaves. "Tell My Father" is sung by Private Sam Taylor.

CHARACTER: Sam Taylor is the brother of a young soldier who has been shot and killed in battle. Since *The Civil War* does not have a through story line with characters, it is an creative opportunity for the actor playing Sam to fabricate his own background and how he feels about his brother, and his father, according to the surrounding circumstances.

CONTEXT: The song is placed near the opening of the show; it is the fourth piece. It follows "Sons of Dixie," sung by the Armies. Sam opens a letter from his brother, which was written before he was killed. His brother fought for the Union army, and he implores Sam: "Please tell him I fought bravely. His pride will make this pass easier."

CONTENT: The song begins with a simple melodic motive of two measures, repeated twice. It is played by a lonely fiddle, and then the voice enters, a cappella. The melody is simple and folk-like, sung in the lower-middle register. The song is poignant and plaintive when sung straightforwardly. The form is two simple, short choruses, followed by a bridge that begins higher in the voice, at the top of the staff, of eight measures in length. The bridge is followed by one more chorus, sung with more meaning and weight, and slows with the words "I will say you wore the blue proud and true like he taught you," before the final line: "I'll tell father not to cry . . . then say [fermata] good-bye," as the song ends, marked "piano."

VOICE: The song requires a simple, straightforward delivery that is without any artifice of emotion whatsoever. The performer does not need to add any emotion or artificial energy which would ring false. The singer should observe the correct rhythmic values, and there are some dotted rhythms that vary from verse to verse, which gives the song variety and momentum. The song does not require powerful tone, but instead should be sung lyrically in a folk style, with unforced, natural vocal production. The opening phrases sustain middle-range tones, of A and B, ascending through middle C to D. The composer and lyricist chose singer-friendly words to sustain, including "son," "run," "pride," "tried," and "re-mem-ber," all centered on vowels that will open the jaw and free the tone, as long as the singer does not add diphthongs. There are two verses before the bridge, which is pitched higher (E and F-sharp at the top of the staff). These bridge phrases are also repeated before returning to another singing of the verse. There is a brief interlude, as the accompaniment plays the melody alone before the singer sings one last repetition of the phrase closing the verse, concluding with a fermata in the last three measures to indicate the ending phrases of the song.

BEHIND THE SCENES WITH THE ARTISTS: FRANK WILDHORN, COMPOSER

Mr. Wildhorn points out that *The Civil War* has been presented in many different formats. "It does not tell a linear story, but instead presents characters out of story context that set an environment and provide a frame in which real letters are sung, not acted." Frank points out that the singers "shouldn't act, but instead should tell the truth." Furthermore, this song in particular is sung by a young soldier, who sings the song with a sincerity and earnestness that fit the situation, because he is recounting his brother's words that are intended for their father. Frank told me that the voice does not need to be specifically tenor or baritone, and in fact does not require specialized training to sing dramatically or in a high range. "The voice should not be too *bold*," he said. Frank also pointed out that he comes from the pop world of songwriting, having tailored song to singers' individual styles, not to fit into a story line where singers were later "plugged in." That means that his songs have always "framed the singer and his or her style."

You Walk with Me

The Full Monty

"I was taken by this beautiful song that David Yazbek 'uncorked' for the occasion, sung by Jason Danieley."
—Jack O'Brien, the original director of *The Full Monty*

CHARACTER: Malcolm

MUSIC AND LYRICS: David Yazbek

BOOK: Terrence McNally

BASED ON: The film of the same title

SETTING: Buffalo, New York

BROADWAY PREMIERE: 2000

CLASSIFICATION: Lyric song for tenor

RANGE: 

TESSITURA: Above the staff

TIME: 3:06

PLOT: Based on the 1997 British film, the musical is transplanted to depressed Buffalo, where the once-active steel mills have shut down. Six of the unemployed and low salaried men decide to create their own strip act, when it is revealed that their wives are enthusiastic about a Chippendales club in the town.

CHARACTER: Malcolm is an awkward and lonely security guard at the plant. He lives with his domineering mother, who is an invalid. He tries to commit suicide in his car by carbon monoxide poisoning. He is saved by friends Jerry and Dave and is eventually brought into the strip act. Ethan Girard longs to dance like Donald O'Connor and auditions for the act. Malcolm's mother dies, and the two men are brought together at her funeral. "You Walk with Me" becomes a duet as Ethan comforts his friend, making clear the nature of Ethan and Malcolm's romantic relationship. The song can be sung as a standalone solo, following Malcolm's line throughout the duet section.

CONTEXT: The song is sung at the cemetery on a dreary, rainy day at the graveside of Malcolm's mother at her burial. Malcolm and his friends are standing by the grave, and the priest is speaking. Although this is a somber scene, the vision of the friends unconsciously gyrating their hips to the music elicits laughs. In the film, Jack O'Brien told me, this comic touch occurs in a different section of the movie, but the juxtaposition with the touching vulnerability of Malcolm singing the song is a brilliant touch. The priest asks Malcolm at the graveside, "Do you want to say anything?" at which point Malcolm begins the song after a two-measure introduction.

CONTENT: The beautiful lyrics to the song—"Is it the wind there over my shoulder? Is it your voice calling quietly?"—are simple, poignant, and moving. There is a countermelody in the orchestra played by oboe, which adds a plaintive, mournful musical color. The moving parts of the accompaniment in the keyboard are both written in the treble clef and feature a flowing, moving, active-rhythmic support. The first two melodic sections are similar, but in the second section, as Malcolm sings "Over the hilltop," the line arches up to a high A-natural, and then descends again, in an example of textural painting in the music. In the second verse, when Ethan joins in, the accompaniment becomes a little thicker in texture. Instead of delicate eighth-note/sixteenth-note rhythms, the pattern becomes simply a quarter/eighth rhythm, repeated, to thicken the chordal texture. After the second verse, there is a short interlude of one measure, which sets up the final phrase, marked "ritard": "Never alone for you walk," with a caesura for a dramatic pause, and then he sings "with [sustained fermata] me," as the accompaniment continues, a tempo, with a rhythmic pattern, marked "piano," to the final chord. There are no key changes in the piece, just some exposed accidentals in the vocal line. The song is hauntingly beautiful.

VOICE: The text and vocal lines are lyrical and delicately inflected, as is the text. Many of the vocal lines begin at the higher pitch level, then descend. This means that each line needs to be approached lightly, lyrically, as the phrase moves toward the important, inflected pitches at the middle and end of the text. The piece is not without accidentals, which need to be carefully negotiated and tuned. The entire song is sung lightly, reverently, poignantly. "No, not alone," can be sung with a little more authority and security, suggesting hopeful confidence. It follows the line "Will I be alone... there in the darkness?" All text needs to have a freed, open jaw, so that the sequence of vowels in the text can flow without the singer "chewing" the words. The articulation of the text, even when sung softly, can involve strong initial and final consonants. Be careful of glottal attacks when attempting to articulate when the word begins with a vowel, such as: "*Is* it the wind?" at the beginning of the song, and: "*Are* you alone?" When the attack begins with a vowel, make sure that the breath supports the onset with a breath flow that precedes phonation, and do not close the vocal folds to begin to phonate the vowel (glottal attack), which is not a healthy vocal habit, in any case.

BEHIND THE SCENES WITH THE ARTISTS: JACK O'BRIEN, THE ORIGINAL DIRECTOR

Jack points out that in the film, when Malcolm's friends discover that he is gay, it is more of a surprise than in the musical, but in the course of singing this song, it is a beautiful opportunity for the nature of Malcolm's relationship with Ethan to be revealed. It is a rare moment for the guarded Malcolm to reveal his pain and vulnerability in being alone in these circumstances at graveside, and the perfect time for Ethan to comfort him, as Malcolm chokes up during the song, making it difficult for him to continue. This is also the opportunity for Ethan to sing along to support him further. In the original construction of the show, Jack recalls, he "was taken by this beautiful song that David Yazbek 'uncorked' for the occasion." He thought it was beautiful, but also kind of odd, in that it is not a hymn or any other "type" of a song you will hear usually in a musical. However, the lovely melody and odd harmonies and countermelodies work in "capturing Malcolm's pain, his need to be comforted, and Ethan's support as he reveals his feelings for Malcolm with friends standing by at the graveside of Malcolm's mother."

At the Fountain

Sweet Smell of Success

"Never underestimate what you can bring to the table."
—Brian Darcy James, the original Sidney

CHARACTER: Sidney Falcone

MUSIC: Marvin Hamlisch

LYRICS: Craig Carnelia

BOOK: John Guare

SETTING: New York, 1952

PREMIERE: 2002

CLASSIFICATION: Belt song for tenor

RANGE: 

TESSITURA: Top of the staff

TIME: 3:53

PLOT: The show is the story of a powerful New York columnist, J. J. Hunsecker (based on Walter Winchell), who uses his underworld connections to ruin the relationship of his sister Susan to a man Hunsecker does not like. J. J. has the dirt on everyone, from politicians to starlets. J. J. can make or break you in his column.

CHARACTER: Sidney is a struggling press agent with one client, the Club Voodoo, a two-bit joint. He is a small-time hustler in a cheap suit with big-time dreams. However, the owner of the club warns Sidney: unless the establishment appears in Hunsecker's column soon (a PR coup for the struggling club), Falcone will be left with no clients.

CONTEXT: The only customer in the Club Voodoo this night is a woman by the name of Susan. She is there to listen to Dallas, the talented piano player, and they are attracted to each other. But there is someone who wouldn't like it, she cryptically remarks to Dallas. Sidney, loitering at the club, tries to recruit the gifted Dallas as a client, but the piano player is not interested. Sidney was going to try to pick up Susan, but he can now see that Dallas and Susan are attracted to each other. Sidney feels like a loser. At this moment in bursts J. J. Hunsecker, who—to Sidney's surprise—happens to be Susan's older brother. To distract J. J. and keep him from finding out about her relationship with Dallas, Susan claims that Sidney is in her acting class and is a friend of hers. To get close to a friend of Susan for the purpose of keeping an eye on her, J. J. helps Sidney in his career, including buying him a new suit, while getting a new job for Sidney's waitress girlfriend. Sidney believes his ship has come in, and joyfully sings "At the Fountain."

CONTENT: "At the Fountain" refers to the Hollywood legend of Lana Turner, who was discovered at the soda fountain as a nobody, eventually becoming a big movie star. Sidney Falcone is going to be "that" press agent and be mentioned in the same breath someday as the agent who discovered Lana Turner.

The song begins excitedly, with Sidney repeating some text for emphasis ("You take the whole damn past and cash it in, cash the whole thing in," in the opening phrases. He can hardly believe his good luck. The delivery of the song is in excited, clipped, staccato-like syllables. There were so many obstacles in his path before; maybe this is his shot" at success. Phrases are short at first, as if he is short of breath with excitement, but then the melody begins to unfold and extend with sustained notes at the end of the vocal lines. "Hey Sidney, you finally found some luck!" he crows, and his confidence grows. He begins to believe that he actually deserves his success. The song stops, and he speaks in dialogue, recounting the story of "Lana Turner, sitting at the soda fountain." The mood suddenly changes, and Sidney sings in a dream-like waltz meter. "Maybe I'm at the fountain," he sings. This is perfect timing, and it "feels like a work of art," he croons. This is his big break, he says. Then the song launches into the same rhythm and energy as at the beginning. People change; is it possible for his career to change, too? Falcone now imagines he is at the fountain, he sings, with Tchaikovsky-like chords arpeggiated up and down the piano, again in the triple meter, as the song builds to the high A before the words "So let my life story start" at the climactic ending to the song.

VOICE: Sidney feels as if he just won the lottery, and this is conveyed by a supremely confident vocal delivery with syncopated rhythms that swing and celebrate his good luck. The rhythms are tricky in their off-the-beat syncopated accents, and need to reflect his newfound confidence. The piano is playing an eighth-note rhythm pattern that sets up the vocal line nicely. The singer needs to be "on top" of the beat and in control of the rhythms, and to lead the accompanist without running away with the tempo. In the opening, which is joyously delivered, Sidney also needs to implode the consonants with full abdominal breath support that start the words "half a *chance, cash* the whole thing, *Keep* the O." When he sings in waltz time as he recalls the story of Lana Turner, Sidney changes the direction of the song to a more lyrical approach with quarter note/half note combination that is more "dreamy" and crooned in its delivery. The last section recaps the opening, which builds with a strong vocal momentum to the end, as he sustains a high A at the top, which is sung on the *o* vowel ("s*o*ar").

BEHIND THE SCENES WITH THE ARTISTS: BRIAN DARCY JAMES, THE ORIGINAL SIDNEY FALCONE

Brian watched the source film (*Sweet Smell of Success*) two times, once with the cast. This being a new production, there was an opportunity for him to mold the character of Sidney Falcone with the aid of a fantastic creative team. He equates working with such a talented team with being fitted for a custom-made suit. After reading through the script with the cast in workshop and beginning to put it on its feet, the team knew that it was important to mold the character and to try to find a likeable core in the character, even though Sydney was ambitious and did not always make the right choices. The audience would need to see him through the show and want him to succeed. What was it about him that was likeable? Was it the naïveté? And here it was right in front of them, Sidney looking up to J. J. (the Walter Winchell character); J. J. Hunsecker was everything that Sidney wanted to be, so he became a "puppy dog" in J. J.'s presence, and Sidney's sympathetic character was revealed to the audience.

Brian told me that he made a quiet promise to himself to take as many original roles as he could (he has created many roles). The creative process of putting a show on its feet proves to him that the creative spark from many composers, lyricists, and others on the creative team continues to bring new, exciting works to the public. Some final advice for young singers from Brian: "Never underestimate what you bring to the table."

I Miss the Music

Curtains

"I get the added 'loaded emotional gun' of knowing that it is also about Marin and me and John and Fred."
—Jason Danieley, the original Aaron Fox

CHARACTER: Aaron Fox

MUSIC: John Kander

LYRICS: Fred Ebb (completed by Rupert Holmes)

BOOK: Rupert Holmes

SETTING: Boston, Massachusetts, 1959

BROADWAY PREMIERE: 2006

CLASSIFICATION: Lyric tenor

RANGE: 

TESSITURA: Middle of the staff

TIME: 3:15

PLOT: This musical was inspired by backstage murder stories. When the untalented star of *Robbin' Hood of the Old West* (a fictional Western version of Robin Hood) is murdered during the opening night curtain call, a police detective (a musical theatre fan) wants to solve the case before the show reopens. After the crime, everyone in the cast believes that one of them must be the murderer.

CHARACTER: The fictional songwriting team who created the new musical is made up of the divorced creative duo of composer Aaron Fox and Georgia Hendricks. Aaron is described as a charming ladies' man in his forties. Aaron and Georgia now argue because he wonders why his ex-wife signed on for the show's run. He claims that she only wanted to be close to the show's choreographer, Georgia's ex-boyfriend Bobby. Since the leading lady has been murdered, and the show must go on, the producers cast Georgia as the lead to replace the star.

CONTEXT: The detective Lieutenant Frank Cioffi, trying to solve the murder, who is an amateur performer himself, saw the show and loved it (but not the leading lady). He encourages the cast to continue the run of performances, even though the reviews of the show have not been good, mostly due to the leading lady, now deceased. The production staff talks about some revisions. The composer, Aaron, now alone with the lieutenant, tells him that the process of composing a song is difficult and proceeds to sing "I Miss the Music."

CONTENT: The introduction in orchestra is only three measures, and is marked "freely," and the dynamic is pianissimo. Aaron begins to sing lyrically as he talks about "missing the music I write with her." The dotted-quarter-note rhythms in the melody add momentum to the vocal line. With wistful lyrics, the melody has a beautiful shape as it unfolds. "I've lost the music, I don't know why," he sings. He repeats the refrain. The middle section is quite different, more about the text than the music, and the piano accompaniment lends a light, jaunty rhythmic style as Aaron describes the collaborative writing process, and then continues to explain what it is like to write without a partner. "No one makes you better than you are," he remarks. The last section is a recapitulation of the A section, but modulates up a half step to the key of F-sharp in an expression of longing and regret, especially on some of the sustained higher tones. The song ends softly, lyrically. He misses making the music, making the music with her...

VOICE: This song requires an easy, lyric top voice (though the range is not extraordinarily high throughout the song) and the ability to underline and deliver words while telling a story. Vocal control and beautiful legato singing is important. The originator of the role, Jason Danieley, was able to combine the vocal qualities of lyricism with dramatic expression while delivering the text with clarity, expression, and passion. The song has high E and Fs at the top of the staff, and high F-sharp in the last chorus, but the text cannot be compromised. Words must be enunciated and communicated, and sung freely, without tension, to convey the full expression of Fox's emotions.

BEHIND THE SCENES WITH THE ARTISTS: JOHN KANDER, COMPOSER OF *CURTAINS*

Mr. Kander said that the song was originally written for Jason Danieley, who created the role of Aaron Fox. "It was an important addition for the character and the dramatic situation," Mr. Kander said. Before the musical premiered on Broadway in 2006, the lyricist Fred Ebb, who had created with Kander the music/lyrics for *Chicago* and *Cabaret* as well as other successful musicals, died suddenly of a heart attack in 2004. Rupert Holmes finished the lyrics of a number of the songs. With regard to "I Miss the Music," Mr. Kander at first rejected the idea that the song was written about his departed writing partner. However, later in the songwriting process, Mr. Kander realized that the claim was true. And at that point, he had completed the song, finishing with the middle of the piece, the bridge. He remarked that no one sings this song as well as the creator of the Aaron Fox role, Jason Danieley.

Jason Danieley: As director Scott Ellis told Jason, he had been after Kander for a while to write a song for that spot in the show. "After I was on board to play Aaron, John supposedly said, 'I have to write a song for Jason.'" Jason describes hearing the song the first time. Music director David Loud played it, and Jason sight-read it over his shoulder. "We were both very moved by what we perceived to be an homage to Fred. I told John Kander how David and I were in near tears after the first read and what a beautiful tribute this song is to the spirit of their collaboration and friendship. John looked genuinely surprised by our observation. He said he hadn't written it with that in mind." The composer went on to tell Jason who he was thinking of when creating the song: "First of all it was about Aaron and Georgia's relationship, but secondly he wrote it with me and Marin Mazzie [Jason Danieley's wife)] in mind—what it would possibly mean to us if either of us were not in the relationship anymore. John later said he added the bridge to the song, which as you can hear in the text reflects a more direct influence attributed to his creative relationship with his longtime friend, Fred Ebb."

This is what the song ultimately means to Jason: "Not only is it a personal highlight in my professional life to have John Kander write a song for me to perform in an original Broadway show for a role I created, but I also get the added 'loaded emotional gun' of knowing that it is also about Marin and me and John and Fred."

All That's Known

Spring Awakening

"The words 'radical' and 'rebel' were burned into
my mind as I found my way into the song."
—Jonathan Groff, the original Melchior

CHARACTER: Melchior

MUSIC: Duncan Sheik

BOOK AND LYRICS: Steven Sater

BASED ON: A German play by Frank Wedekind

SETTING: Germany

PREMIERE: 2006

CLASSIFICATION: Upbeat, angry/lyric tenor/high baritone

RANGE: 

TESSITURA: Upper-middle staff

TIME: 2:02

PLOT: The musical *Spring Awakening* is based on a controversial play written in the late nineteenth century in Germany. The story is about teenagers discovering the confused feelings of emerging sexuality and repression. In the show, a rock-infused score lends a dramatic edge to the characters and situations.

CHARACTER: Melchior is headstrong, handsome, and a charismatic leader. He reads books and soaks up knowledge. He mentors his good friend Moritz in the mystery of sex. He sees corruption in society. He falls in love with Wendla, a girl whose mother has not been able to tell her about the facts of life and has tried to suppress her daughter's sexuality. Melchior's mother, Fanny, also has a strong personality. She has an open mind and tries to counsel and guide him in his sexuality; she also tries to help his friend Moritz. Fanny intends to send Melchior away before he finds out that Wendla is pregnant.

CONTEXT: In a schoolroom (act I, scene 2), male teenage students are reciting their Latin exercises when Moritz Stiefel, a very nervous and insecure young man, misquotes a line. The teacher berates Moritz, and his friend Melchior tries to come to his aid. In response, the instructor strikes Melchior with a stick. Melchior muses upon the narrow mindedness of school and its rules, and he is frustrated that he cannot openly respond.

CONTENT: At the opening of the scene, Melchior displays his youthful idealism in standing up for a friend and taking chances for the sake of his principles. The boys continue to chant in Latin as Melchior begins his inner monologue and manifesto. The song is marked "hypnotically, at a moderate tempo." The key is G minor, and while the melody begins with a narrow range, it soon widens its intervals. Rhythmically, the melody in written mostly in eighth-note rhythms, but begins to include sixteenth-notes in a variety of syncopated patterns. The treble of the accompaniment is composed in all eighth-note values to simulate the rhythm of a steady heartbeat. It is an unusual song in that it does not feature a recognizable tune. The song introduces the character of Melchior, so it needs to strongly reflect many of his qualities as radical rebel and capture his repressed anger. There is a driving beat, but also a lyric cello line heard underneath. "Money is their idol"; "thought is suspect." "You watch me"; "you just watch me," he repeats. "One day all will know," And even though it is an inner-monologue "freeze" as performed in the original production, Melchior in his delivery needs to portray the passion of his convictions with energy.

VOICE: This is an angry song, but it is also intended to be bound up with repressed emotion and intense feelings. What is needed vocally is a strong delivery in a rock-style, middle-ranged tenor voice. There are no pitches written higher than a passing E natural, and the top sustained pitch is D. Jonathan Groff, who created the role of Melchior, explained that since the composer, Duncan Sheik, preferred the song sung without vibrato in more of a "rock-singing style," he worked with the show's vocal coach to sing the song with more of a "straight-tone" delivery. The singer needs to repress the vibrato (which tends to bring out the warmth in a voice) by using intensity of breath-support voice connection. Healthy vocal habits while singing the song are important. Check for throat tension, as intensity and removal of the vibrato should not be accomplished by constriction in the throat. Also: note the entrances are not on the beat, but are instead written to be sung off the beat, each vocal entrance alternating between an entrance after an eighth-beat and after a quarter-beat rest.

BEHIND THE SCENES WITH THE ARTISTS: JONATHAN GROFF, WHO CREATED THE ROLE OF MELCHIOR

Jonathan described the journey of taking the show from workshop to finished form on Broadway. "Through rewrites and discussion, the director decided that he wanted Melchior to be a 'rebel' or 'radical,' as he is called by the girls later in the play. They rewrote the first scene so that Melchior stood up for Moritz in the class room, and composer Duncan Sheik and lyricist Steven Sater wrote the song 'All That's Known,' which the creative team wanted to serve two major purposes: give Melchior an 'I want' song and establish him as a rebel." Jonathan admits that he had some difficulty in finding the character early on in the show: "Michael [Mayer, the director] told us all at the beginning that the songs are interior monologues, and that they are there as expression of a moment frozen in time, not really to further the story. But, in the [singing] of 'All That's Known' I found it easier to act it as I would a traditional musical theatre song. This truly is the 'I want' song that every great character in a musical gets to sing at the top of the show to let the audience know what he's after." Jonathan explained that "the words 'radical' and 'rebel' were burned into my mind as I found my way into the song, and the scene right before is full of so much deeply repressed anger about what just happened in class that it felt completely natural to whip the mic out of my coat and express myself."

Absalom

The Glorious Ones

"In order to be whole and fully formed artists, we need to shed our past and move on from our teachers. That is a heavy sentiment. And that is where I begin when I think about singing Absalom."
—Jeremy Webb, the original Francesco Andreini

CHARACTER: Francesco Andreini

MUSIC: Stephen Flaherty

BOOK AND LYRICS: Lynn Ahrens

BASED ON: The historical novel *The Glorious Ones* by Francine Prose (2000)

SETTING: A beautiful spring day in Venice in the late 1500s

PREMIERE: 2007 at Lincoln Center

CLASSIFICATION: Middle-voice lyric tenor

RANGE: 

TESSITURA: Middle of staff

TIME: 2:38

PLOT: The musical, which is set in sixteenth-century Italy, tells the story of a traveling band of actors, including the young Francesco Andreini, performing commedia dell'arte, a popular style of entertainment at the time. Each character in the show has its own archetypal type from the Italian commedia dell'arte form. These characters include the sly harlequin (Francesco); the quack "dottore" Graziano; the old miser Pantalone; the voluptuous leading lady, gossip-loving Columbina; evil-minded Brighella; and the devoted dwarf, sunny Armanda. The troupe, called the Glorious

Ones, is led by the ingenious madman Flaminio Scala, who actually lived (as did Francesco Andreini) in sixteenth-century Italy and was integral in the effort to codify commedia dell'arte. The style of the commedia was improvisational, but it had guidelines and rules.

CHARACTER: Francesco is a talented young comic—youthful, energetic, and street smart. The boy becomes a man in the course of the show. "He learns from the leader, Flaminio, then exploits," according to Jeremy Webb, the original Francesco. Flaminio is inspired by the many patches on Francesco's clothes, designing a costume that defines Arlecchino, the clown, the sly trickster. Francesco becomes a featured actor in the troupe. His wife, Isabella, is also a member of the Glorious Ones.

CONTEXT: Earlier in the show the troupe finds Francesco in the street. The song appears midway through the first act. Jeremy Webb talks about the format of the show's construction: "In the play and the staging we created for the original production, the verses of the song were interspersed with scenes where you saw Flaminio teaching Francesco how to play the archetype commedia character Arlecchino. But the story Francesco relays to the audience is about his own ambition."

CONTENT: The song tells the story about Absalom and his son and is a lyric narrative. In the Bible, Absalom was the third son of King David. The book of Samuel in the Old Testament describes him as "the most handsome man in the kingdom." Absalom was a favorite of his father as well as the people, but eventually rebelled against his father. "The song is an intimate confession, even as it is shared with the audience," says Jeremy Webb.

The song begins with an eight-measure introduction in cut time, then alternates between 4/4 and 3/2 meter, as dictated by the setting of the text. The accompaniment is not especially challenging to play. Much of the accompaniment texture is homophonic, with occasional countermelodies, rhythmically syncopated. At times during the song the accompaniment doubles the vocal line. The attractive melody and text are in verse form as Francesco tells the story. There is rhythmic variety in each verse of the vocal line, again dictated by the text. There are many sustained tones at the end of phrases, which are cleverly contrasted with simultaneously moving imitative phrases and rhythmic activity in the accompaniment. After the second verse, the tonality modulates briefly from E-flat major through a transitional verse, progressing through a number of key areas before returning to E-flat major for the last verse: "We would stroll in the fields at night," which is an example of the poignant and meaningful melody/text in the song.

VOICE: The song is not demanding vocally for the tenor. Its melody is composed lyrically in relating his story. The singer's vocal technique contributes to characterization. For example, Francesco can convey confidence by not vocally straining in the intervallic fourth up to E-flat (top space of the staff), or the ascending scale line ("and I recall"), also carried up to E-flat. These are not high pitches for tenors to sing, but because of the need to enunciate the important text, "chewing" the words can result in vocal tension. Clear enunciation of the text is best projected and energized by a commitment to defined consonants in telling the story. Although the tempo marking is 'moderato, casual (in two)," the gently syncopated rhythms in every phrase signify the energy of the young Francesco and delineate his character from the older, more mature Flaminio, the leader of the troupe. There also is an ease to Francesco's delivery of the song that displays his confidence that all things come easily to him.

BEHIND THE SCENES WITH THE ARTISTS: JEREMY WEBB, THE ORIGINAL FRANCESCO

Mr. Webb has a number of resources to draw upon when creating this character: "Francesco Andreini was a real person, an actor who started out in Flaminio Scala's commedia dell'arte troupe but ended up having his own very successful acting company with his wife, the actress Isabella Andreini, who is also a character in the play." The play is based on these characters as imagined by the novelist Francine Prose, whose book of the same name the musical is based upon. "The book is incredible, and a great resource for this song, because the lyrics of Absalom are all in the character Francesco as imagined by Prose." In approaching the performance of the song, Jeremy felt that the song, although lyric in sections, was text-driven: "For me the song 'Absalom' starts and finishes with the text, and that was my approach when I worked on the original production of the show." He realized how much meaning was packed into each word and phrase by lyricist Lynn Ahrens. "It's more than just the telling of a story. Preparing to sing Absalom is about wrapping your head around that axiom that we all must one day supersede and abandon and leave our artistic mentors, the sources of light and knowledge in our lives. In order to be whole and fully formed artists, we need to shed our past and move on from our teachers. That is a heavy sentiment. And that is where I begin when I think about singing Absalom."

Beautiful City

Godspell

"The newest version, with the new lyrics and vocal arrangement . . . ,
is the version that I prefer."
—Stephen Schwartz, composer

CHARACTER: Jesus of Nazareth

MUSIC AND LYRICS: Stephen Schwartz

BOOK: George Furth

SETTING: Roman Judea

BROADWAY PREMIERE: 2011 (revival) 1971 (off-Broadway)

CLASSIFICATION: Tenor anthem

RANGE: 

TESSITURA: Upper staff

TIME: 3:55

PLOT: *Godspell* is the story of Jesus and his disciples, inspired in form by Jesus's parables in the Gospels. The introductions of the stories are in a decidedly contemporary context, with topical cultural references according to that which is timely at the time of the production one is seeing. The scenes after the opening song, "Prepare the Way of the Lord," include Jesus gathering his disciples and presenting the parables of the widow and the judge, the Pharisees and the money changers in the temple, the good Samaritan, Lazarus and the rich man, and so forth. The presentations are mostly light-hearted, quick moving, and clever.

CHARACTER: Stephen Schwartz writes: "The main thing to remember is that the story of the show is that Jesus comes into a group of disparate and desperate individuals and leads them into becoming a community. The word 'leads' is important—he is the driving force in the show; therefore he needs to have the most energy, the most humor, and the most willpower of all the characters. He starts the games, he teaches the lessons, he motivates the action. When the show goes wrong it is usually because Jesus is played too reverently, standing off to the sidelines watching beatifically as the rest of the cast clowns around. The exact opposite is what is needed." Quote from composer Stephen Schwartz on his website, stephenschwartz.com.

CONTEXT: In Act II, after a few lighter sequences (separating the sheep from the goats), the tone turns more serious. In the earlier productions, the cast members, after being recruited as disciples by Jesus earlier in the play, applied clown makeup; at this point of the play, toward the end of Act II, the makeup is removed before a recreation of the Last Supper takes place, followed by the betrayal of Jesus and the Crucifixion. A new song was added to the film version to be sung by Jesus in act II after "By My Side," referring to the return of Jesus, "Beautiful City." As written for the 1972 film, it is celebratory in tone. Later, the song was rewritten after the Los Angeles riots in 1992. It is an inspirational, lyric, anthem-like prayer song which reflects an optimism regarding the hopes and dreams that Jesus has for the people he has left to carry on his mission. Subsequently, the song had an important place in the 2011 Broadway revival, sung as a slow ballad by Jesus to his followers before the Last Supper. As a prelude to the Last Supper, the song can be especially meaningful.

CONTENT: The introduction is simply four measures of four quarter-note block chords. Jesus begins by painting a picture of hope emerging from "ruins and rubble." Only after smoke and struggle can we finally see "a ray of hope," he sings, as he sustains higher pitches (E and F-sharp at the top of the staff). This verse merges into the chorus of "We can build a beautiful city…not a city of angels, but of men." The melody of the chorus has an interesting sound quality that is unusual and different. This is possibly because the chorus melody is "detached" from the normal beginning or quick-phrase return to the tonic base tones in the key. In fact, the melody only goes home to the tonic at the end of the chorus. Another compelling device is the chord progression, which alternates between major and minor chords.

The second verse suggests that we may not find the end of the chaos, but can start to resolve it. The mending might be "brick-by-brick," and "heart-by-heart." We have to take an attitude that we need to "learn how," as the song moves into another chorus. The melody is compelling, and should be simply sung in the higher register without effort or strain for best results.

The B section is more intimate and direct in tone, saying that, when your faith and trust are in question, "you can give up, or slowly start to build," sustaining the word "build" as the song spills into the chorus of "a beautiful city" to complete the statement. The accompaniment in the B section is again the block-chord quarter notes, emphatic and insistent in their support. There is a tag at the end of the song that is peaceful, calming, and confident, as the quarter-note block chords play on in their simple progression to symbolize a continuation of the hopes for building the future of the "city of men."

VOICE: The song calls for a voice that is free, not strained at any point of the song. However, the singer needs to possess energy and emotion. Although much of the song lies at the intersection of the head and chest voice for the male range, the nature and style of the song does not allow the singer to croon or lyrically "float" the phrases. The emotional tone of the song needs the quality and color of warmth and empathizes for what he sees man has done to man. Still, the song is hopeful, and must have momentum, so as not to sound too heavy or be too self-important. Although the tempo is essentially slow and lyric, there is some subtle rhythmic variety in the vocal line that should be observed and sung correctly. The singer should be assertive in his delivery and articulation of rhythms to lead the song forward, because the quarter-note rhythm accompaniment notated in block chords continues in the treble throughout the song.

BEHIND THE SCENES WITH THE ARTISTS: STEPHEN SCHWARTZ, COMPOSER

Mr. Schwartz told me that the song as written for the movie is not his preferred version. He felt that the lyrics were "goopy"—in other words, they have a soft edge, and the 6/8 meter the song was originally composed in felt dated. He rewrote the lyrics and changed the meter. The version in his most recent Broadway revival of *Godspell,* with a minor adjustment of the chords, is the arrangement that Mr. Schwartz prefers above all others.

Goodbye

Catch Me If You Can

"In all musical theatre there is a performance element that requires of the character a reason to sing."

—Jack O'Brien, director of the first Broadway production

CHARACTER: Frank Abagnale

MUSIC: Marc Shaiman and Scott Wittman

BOOK AND LYRICS: Terrence McNally

BASED ON: A 2002 film of the same title and the 1980 autobiography of con artist Frank Abagnale Jr.

SETTING: The 1960s

BROADWAY PREMIERE: 2011

CLASSIFICATION: High lyric tenor

RANGE: 

TESSITURA: Easy top of staff

TIME: 3:34

PLOT: See "Fly, Fly Away."

CHARACTER: Frank's character, of course, is rather secretive, and he is reluctant to let down his guard while he is on the run. He has had a troubled youth and ran away from home at a young age. He survives by writing fake checks, eventually for millions of dollars. He is obviously talented and has the capacity to do great things, so there is also a tragic element in the story. There are times in the play when Frank reveals the loneliness of his chosen life, and he develops a strange bond with Hanratty, the detective who is chasing him. He will eventually become a sort of surrogate father to Frank.

CONTEXT: At the end of the show, the show returns to the opening sequence, when Frank is cornered in the Miami airport. A key song is "Goodbye," in which Frank addresses the audience to tell them, and the world, that he has had enough.

CONTENT: The introduction is four measures of bass-line eighth notes on A-flat, with unexpected accents marked on and off the beat. When the treble enters, syncopated chords are written with matching accents. Frank says he is writing his own "happy ending." It is time for "the spotlight man to turn off my light," he says. Frank continues to sing off-the-beat rhythms in the key of A-flat major, flatting the C for a minor-third inflection in the voice. He is cornered and there is no escape; does he really think that he can say goodbye and run off into the sunset? He is saying farewell to his scams, his lies, his made-up characters—and in a way his stage character as well. The "band has no more songs to play," he says, so he will now say "goodbye," as he sustains the farewell on E-flat. Frank doesn't even get a chance to take a breath until he finishes his "goodbyes." The interlude between verses remains in the key of A-flat, this time notated in the treble clef with the same accents as the verse before. In the second verse, Frank sings, "I hope you got your money's worth." "Gonna stop the show now," he remarks. He is hopeful that he can start anew, "cause I wanna leave on top," and he is confident that he can do so. At the end of this verse he sustains the "goodbye" on a high A-flat. Before the final build to the modulation, there is a short transition of eighteen measures. The song modulates to the key of B-flat major and adds more instruments to the orchestration and notes to the chords before the last, sustained high note, the stratospheric high B-flat as Frank sings one more, final "good-bye."

VOICE: The song requires an easy high range that when syncopated and energized does not cause the singer to strain. The tenor should not have to push the voice on any of these lines, and should start in a mezzo forte dynamic and then build. Everything, including singing this song, is easy for Frank. Some of the off-the-beat entrances are tricky, and the rhythms are determined more by text and word inflection than arbitrary rhythmic choices. The text needs to come through the rock textures, and the singer needs to be in command, pushing the song forward to its conclusion with confidence, brashness, talent, sarcasm, youth, and energy. The only notes that are sustained are set on the word "goodbye" at the top of the staff (except for one other place, landing on the word "me"). While *i* is a very bright vowel, "bye," which he also sustains, is a more open vowel to sing without straining. The singer should energize the sustained notes with a crescendo for forward momentum and excitement. And if the singer cannot crescendo on the sustained tones, it means that there is too much tension in the jaw and/or throat, and the jaw needs to be released.

BEHIND THE SCENES WITH THE ARTISTS: JACK O'BRIEN, THE ORIGINAL DIRECTOR

Jack notes that most of the songs for the show, by Marc Shaiman and Scott Wittman, were written before the show was constructed. The songs were originally conceived to be in more of a 1960s showcase of numbers in the style of the time. However, when we get to the end of the show and Frank is at the end of his rope, so to speak, Jack told the composer and lyricist that there needed to be a song that would capture Frank's frustration. He had to have an opportunity to break down the fourth wall and tell the audience that he had had enough and was through—"done with it all," and it was time to sing "Goodbye." In all musical theatre there is a performance element that requires the character to have a reason to sing, which Frank certainly possessed at that point of the show. Jack confided to me that he became emotional when he heard the song the first time; he felt that as Shaiman performed the song, at the climactic point in which the music modulated into the final chorus, the frantic energy of the piece captured perfectly Frank's emotions at that time in the show and his need to sing "Goodbye."

Lyricist Scott Wittman told me that he came up with the concept of this particular song while recalling a story about the great actor Daniel Day-Lewis and his 1987 performance of *Hamlet* onstage in London. Scott recalls that he heard that Day-Lewis had said, "Goodbye," and proceeded to walk offstage in midperformance never to return to acting in live theatre. That became the germ of this song, as Frank says "enough" and disappears, after singing "Goodbye."

Santa Fe (Prologue)

Newsies

"He holds on to the *hope,* which is playing tug-of-war with the thought-probably can't."
—Jeremy Jordan, the original Jack Kelly

CHARACTER: Jack Kelly

MUSIC: Alan Menken

LYRICS: Jack Feldman

BOOK: Harvey Fierstein

BASED ON: The 1992 film of the same name

SETTING: New York City, 1899

BROADWAY PREMIERE: 2012

CLASSIFICATION: Lyric tenor (with attitude)

RANGE: 

TESSITURA: Upper-middle staff

TIME: 2:02

PLOT: The original film (and stage play) is based on the historical 1899 newspaper strike in New York City. The film and play explore the effects (true and fictional) of the strike on the boys and their relationships.

CHARACTER: Jack Kelly is seventeen years old and is the leader of a group of "newsies," tough kids in New York who deliver newspapers at the turn of the twentieth century.

CONTEXT: We first hear the song at the beginning of the show, when Jack confides in his disabled friend Crutchie, singing "Santa Fe," telling his friend of his dreams to escape New York some day for the exotic place he can picture, though he's never been there.

The extended solo song is placed at the end of act I, when Jack is at a very low point. After a strike is called and there is a violent conflict between the strikers and the police and the strike breakers, an angry and desperate Jack vows that he will soon leave New York City forever. This iteration of the song, because of the circumstances, is sung faster and more desperately than the first time we hear the melody at the opening of the show (prologue), which is the version described in this entry. Jack's friend Crutchie joins in, but the prologue can be sung as a stand-alone solo.

CONTENT: There are two memorable motives in the song. One is the chordal-rhythmic harmonic progression at the opening; the other motive is the vocal interval of the seventh at the beginning of the chorus, ascending to the fourth before the third of the tonic in the key of C. At the beginning of the song, Jack sings after a two-measure (and three-beat) introduction. The opening is marked "pastoral, freely," and is sung in four, rather slowly and dreamlike. Although the first section is slow, the short phrases and direct language reflect Jack's youth and attitude. He's never been there, but he can see Santa Fe when he closes his eyes, which is a marvelous setup for the refrain, beginning in measure twenty of the song, as Jack sings, "Close your eyes. Come with me," to Crutchie. Jack is telling his friend that when he gets there, folks will be so friendly that they will say, "Welcome home, son. Welcome home to Santa Fe." Jack continues to tell Crutchie what he "sees" in his fictional vision, as the chorus (and the signature motive) is sung the second time: "Plantin' crops. Splittin' rails," but on Sunday (which normally is the newspaper boys' heaviest workday), you will "lay around all day" when you live in Santa Fe. Another chorus is now sung, marked more broadly. This chorus is sung more convincingly in a declamatory manner as they sing together: "Santa Fe! You can bet we won't let them bastids beat us." They are going to "work the land. Chase the sun!" They will even swim the Rio Grande. The song closes much the same way as it begins, with Jack going back to tempo I and the same reflective feel as the opening. Jack considers Crutchie part of his family, and he won't let him down. He tells him, "Just hold on, kid. 'til that train makes Santa Fe." The accompaniment doubles the voice throughout the song in the notated sheet music, but this doubling can be easily omitted by the accompanist, since the textural relationship of the piano/instruments to the vocal line is mostly homophonic (chords and melody).

VOICE: The verses are marvelously composed, with accidentals creating the G minor chord in the opening phrase. The vocal line is lightly syncopated, which should be observed by the singer, underlining Jack's youth and energy, and also some rough edges in his personality. When Jack sings below the staff in the opening (and the conclusion), it is important not to press vocally. The text is important here, and the strong attention to consonants again gives his character some edge and attitude. When Jack ascends above the staff, he should also not force his voice. Much of the higher singing at the top of the staff is lyric and should be free of tension. These are his hopes and dreams, and the throat should not be constricted. Make sure the lines are supported by the breath and the jaw is free, and think of finding the center of the vowel without diphthongs to compromise the sustained tones.

BEHIND THE SCENES WITH THE ARTISTS: JEREMY JORDAN, THE ORIGINAL JACK

Mr. Jordan was a fan of the Disney film as he grew up, and by the time he played Jack Kelly in the Broadway show, he felt he already knew the character as played by Christian Bale in the movie. The differences were that in the film the song was pitched lower and the song "Santa Fe" had a different placement in the play; in the film the song is sung just once. Jeremy described Jack's character to me, and the setup of the song "Santa Fe" in the prologue at the beginning of the show. "Jack has learned to live with what he has," Jeremy explained. "They are just trying to get through each night, and it is a tough existence." After the opening number with all the boys, which is joyous and upbeat, we see what life is really like for these poor kids. In the prologue, Jack is also trying to cheer up Crutchie, who is like a little brother to Jack. Crutchie is downtrodden, and Jack is trying to reassure him. Jack is not old enough to know hopelessness yet. He still possesses a measure of optimism, and he encourages his friend Crutchie not to give up, to keep trying. Even though Jack has never been to Santa Fe and has only seen brochures, he imagines it as a place that he can escape to someday soon, although, as Jeremy says, "Deep down Jack knows that he will never get out of the city. He holds on to the *hope*, which is playing tug-of-war with the thought '[I] probably can't.'" As we go through act I, Jack "starts to become the guy who could ditch all of his friends and get out of town by himself, for himself." When he sings the reprise of "Santa Fe" to close act I, he realizes that if he is going to make it on his own, he will need to give up his role as a leader. The reprised, longer "Santa Fe" at the end of act I becomes a song of self-loathing and hate.

PART FOUR

Baritone

If I Loved You

Carousel

"'If I Loved You' is part of that unique American-musical tradition where a person reveals what he feels but in a playful and guarded way."

—Nathan Gunn, baritone

CHARACTER: Billy Bigelow

MUSIC: Richard Rodgers

LYRICS AND BOOK: Oscar Hammerstein II

BASED ON: The play *Liliom* by Ferenc Molnár (1909)

SETTING: A coastal town in Maine, Nettie Fowler's spa, 1873–1888

BROADWAY PREMIERE: 1945

CLASSIFICATION: Anthem for baritone

RANGE: 

TESSITURA: Middle to upper staff

TIME: 1:46

PLOT: The story, transplanted from the novel's setting of Budapest, now takes place on the coast of Maine. Billy Bigelow, a traveling carnival barker who has known many women, has a romance with kind-hearted Julie Jordan. He attempts a robbery hoping to provide for their unborn child, but the robbery goes wrong.

CHARACTER: Billy Bigelow is all man. He comes from the wrong side of the tracks. Nothing is ever given to him, so he takes it. When he muses about his unborn child in "Soliloquy" we see a good man with a full heart. But Billy is flawed and makes bad choices, which turns this story into a tragedy. As the show opens, we are introduced to Billy, who is working at a carnival. We see him onstage flirting with a young lady who he knows is out on a date with another man. Billy is the barker for the carousel, inviting all to climb aboard and take the ride. The opening stage directions clearly direct Billy to speak in a rhythmic cadence that is almost hypnotic in its effect. While all onstage "sway unconsciously," Julie Jordan stands apart from the crowd, seemingly unaffected by the "magic" of Billy's spiel. Although there is a moment of attraction when Billy and Julie's gazes meet and Billy loses his train of thought, it is clear that he has the confidence of a man who knows that he can have any girl he wants.

CONTEXT: "If I Loved You" is part of an extended scene of song and dialogue over orchestral music, a scene that unfolds over time. The song takes place in act I, scene 2. At the opening of the scene, we see a tree-lined path along the shore, near sundown. The description in the script reads: "Through the trees the lights of the amusement park can be seen. The music of the merry-go-round is heard faintly in the distance." There is a park bench just right of center. Julie is seen onstage with her friend Carrie. Billy has just been fired from his job at the carousel for spending too much time with Julie, who he has just met. Billy shows a dangerous temper in his initial reaction to losing his job. After Julie and Billy are left onstage alone, we quickly learn that Julie is quiet and serious, while Billy is talkative and can be bullying. He doesn't seem to care that Julie could lose her job for talking with him, a man who is not "respectable." Julie sings "If I Loved You" in the extended scene first. She makes it clear that "if I love someone," it doesn't matter who they are. However, she also declares that she "will never marry," which appears to pique Billy's interest. Although she definitely does *not* love him, she says, she instinctively knows what it would be like *if* she loved him. Billy remarks that he has it all figured out. "We are all specks in the sky, and don't count at all." However, Julie has a different analogy to nature: "a feathery cloud floatin' by." She is not like the other girls. She throws him off guard and doesn't seem to care if he wants to marry her. He does wonder what it would be like if he loved her, and after she sings the song, he sings it in his own way.

CONTENT: The notation of the song both times Billy and Julie sing it is nearly identical in melody and accompaniment, but not in all dynamic markings. Julie's line "Soon you'd leave me" is marked "piano," while his is not. His last note of the final line, "If I loved you," has a marked crescendo into the dialogue, while hers does not. The expressive nature of the song is especially underlined by the triplet-rhythm figures, which need to be drawn out for their full value both times it is sung.

VOICE: Billy needs to sing the song with an easy lyricism, without pushing. The first line, when he sings the opening "If I loved you," as the line ascends to D-flat on the *u* vowel, can constrict the voice at the top, so the vowel cannot be small and pinched. The jaw needs to be free, the breath supported fully, and the lips rounded to the requisite *u* vowel. Each longer note value at the end of the lines has a connection to the phrase that follows, so that momentum is established and continues to sustain energy in the song. His sustained notes should decrescendo and crescendo. Tension in vocalism is especially evident when the singer cannot crescendo/decrescendo on the flow of the breath. It should be observed that the line that begins with the text "Soon you'd leave me" has a sweet sadness to it, but it continues to the conclusion of "*If* I loved you" which has a marked crescendo that can indicate hopefulness.

Billy has a temper, and he can be a bully and a bore, but he is also alive and is showing Julie that he can be passionately strong in his singing of this classic melody.

BEHIND THE SCENES WITH THE ARTISTS: NATHAN GUNN, BARITONE

"'If I Loved You' is part of that unique American-musical tradition where a person reveals what he feels but in a playful and guarded way. He says what he means to say but in the subjunctive. This began with 'Make Believe' from *Show Boat*. I absolutely love this idea. It adds youth and complexity to the character of Billy that you otherwise would not see."

There but for You Go I

Brigadoon

"Tommy in a nutshell: If it weren't for you, Fiona, I would be a man with bowed head and lost heart who has never known love."
—Martin Vidnovic, Tommy in the 1992 Broadway revival of *Brigadoon*

CHARACTER: Tommy Albright

MUSIC: Frederick Loewe

BOOK AND LYRICS: Alan J. Lerner

SETTING: A mythical Scottish village

BROADWAY PREMIERE: 1947

CLASSIFICATION: Lyric baritone

RANGE: 

TESSITURA: Middle of the staff

TIME: 2:35

PLOT: See "Waitin' for My Dearie."

CHARACTER: Tommy Albright is a thirty-year-old well-to-do New Yorker. The script tells us that he is of medium height and virile looking, with an attractive, sensitive face. While his friend Jeff is more introverted, Tommy appears to be outgoing and is a take-charge kind of guy. Tommy's life seems perfect, including a good job and an engagement to a devoted young lady, Jean Ashton. However, he keeps postponing the wedding. It is telling that when Tommy leaves Brigadoon and goes back to modern life, after leaving his New York job he avoids seeing Jean for four months, even though she remains devoted to him.

CONTEXT: The song occurs in act II, scene 1, on the outskirts of Brigadoon, the mythical village. The sun has fallen, and a mist appears near the ground. Fiona's younger sister, Jean, has married Charlie, which leaves another villager (Harry) despondent because he loves her, too. After the wedding, Harry has made it clear to the entire town that he is leaving the village, which (according to folklore) will cause Brigadoon to disappear forever. To keep him from carrying out his threat, the men chase Harry through the clearing, and as they run offstage Harry falls and hits his head on a rock, which kills him, unbeknownst to the rest of the town. The men agree not to inform the town of Harry's death until the next morning. Against this tragic backdrop Fiona comes onto the stage, thinking that Tommy has gone back to New York. When she sees that he has not left yet, Fiona is relieved and confesses her love for him. Taken aback, Tommy is unable to respond, except to say that he has feelings for her he finds difficult to describe.

CONTENT: "There but for You Go I" is a different song from their earlier "Heather on the Hill" duet, which is a more flirtatiously harmless rhythmically lilting song. The act II song that Tommy sings to Fiona is more lyric, serious, and earnestly sung. It is his way of telling her how much she means to him. The accompaniment throughout is understated, but doubles the vocal line. The song begins haltingly, hesitantly (marked "piano"), as Tommy struggles to find the right words to express his feelings in the seven measure setup of the song, and builds from there to a fervent climactic admission and vow of love for Fiona. Tommy sings the hauntingly beautiful verses, each only nine measures in length. Each verse begins with the same phrase, which glues the song together: "I saw a man." During the bridge, Tommy finally refers to himself as he talks about the "lonely men around me." He would be one of those men if not for her. Tommy realizes that he must articulate his feelings for Fiona at that very moment, with urgency. How much longer do they have? He sings the third verse before an interlude, where there is dialogue between them that is underscored by the orchestra. Their exchange is hurried as they realize that this may be "our last minute together." At the end of their day, Fiona will vanish with the village. Tommy is afraid to be without her, he says. He then sings the last verse, which lead to his line "I thought as I thanked all the stars in the sky / There but for you go I," sung strongly, in tempo, with conviction and commitment.

VOICE: This song is a beautiful, lyric, genuine expression of love. Tommy confesses his feelings through a story of other men who are alone, walking by the sea and, finally, a man who has "never known a love that was all his own." The broadly sung melody is delivered without forcing the voice. The vocal line is rather narrow in range (C to C in C major) until the climactic final phrases, beginning "I thought as I thanked all the stars in the sky," which extends up to high D and E natural (on the word "there") for the climactic final phrase, which only sustains the high E for a quarter-note rhythmic value. However, within the cadence, the vowel is *u*, which can be tightly produced if the singer sings the word ("you") with a closed jaw; the baritone will need to have a free jaw, then round the lips to form the vowel. Even during the ascending last phrase, the singer should be guided in the line by his emotions and the realization of the power of his feelings for her, rather than dramatic, forceful vocal expression. The song is intimately sung, but with emotional power, as the gravity of the situation and the freedom that comes from finally releasing strong feelings must be on the singer's mind.

BEHIND THE SCENES WITH THE ARTISTS: MARTIN VIDNOVIC, WHO SANG THE ROLE OF TOMMY IN THE 1992 BROADWAY REVIVAL

Mr. Vidnovic tells how the director (through a what-if) built up a resistance in Fiona to Tommy's "desires for love and commitment, for fear that it wouldn't work... [given] that Tommy was an outsider who would leave or be left behind when the town (again) vanished... So, instead of simply a lovely ballad about how empty his life is without her, the director created an urgent and forceful 'stopping her' with his words as she tried to escape the hopelessness she felt in the moment. At the end of each of the three verses in which I stopped her to make her hear me—'There but for You Go I'—she would move away, only to have me grab her attention again with the next verse." At the conclusion of the song, finally, he won her over, "for the moment." In this manner each verse began with an impulse, an energy, that kept the song vital and alive.

Luck Be a Lady

Guys and Dolls

"He is really gambling and hopeful but not cocky during this song."
—Peter Gallagher, Sky Masterson in the 1992
Broadway revival of *Guys and Dolls*

CHARACTER: Sky Masterson

MUSIC AND LYRICS: Frank Loesser

BOOK: Jo Swerling and Abe Burrows

BASED ON: "The Idyll of Miss Sarah Brown" and "Blood Pressure," two short stories by Damon Runyon

SETTING: New York City

BROADWAY PREMIERE: 1950

CLASSIFICATION: Up-tempo baritone

RANGE: 

TESSITURA: Upper-middle staff

TIME: 3:14

PLOT: See "If I Were a Bell."

CHARACTER: Sky is worldly and has quite the reputation as a high-rolling gambler. He is nicknamed Sky because when he is involved in a bet, the sky is the limit. He will bet on anything, but only when he has the edge and is in control. Sky is smooth and slick, a ladies' man. As the show begins, Sky has just returned from Las Vegas, where he has won fifty thousand dollars. He's on his way down to Havana, Cuba, "where the action is." Before he meets Sarah Brown of the Save-a-Soul Mission, Sky tells Nathan, "As pleasant as a doll's company may be, she must always take second place to aces back to back." He also says he believes that "all dolls are the same." When Sky meets Sarah Brown of the Save-a-Soul Mission, he is immediately attracted to her (and the challenge she presents), and he finds that his knowledge of the Bible is helpful. Sky knows the Bible so well, he says, because he's spent so many nights in hotel rooms with only a Gideons Bible for company. Observing that sinners are not exactly lining up to be saved by the Save-a-Soul Mission in New York, Sky makes a bet with her: if he can fill one of her meetings with "one dozen genuine sinners who will sit still at the meeting," she will have dinner with him, alone. Sarah doesn't want to bet, but circumstances force her to change her mind. This arrangement does not exactly endear Sky to Sarah, and he is going to have to work to win her.

CONTEXT: In act II, the scene is an important crap game in the sewer below the street. Sky knows that Sarah is under pressure to bring souls to the mission or it may be shut down. To provide the sinners for the meeting, Sky bets his cronies a thousand dollars each against them all showing up at the mission meeting if they lose. It all hinges on a roll of the dice, which occurs at the end of the song "Luck Be a Lady." If he loses the bet, he not only loses the money, he most likely also loses Sarah. But if he wins, he gets to take her out for dinner at "his favorite restaurant" (in Havana, Cuba); In addition, Sarah will get the souls at the meeting and the mission will be saved. At the conclusion of the song, as the tension builds, the dice are rolled. Blackout.

CONTENT: After initially hesitating before rolling the dice before the song begins, Sky explains, "I've got a little more than dough riding on this one." The opening of the song is freely sung as Sky takes control, with caesuras marked after each line, before the refrain begins. Loesser gives the singer an interval of an ascending minor third, then major third, in the vocal line, flavoring the melody with a little jazz-like spice. In the chorus that follows, the tempo is in cut time, and the final notes of each phrase are sustained by the singer. The tempo continues to tick at a fast pace with momentum, as the key modulates up one half step. There is another key change for the bridge, beginning with "A lady doesn't leave her escort," before the key reverts back to the original key of D-flat major. In the original stage version, at this point the chorus of gamblers joins in with a call-and-response, as Sky has gotten the gamblers all stirred up. He changes keys again, modulating up one half step. Another modulation, another bridge ("A lady wouldn't flirt with strangers"), and then Sky finally ends up back in the key of D-flat with the background singers impatiently singing: "What's the matter? Roll the dice" before the all important roll of the dice.

VOICE: Although the phrases in the song are short, Sky can sing with a confident lyricism with edge. The edge is provided by the consonants chosen by Loesser. For instance, the important word "luck" has a strong final consonant, as do the words: "doubt," "out," "lush," "brush," "tonight," "escort," "nice," "dice," "polite," and "sight," and as these words repeat with ascending modulations, the final consonants create more of a "bite" that forms an interesting contrast to the smooth, confident vocal lyricism. Many of the final words of the sung phrases are sustained in the notated music, but Sky will at times cut them short for the sake of a strong consonant, with the exceptions of words ending with vowels and the final D-flat, as Sky crescendos to sustain the pitch.

BEHIND THE SCENES WITH THE ARTISTS: PETER GALLAGHER, SKY MASTERSON IN THE 1992 BROADWAY REVIVAL

Sky Masterson is a smooth operator, but Peter Gallagher does not feel this song should be sung "in a cocky way," and it is a mistake for the actor not to find the real reason why he is singing this song. "Sky is confident, smart, knows the odds, and is a student of human nature." Peter offers more insight into Sky's character: "He is a gambler, and he cares more about the outcome at this point. For the first time in his life, he is admitting that he is powerless in the outcome."

If Ever I Would Leave You

Camelot

"This song is sung 'without armor.'"
—Nathan Gunn, Lancelot in the Live from Lincoln Center revival of *Camelot*

CHARACTER: Sir Lancelot

MUSIC: Frederick Loewe

LYRICS: Alan J. Lerner

BASED ON: The King Arthur legend as adapted in the T. H. White novel *The Once and Future King*

SETTING: The medieval castle of Camelot

BROADWAY PREMIERE: 1960

CLASSIFICATION: Romantic lyric ballad for baritone

RANGE: 

TESSITURA: Middle of baritone range

TIME: 3:32

PLOT: The plot of the beautifully scored musical by Lerner and Loewe centers on the classic legend of King Arthur, his wife Guinevere, and the Knights of the Round Table. At the beginning of the play the young King Arthur is seen with his mentor, the wizard Merlyn. He meets the lovely Guinevere; their marriage has already been arranged. Arthur is a kind and caring ruler, unspoiled and unassuming, even at a young age. His nickname as a child was "Wart." Arthur grows to love Guinevere, his trusted French knight Lancelot (after a difficult first meeting), and the people of his kingdom—which leads to heartbreak when realizing he is betrayed by the two people he is closest to and trusts most.

CHARACTER: Lancelot is initially described as a "striking figure of a young man, with a stern jaw and burning eyes. His face is unlined because he has never smiled." Lancelot is a French knight who lives according to a clear code of behavior. He approaches Camelot on the first of May and fervently and devoutly sings about "hearing the call of Camelot." He is a serious young man who does not lack in confidence. After all, he sings "C'est Moi" when first introduced to the audience. When Lancelot first meets Guinevere she is struck by his passionate, high-minded idealism in describing his vision for the kingdom.

CONTEXT: "If Ever I Would Leave You" is sung at the beginning of act II, in the afternoon on the main terrace of the castle, a few years after the arrival of Lancelot. In the rear of the stage, beyond the flower-covered walls, is a backdrop showing the rolling, green English countryside. In the distance can be seen the tree in which Arthur hid in as a boy. Lancelot tellingly waits for people to pass before beginning to sing after the musical introduction. He sings a translated French poem ("Madrigal"), the final line of which is: "The reason to live is only to love a goddess on earth and a God above." The dialogue continues over the introduction to "If Ever I Would Leave You," as Guinevere wonders aloud why his poems are always about him. "Why don't you write about me?" she asks. He answers that he loves her too much. "I should leave you and never come back," he says, before he begins to sing the familiar melody.

CONTENT: In the introduction, under the dialogue, the keys modulate to the home key of the song, B-flat major, coming to a caesura before the melody begins. The strings double the vocal line. The famous song is a classic "misdirect" love song. He doesn't say "I love you so I can't ever leave you"; he says, "*If ever I would leave you . . .*" Continuing from the title line he continues: "If I *would*," not *when*. The melody unfolds from the very low-pitched, almost spoken phrase at its opening words, rising in pitch and fullness and culminating with a passionate high declaration at the D in longer note values. The form of the song is: main melody, with the simple phrase "If ever I would leave you" followed by different texts in each verse (in the first verse: "it wouldn't be in summer"; in the second verse: "it couldn't be in autumn"), after which there is a bridge, which picks up in tempo a little for dramatic fervor. The melody line slows a little at the cadence with "Or [leave] on a wintry evening when you catch the fire's glow," which is followed by a caesura. The sudden silence can be very dramatic. With the final verse it is clear that he absolutely cannot leave in springtime, and for that matter, not in "Summer, winter or fall," in the climactic phrase before a final caesura at the cutoff before the last, poignant phrase. Finally Lancelot sings, "No, *never* could I leave you at all" over the final cadence. Sung alone (unstaged), the singer will usually sing one final chorus (song duration is 2:24). In the full staged version (3:32), there is an interlude after the final chorus without slowing the cadence. After the interlude, there is a final repeat of the chorus, with full cadence and observed markings.

VOICE: Each verse begins in the low register of the baritone voice. It is important that the singer does not "growl" the low tones or try to vocalize the notes too lyrically. The song needs to be sung "on the breath," but still have intensity and focus, so that there is no breathiness, or crooning, which cannot substitute for true legato lyricism. The text is beautiful and important, with proper inflections needed for dramatic meaning. The singer needs to clearly mark the phrasing (where the breath commas/punctuation are observed) to successfully sing the climactic phrases without running out of breath. The important initial consonants, especially for "Fall, Summer, Springtime, and Winter" should be fully supported. Passion and urgency is very important. The couple is in the open air, and before anyone else can come onto the scene and hear his treasonous declaration of love, Lancelot must express his long-pent-up feelings, so the song should not be sung too slowly, not too self-importantly. Finally, the song is about *her*, not *him*. Each vocal phrase, as it builds, should move with momentum toward the sustained D near the top of the staff. The vowels of the lyrics that are sustained happen to be the sustained *o* ("go," "know," "so")—and finally "you" sustained in the final phrase (*u*). Coming to the final phrase of the song, he stops at the caesura, and then after a moment of silence sings: "No, never would I leave *you* (//) at all." He begins the climactic phrase at the top of the song's range a cappella. The phrase is exposed, and the singer must enter with tenderness, singing softly (marked "piano"), as the orchestra crescendos with strong triplet-rhythm chords to the final whole-note chord, and Lancelot must also crescendo with the accompaniment.

BEHIND THE SCENES WITH THE ARTISTS: NATHAN GUNN, LANCELOT IN THE LIVE FROM LINCOLN CENTER REVIVAL OF *CAMELOT*

Nathan knew the well-known song before singing it in the show. What struck him most about it was how different it was musically from "C'est Moi," Lancelot's first song, when he is introduced in the play. "'If Ever I Would Leave You' is a song without armor," Nathan explained. "Lancelot is baring his soul, and that why it is so emotional." The song seems more contemporary next to the more medieval-sounding "Madrigal", because "it's a modern love song in which Lancelot discovers how he truly feels about Jenny."

Once Upon a Time

All American

"I think first loves are among the most indelible memories one has all one's life."
—Charles Strouse, composer

CHARACTER: Professor Fodorski

MUSIC: Charles Strouse

BOOK: Mel Brooks

LYRICS: Lee Adams

BASED ON: The Robert Lewis Taylor novel *Professor Fodorski*

SETTING: A fictional campus in the south

BROADWAY PREMIERE: 1962

CLASSIFICATION: Ballad for baritone

RANGE: 

TESSITURA: Upper-middle baritone

TIME: 2:32

PLOT: Immigrant professor Fodorski teaches at the fictional Southern Baptist Institute of Technology. Fodorski teaches engineering, and the story is about how applying engineering principles to football results in a winning team for the school. Of course, the commercial world of Madison Avenue intrudes, hoping to cash in on the phenomenon. The show was intended to be an old-fashioned musical showcasing the talents of Ray Bolger, playing the role of Fodorski.

CHARACTER: Professor Fodorski is from Hungary, and the story is about how this man, thrown into the culture of the South, becomes an American.

It is also about him falling in love with Elizabeth, the dean of students at the college.

CONTEXT: As the show begins, Fodorski is seen teaching at the university. At first, the students do not treat him well, and his transition to teaching college in the United States is not a smooth one. However, he is attracted to the dean of students, Elizabeth Hawkes Bullock. As the story unfolds in the first act, Fodorski is encouraged by the students' newly favorable attitude to him, after he demonstrates that engineering principles can be applied to football, and the team put it into practice, winning games. Fodorski is elated, but Elizabeth, recognizing that he is a gifted teacher, feels that his scholarly knowledge is better applied to the classroom, rather than the novelty of helping the team win. In this scene, on Elizabeth's porch, it is evening. She tells him that he is responsible for bringing a new educational climate to the campus. "You can feel it in the air," she says. "You've helped me," he replies, and he impulsively takes her hand. "I don't know why I did that," he says. She remarks that no one has taken her hand for a long time. He thinks back, to his first love twenty-five years ago in a small village in Hungary, and the musical introduction to "Once Upon a Time" begins.

CONTENT: The song opens with a four-measure introduction, with an attractive motive that ties the song together with its repetition between verses. In the solo version, the singer, male or female. will sing two verses, a bridge, and a final verse to end. In the duet written for the stage version, the male sings the entirety of the song, and the female then sings the same song through with a different text.

VOICE: This beautiful song requires a legato smoothness that also underlines and brings out key words in the text through inflection and the natural shape of the pitches in the vocal line. The melody should be sung with a warmth and expressiveness that is strongly supported with the breath support throughout, especially since many of the key words are at the end of the phrases, which descend to D at the bottom of the staff, and are set on sustained pitches. The contrasting bridge section ("How the breeze ruffled through her hair") is marked "a little faster," which provides momentum. "Where did it go?" at the end of the bridge is marked "poco ritardando," and is a transition into the final chorus, which is the most bittersweet and poignant one. The baritone (or lyric mezzo) who sings this song will need an easy D at the top of the staff, which is sustained in the first line of each verse. The word "time" is easy to open at that pitch, but "hill" needs to be open as it is sustained, with no thought of closing to the consonant (*l*) until the final beat, at which time the tongue is placed behind the top teeth for consonant identification and is not swallowed. The performer will need a low B-flat below the staff as well, which needs to be sung freely with warmth and resonance.

BEHIND THE SCENES WITH THE ARTISTS: CHARLES STROUSE, COMPOSER

"Lee [Adams] and I had originally written a version of that song when we worked together earlier—never quite finished it—and when the dramatic opportunity arose ('an elderly couple trying to remember and reminisce') and cutting out a scene that Mel [Brooks] had written that we all felt didn't work, we summoned up this song, rewrote it, and it fortunately became a standard. Personally, it brings up real feelings I've had all my life about my *own* first love—which I still recall." He added, "I think first loves are among the most indelible memories one has all one's life."

Rain Song

110 in the Shade

"It made sense to write funky and jazzy music for 'Rain Song,' since Starbuck is such an impertinent character."
—Harvey Schmidt, composer

CHARACTER: Bill Starbuck

MUSIC: Harvey Schmidt

LYRICS: Tom Jones

BOOK: N. Richard Nash

BASED ON: Nash's play *The Rainmaker* (1954)

SETTING: The town Three Point in the southwestern United States, 1936

BROADWAY PREMIERE: 1963

CLASSIFICATION: Baritone

RANGE: 

TESSITURA: C–E-flat; not stable

TIME: 3:06

PLOT: See "Is It Really Me?"

CHARACTER: Bill Starbuck is a big man, but lithe and agile. He is a loud braggart, a gentle dreamer. He carries a short hickory stick. "It is his weapon as well as his tool—his pointer, magic wand, his pride of manhood," says actor Ron Raines.

CONTEXT: The song is placed toward the beginning of the show and introduces the character of Starbuck. Before "Rain Song," the women are singing, "Fix a basket of food for the hungry men," in a repeated mantra of what they do in in the small town, their "job." There is a weariness in the repetition, especially since it is so hot and dry.

CONTENT: The setup for the song comes from bystanders Jim and H. C., who ask Starbuck (after he claims that he can produce rain in the parched town): "How you gonna bring it? How will you make it?" and Starbuck begins to speak in a rhythmic cadence (with music underneath) words that begin to hypnotize the townspeople, all except the skeptical Lizzie, who heckles: "In other words, bunk!" Starbuck is not thrown and responds: "Lady, you're right." After she asks what scientific methods he uses to bring rain, the music moves into a new key in a blues tempo, and Starbuck sings in a soft, seductive tone to draw in his audience further: "You wanna hear my deal?" he says. Once his audience is hooked, he moves into a cut-time, allegro section, moving toward a new key area. He sings in a confident experienced-salesman-style as he describes his method while continuing his hypnotic rhythmic cadence. The accompaniment underneath contributes its own rhythmic energy. Finally, Starbuck moves in transition toward a gospel-like chorus ("It's gonna rain all through the night") and sustains the high E-flat with rhythmic accompaniment underneath in an ecstatic celebration of the magnificent ability of moisture to save the crops and their "souls." He sings, "There's a big rain comin'!" softly, rhythmically, in the low part of his range, inspiring the chorus to join in, singing the same rhythm, then Starbuck takes a preacher-style approach in the next section ("may be shouted") in which he alludes to the Old Testament and continues to extol the glories of water. By the time Starbuck repeats the chorus ("It's gonna rain all day tomorrow"), all of the townspeople believe it really could storm. Not only will it rain, but "rivers will overflow," and "dyin' cattle will rise right up and live," as the song moves toward a final chorus which has the church-like call-and-response leading to the final altar call, so to speak, as Starbuck rises up in song to produce a sustained and exposed high A-flat.

VOICE: The singer must sing this extended piece with a salesman-like detachment, and not get too involved vocally and exhaust his resources too early. The song builds, and the actor will find that he can capture the audience's attention as effectively by singing softly with intensity and powerful, committed consonants as by oversinging (or yelling) in the opening. It is also wise to sing the E-flats at the top space in the staff (and there are many of them) with freedom from constriction and low larynx position. Apply slight crescendos on sustained tones to keep them free from tension, and on the word "rain," keep away from the diphthong *e* migrating to *i* until the end of the value, so that the jaw does not close. As a salesman, Starbuck has the benefit of a certain professional detachment that comes from repeated performances of his spiel in countless towns. At the same time, he recognizes that Lizzie is the one person who remains skeptical, and he has to try harder to convince her that he can make good on his claims.

BEHIND THE SCENES WITH THE ARTISTS: SINGER RON RAINES AND COMPOSER HARVEY SCHMIDT

Ron Raines sang the part of Bill Starbuck in the recording of the show with symphony orchestra. Presiding in the recording booth were composer Harvey Schmidt and lyricist Tom Jones. Ron remembers that he felt "right in the role," since he hails from Texas, and the bravado and swagger that Starbuck possesses felt natural to him. Ron also said that he sang "Rain Song," with its many styles (blues, gospel) and dialogue above the chorus and sustained high notes (up to A-flat) in his "own voice," meaning he did not change his means of vocal production to "make different voices" to match the style indicated in the score. Ron feels that this can be the downfall of many singers and can shorten their singing career.

Composer Harvey Schmidt comments that since Starbuck is a "saucy, sassy character," it made sense to write "funky and jazzy" music for "Rain Song." Mr. Schmidt is also a Texan, and "loves to write the big chorus scenes," he says. As the song moves forward, the music "becomes more *serioso* in tone, as the song becomes triumphal in spirit celebrating the *possibility* of rain and what it would mean to the town."

It Only Takes a Moment

Hello, Dolly!

"He is susceptible to [love] because he is young and romantic, has gone to New York City for a good time, not a relationship."

—Jerry Herman, composer

CHARACTER: Cornelius Hackl

MUSIC AND LYRICS: Jerry Herman

BOOK: Michael Stewart

BASED ON: The 1938 farce *The Merchant of Yonkers* by Thornton Wilder, which Wilder revised and retitled *The Matchmaker* in 1955

SETTING: New York City, turn of the twentieth century

BROADWAY PREMIERE: 1964

CLASSIFICATION: Baritone lyric

RANGE: 

TESSITURA: Middle of staff

TIME: 3:03

PLOT: The show begins in the small town of Yonkers, just north of New York City, in a hay and feed store. The store is owned by grumpy Horace Vandergelder, a prominent citizen and a "half-a-millionaire." Dolly Levi, a well-known matchmaker in New York City, plans to marry Horace herself. However, he plans to marry Irene Malloy, a young widow in New York, until Dolly intimates to Horace that she has heard that Irene's late husband might not have died of natural causes. Horace goes to New York, telling his employees Cornelius and Barnaby to mind the store while he is away. After Horace leaves, the young men decide that they want to go to the big city for an adventure on their own, so they close the feed store and head off to New York City.

CHARACTER: Cornelius Hackl is a young, naïve clerk in the Vandergelder hay and feed store in Yonkers, New York. He has never strayed from the small town of Yonkers. He is wide-eyed when he sees New York City for the first time. He is energetic, enthusiastic, and longs for an adventure.

CONTEXT: The two young men plan to go to the city only for a meal and a good time, but on Dolly's recommendation they go to visit Irene and her assistant, Minnie Fay, at Irene's hat shop. Cornelius and Barnaby visit the shop and, after hiding in the store when Horace visits Irene, they invite the young ladies to dinner. Both young men pretend to be rich. The charade continues throughout the day, but finally after dinner in act II, where there is a commotion caused by all characters running into each other at the restaurant, the group is hustled off to night court by the police. It is there that Cornelius and Barnaby confess that they are poor clerks from Yonkers and are hardly worldly: they have never even been to New York City before. Cornelius tells Irene that even if he has to dig ditches the rest of his life, it is worth it because he has met her. He further professes his love for her in the song "It Only Takes a Moment." The song is set up very cleverly in dialogue by bystanders, when Cornelius asked if he could really fall in love in just a day. "It was much faster than a day," Cornelius says, searching for the words to express himself, which then becomes the kernel of the song. He introduces the melody of the classic song, which is soon sung by the entire chorus in response.

CONTENT: After a very brief two-measure introduction (marked "slowly"), Cornelius begins to sing the simple melody, slowly in the middle-low range and not doubled in the accompaniment. The music is marked "piano" and is sung lyrically, sensitively. The song unfolds as Cornelius gains confidence, and the intervals and range of the pitches expand. After the melody is sung through one time, there are a few lines of monologue before the chorus takes up the melody and sings the chorus in four vocal harmony parts. Irene joins in as the chorus modulates into a higher key. Cornelius and Irene trade lines and, as they fall in love, finally sing in harmony together.

VOICE: The song should be delivered with a lyric, even tone, capturing the stunned awe of a young man in love. It should not be sung with emotive frills or embellishments, just the genuine honesty and amazement of a young man realizing that this is the first time he has been in love. The song does not have many rhythmic or range demands or other challenges; it just calls for in-tune, lyric singing, and is a classic "moment" song in musical theatre. If the final climactic line of the song feels tight in the throat, jaw, and facial muscles, then consider loosening the jaw and letting go of the words more, as if you were declaring and projecting these emotions to someone across the street. Do not be concerned about getting across the text at this point; you have already sung "It Only Takes a Moment" at the beginning of the song. Now you are framing it.

BEHIND THE SCENES WITH THE ARTISTS: COMPOSER JERRY HERMAN

"Cornelius is a young man who falls in love. He is susceptible to it because he is young and romantic, has gone to New York City for a good time, not a relationship."

Dulcinea

Man of La Mancha

"The essence of life is not found in the answers; the essence of life is found in the *questions*. Life's greatest answers are found in the journey, not in the destination. That is the secret of any great pilgrimage. And life itself—every individual's life—is the greatest pilgrimage."

—Brian Stokes Mitchell, Don Quixote in the 2002 Broadway revival

CHARACTER: Don Quixote

MUSIC: Mitch Leigh

LYRICS: Joe Darion

BOOK: Dale Wasserman

ADAPTED FROM: Wasserman's nonmusical teleplay *Don Quixote*

BASED ON: Miguel de Cervantes's seventeenth-century novel *Don Quixote*

SETTING: Spain, late sixteenth century

BROADWAY PREMIERE: 1965

CLASSIFICATION: Baritone lyric

RANGE: 

TESSITURA: Lower middle of staff

TIME: 3:50

PLOT: See "Aldonza."

CHARACTER: The original character of Quixote (in the novel by Cervantes) is both a tragic and comic figure. His major quest in life is to restore the code and ethics of knighthood to a world bereft of chivalry. He is proud and dignified, and sees only what he wishes, seeing the world very differently than most people. He addresses Aldonza as Dulcinea. The word "dulcinea" comes from the name of Don Quixote's mistress in the Cervantes's novel Dulcinea del Tobaso. The English word "Dulcinea" is derived from the Spanish word *dulce* (sweet), and means "a female sweetheart."

CONTEXT: The setting is an inn. The muleteers are present, watching the proceedings and heckling in response. The song is placed in act I, toward the beginning of the show. It is the first song in the play that is lyric and ballad-like, after the faster paced and dramatic songs "Man of La Mancha," and "It's All the Same." The song occurs after Aldonza sings her song, which is a raw response to his formal and poetic addressing of her as "milady." He continues to rhapsodize poetically after her song as he declaims: "Ah, sweet sovereign of my captive heart . . . I shall not fail thee, for I know ..." and proceeds to sing "Dulcinea."

CONTENT: The song begins moderately, with a lilt to it that is not too slow, in 6/8 meter. There is a guitar-like strum in the accompaniment, a rhythmic pattern of eighth and sixteenth notes. The first verse is formalized in its text delivery, while the second is more personal: "If I reach out to thee," Quixote sings. The song continues to flow in 6/8, sometimes changing to 3/4 meter, which changes some of the singer's sustained rhythmic values, and keeps interest in the line so that it is not so predictable in its delivery. The last two times he sings the name he has given her ("Dulcinea"), the markings are rallentando, and then a tempo the final time, as the muleteers are about to sing their jeering, up-tempo version repeat of the song's chorus to make fun of the specter of this "knight of woeful countenance." The men have just observed the knight sing such lofty and delicate poetry in tribute to this lowly prostitute they all know as Aldonza.

VOICE: The phrases in this song are very short until the top of the chorus, as Quixote sings: "And thy name is like a prayer an angel whispers," which takes strong breath support and dynamic control to sing. The beginning of the song is low in range, and then builds to the chorus, in which Ds are needed to be sustained at the top, produced with freedom and lyricism. When he sings the name Dulcinea, the ay (*e*) vowel of her name is at the top, and the singer will have to determine whether he will sing the vowel open, with chest resonance predominant, or closed, with more head resonance, which is easier to sing with a softer, lighter, more lyrical vocal production. If the Quixote is more a bass-baritone, then closed (toward the *i* vowel) is best, while the true baritone can sing it open easily, without tension, and at the proper dynamic.

BEHIND THE SCENES WITH THE ARTISTS: BRIAN STOKES MITCHELL, DON QUIXOTE IN THE 2002 BROADWAY REVIVAL

I asked Mr. Mitchell whether he thinks Don Quixote is actually delusional and crazy or merely acting the fool in order to bring out the best in others. With either choice, how does that affect the singing of the song "Dulcinea" to Aldonza? He responded, "Don Quixote is not singing the song to Aldonza. Instead he is singing "directly to her spirit, her soul, to her ESSENCE. If he shows her what he sees in her, perhaps she will see it, too.... We wonder if he is aware that she is who she says she is: What is important is who she REALLY is." He continues: "Don Quixote sees people's true/higher selves (and occasionally their lower, baser selves that the Muleteers represent), and his vision of people, their essence, allows others to see it in themselves. Not only Aldonza, but also his servant Sancho, the barber, the innkeeper and his wife, and anyone else who has been imprisoned by their own limited point of view, or by their limited view of others. This is the important thing, what he opens up in others." I then asked him about Quixote's motives and what he really wants. This, he pointed out, "is answered later in 'The Impossible Dream.'" Mr. Mitchell explained that "the essence of life is not found in the answers; the essence of life is found in the *questions*. Life's greatest answers are found in the journey, not in the destination. That is the secret of any great pilgrimage. And life itself—every individual's life—is the greatest pilgrimage"

Being Alive

Company

"We had watched [Bobby] watching all night—and now he was taking the risk of participating, taking the risk of 'being alive.'"
—John Doyle, director

CHARACTER: Robert (Bobby)

MUSIC: Tom Kitt

BOOK AND LYRICS: Stephen Sondheim

BOOK: George Furth

BASED ON: The 1934 play of the same name by George S. Kaufman and Moss Hart

SETTING: New York City, 1960s

BROADWAY PREMIERE: 1970

CLASSIFICATION: High baritone anthem

RANGE:

TESSITURA: Upper-middle staff (the 1996 revival version is pitched a minor third below the original low F to high Ab) low D to high F

TIME: 3:09

PLOT: The song "Being Alive" is sung by Bobby, a single man in New York City who is celebrating his thirty-fifth birthday in the late 1960s. Joining him are five married couples at a surprise party in Bobby's apartment, all in complicated relationships, and his three girlfriends. He tries to blow out his birthday candles, but they stay lit. "What was his wish?" they wonder. What follows are flashback scenes that feature Bobby and his married "friends," who are not particularly personally close to him.

CHARACTER: Bobby is single in New York City, with many past relationships. His married friends all have extremely complicated relationships, which discourages him from wanting to get married. He is in reality looking for that perfect woman, and not for a relationship. By the end of the show, he is still alone, still searching.

CONTEXT: "Being Alive," sung by Bobby, is the final solo song in the show. The song is preceded by his friends incessantly chanting his name, and saying, "We have something to tell you." Bobby asks them to stop, and then yells, "STOP!!" followed by silence, before the song begins.

CONTENT: Opening block chords introduce the song, which begins half sung, half spoken by Bobby. As the song unfolds and builds, the accompaniment is increasingly active rhythmically. The melody is in seven short verses, which are punctuated by Bobby's friends speaking in the darkness as if they are the voices in his head. The voices attempt to provoke him to action, and other times encourage, as they say that he does not have a reason for being alone, he's not a kid anymore, "C'mon, you're on to something!" they say. These remarks stimulate the verses and let Bobby know what it would be like for him to "be alive," not just watching from the sidelines. The song builds in its verses through upward modulation, from the key of E-flat major to the bright key of E-natural major. What it would mean for Bobby to "be alive" is the culmination many emotions, unpleasant as well as positive. All of these feelings accumulate and give the song momentum, emotion, and power. "Want *something*," says Amy.

The "stand alone" version of this song necessitates imagining the voices of Bobby's friends in his head, those "inner voices," even out of the context of the show. It is important that these lines are "heard" by the actor singing the song, so that Bobby can move with intent into the verses. The song requires a singer with good range, including a strong middle and upper voice, that can articulate text on higher pitches. It is important that the text is clearly enunciated in every verse. Also, with the repetition of verses, the actor will need to color differently all of the words, all of the emotions, that are generated by different meanings to the performer of what "being alive" means.

VOICE: Bobby starts the first verse haltingly. The phrases are very short, but the composer has interlocked the phrases to create a longer line, as Bobby yearns for a connection with someone. When he hears the words (after he blows out his birthday candles) "Want something," the song comes to life. Connecting the phrases also brings a momentum to the piece, and it is important to keep it moving and energized. Some anger and dramatic color comes into the voice with the words "Someone to know you too well," and "Someone to put you through hell." Now the song's range ascends into higher tenor territory, to remain in the high tessitura at the top of the staff: "Make me confused, mock me with praise," as the singer accelerates and moves forward. In the climactic phrases, Bobby sustains the high F on the word "a-live" over sixteen beats, and finishes with a high sustained A to resolve to the tonic pitch (F, top line of the staff).

BEHIND THE SCENES WITH THE ARTISTS: JOHN DOYLE, DIRECTOR OF THE 2005 REVIVAL, AND MATT CASTLE, SINGER/ACTOR/PIANIST

The director had an interesting approach to the play. All of the actors played instruments, similar to the director's concept in his earlier work directing *Sweeney Todd.* One of the actors was singer/actor/pianist Matt Castle, who describes the rehearsal process, which was unlike anything Matt had previously experienced. The cast usually spent half a day singing and playing a song, then would immediately "get on [their] feet and start staging." No one was completely off-book, and there were, Mr. Castle says, "constant musical mistakes because everyone has only a vague grasp of the material. John's approach to staging is unusual: he starts with a very simple framework, often with spatial relationships based on the dynamics of the scene. Then we repeat and repeat. The repetition gives everyone a chance to become fluent in the music, makes the scene feel lived-in, and of course, gives the staging time to evolve." Matt noted, "This kind of process takes time and requires actors who want to play. . . . Everyone has to participate; it's not a process for the passive or for followers. Also, this way of working requires strong technique because there's so much repetition."

Director John Doyle: "Because the musical was performed by actor-musicians, this threw a different light upon performance style. It allowed for things to be a little more stylized, and certainly the whole aesthetic of the show was one of minimalism and restraint. Bobby was staged to be the 'outsider looking in,' the one actor who seemingly didn't play an instrument. The guy who couldn't join the band and couldn't make music. Then, when he 'broke' towards the end of the evening, asking his friends to leave him alone, he went to the piano and falteringly played the beginning of 'Being Alive' to accompany himself. He was then slowly joined by the orchestral support of his friends, his 'company.'" This made for quite an effect theatrically. "We had watched this man watching all night—and now he was taking the risk of participating, taking the risk of 'being alive.'"

I Won't Send Roses

Mack and Mabel

"While I greatly admire the famous composer/lyricist teams in musical theatre history, for myself I cannot imagine writing only the music. I find that music and text are creatively inseparable."
—Jerry Herman, composer

CHARACTER: Mack Sennett

MUSIC AND LYRICS: Jerry Herman

BOOK: Michael Stewart

SETTING: Hollywood, 1911, at the Keystone Studios

PREMIERE: 1974

CLASSIFICATION: Baritone ballad

RANGE: 

TESSITURA: Middle of staff

TIME: 3:04

PLOT: See "Time Heals Everything."

CHARACTER: Sennett, originally a performer in burlesque and vaudeville, was a silent film pioneer, first known for producing and directing short slapstick classics such as the Keystone Cops films. He generated hundreds of short comedy films during the height of his productivity, which was about the time he met Mabel Normand in 1911, the glory years for his Keystone Studios. He was a powerful studio head and a control freak who was hands-on in all aspects of casting and film production. He was an extremely hands-on studio boss, personally supervising every shot, cut, gag, and title card of every film that carried his name. In 1915 his film distribution company went bankrupt because of employee embezzlement, and the studio did not survive the depression. Although he did make the transition to sound movies later in his career and foresaw the use of color, he knew that his greatest contribution was comedy film shorts, which were what he did best. After Mabel became a star in Mack's studio, she wanted to try her hand at dramatic roles in film. Furthermore, she wanted Sennett's studio to produce more serious fare, but Mack resisted.

CONTEXT: As the studio grows early in the show, Mabel, who is starring in Mack's movies, pursues him romantically. Mack resists, as he is a workaholic director and producer with no time for romance, and sings "I Won't Send Roses" in act I, after Mabel invites him to her train compartment for a private dinner.

CONTENT: There is a repeated chordal pattern with vamp-like repetition in the accompaniment before Mack enters, singing three verses. The accompaniment does not double the vocal line. The attractive melody, despite its short phrases, which reflect Mack's no-nonsense approach to the subject, eventually reflects his true feelings for Mabel. However, the lyrics contain phrases such as "the lack of romance in my soul," and "Should I love you, you would be the last to know." The violins in the orchestra enter after the words "Stay away, kid," perhaps revealing some hidden feelings he is trying to deny. Mack's delivery of the music and lyrics in the first two verses is blunt and direct, and after his second verse there is dialogue with musical underscoring during the seventeen-measure interlude. The dialogue demonstrates that Mabel is not going to be put off by his warnings. She is clearly headstrong and stubborn, determined to draw him into a relationship. The third verse, beginning with the words "My pace is frantic, my temper's cross," is at a quicker tempo, almost as if Mack is trying to say he doesn't have time for this sentimental stuff. The singer should remember that she is pursuing him, which makes him uncomfortable. The last notes of the third verse are extended and sustained up to the final C.

VOICE: This classic melody is sung in the male lower range down to a repeated low G (until the climactic final phrase of the song). Mack wants to sing the song brusquely and curtly and be straightforward with her. Notice that Mack addresses her as "kid" in the song two times, which is a word that should not be vocalized—it should almost be spoken, and it should sound curt, dismissive, and brusque. He goes out of his way not to reveal his feelings, which would be exposed if the singer sings with a legato tone early in the song. However, the final phrases are earnest and sincerely sung, when he can no longer hide his affections.

In the line "Forget my shoulder, when you're in need," he sings the note on the word "need" (middle G) with full value, extending and sweetly sustaining the note expressively, beginning to reveal his true feelings. At the final phrase of the song, Mack sings the final measures in the upper octave, up to the C and D toward the top of the staff, and sustains the tones more. Here he betrays his true feelings, but the singer should not only think of voice and breath-supported tone; the important thing is to focus on sincerity and warmth, perhaps giving in to the longing for a relationship with her.

BEHIND THE SCENES WITH THE ARTISTS: JERRY HERMAN, COMPOSER

Jerry Herman wrote the music for *Mack and Mabel* with the historical characters and their relationship in mind as well as a measure of fantasy. He wrote the song "I Won't Send Roses" very late in the composing process, almost torturing himself in trying to think of the right song, a romantic song that would capture character and the nature of their relationship. He finally came up with "I Won't Send Roses," and after the initial idea and main melody came to him, he wrote the rest in a short burst of creative energy. Although the song itself came late in the creative process, the melodic motive of the song eventually was used throughout the score to connect the show.

Mr. Herman offered some important advice on singing the song successfully: "It should be the 'anti-romantic' ballad," he said. "Mack is telling it to her straight, until the last line: 'I won't send roses, and roses suit you so.' Furthermore, this song is a great exercise for the young singer," Mr. Herman remarked. "The last line, when it is sung suddenly sweet and loving, makes for a beautiful effect."

Robert Preston created the role of Mack, but the composer did not write the song for him. Instead, Mr. Herman wrote it for the character, as he does with all his songs. However, he did feel that Preston was perfect for the role: "He had the right measure of dynamic energy and charm, and really worked on the role." Addressing Robert Preston's attitude toward the song, Mr. Herman proudly states, "Bob loved the song from the beginning."

All I Care About Is Love

Chicago

"Delicious."
—James Naughton, on playing the role of Billy Flynn

CHARACTER: Billy Flynn

MUSIC: John Kander

LYRICS: Fred Ebb

BOOK: Fred Ebb and Bob Fosse

BASED ON: A 1926 play of the same name by reporter Maurine Dallas Watkins, based on real events

SETTING: Chicago, 1924

BROADWAY PREMIERE: 1975

CLASSIFICATION: Smooth lyric baritone

RANGE: 

TESSITURA: Upper-middle staff

TIME: 2:04

PLOT: *Chicago* is a satiric take on American gangster life in 1920s. The play is called a "musical vaudeville" and is based on popular entertainers of the time. Billy Flynn's character is based on bandleader Ted Lewis, whose catchphrase was "Is everybody happy?" "All I Care About Is Love" is Billy's anthem, and is accompanied by dancers.

CHARACTER: Billy Flynn is a smooth-talking, extremely confident, wise-cracking, straightforward attorney in Chicago. He has a reputation for keeping his murder clients out of the electric chair. He is cynical about his work, loves the attention he generates, and is hardly discreet about his attitude toward women.

CONTEXT: Scene 7. The Master of Ceremonies introduces Billy as "the Silver Tongued Prince of the Courtroom," as the girls call for him. Six women sing slowly and languidly the repeated mantra "We love Billy" in unison. They are clearly dancer-showgirls and display large feather fans that they flourish as they gather around him. Billy is elegantly dressed. The directions in the script further state that, following the fan dance with the girls, he strips to his underwear while singing. "Is everybody here? Is everybody ready?" Billy asks as he walks toward the audience and sings his song.

Jerry Orbach, who created the role, would enter holding a cigar and would gesture with it while singing, then, in a very nonchalant way, without a trace of self-consciousness, he would begin to undress while singing.

CONTENT: The song is sung in verses. Billy's anthem begins with his declaration that he doesn't care about a rich style (which he nevertheless embodies and enjoys); instead, he only cares about love. The melody line is sung with a lilt that comes from a combination of smooth vocal timbre and rhythms in the vocal line that are a string of quarter-note values followed by eighth-note rhythms, then repeated, contributing to the momentum of the line. Added triplet-rhythm figures underline the smooth, debonair quality of Billy's character. After the second verse, continuing along these lines, he speaks with a heightened vocal energy, declaring that there are "other kinds of love" besides physical love, such as "love for your fellow man." He ends the list by adding, "And physical love ain't so bad either." The next verse begins with the melody sung on scat syllables, which hearkens back to the style of the Jazz Age. Billy ends the song with the big finish, with the half-sung, declamatory Al Jolson delivery. The last phrases are commonly sung an octave above the other verses, which includes the optional high F-sharp at the top of the staff.

VOICE: The singer needs to sing with a smooth delivery to resonate with the style intended by the composer. This also includes a classic crooning approach used by the early Jazz singers as they caressed the microphone on the stand. These singers sang with less support and vocal tension than singers without amplification traditionally use. However, the rhythmic variety in the melody that John Kander chooses defines a character that projects more energy, perhaps, than the languid, laid-back delivery of the original band singers. This energy, which builds during the song, is underlined during the phrase in which he sings: "Give me *two* eyes of *blue*," which requires Billy to sing toward the top of the staff, ending each phrase on the u vowel, needing more supportive energy. Billy can phrase the song with a little punch to the words at times to give some edge to his personality. With this choice, Billy may not want to sustain pitches at the end of the phrases until the end of the song.

BEHIND THE SCENES WITH THE ARTISTS: ACTOR JAMES NAUGHTON AND COMPOSER JOHN KANDER

Actor (and Tony Award–winner) James Naughton spoke with me about his experience in reviving the role of Billy Flynn in the popular 1996 revival production; Mr. Naughton summed up the role in one word: "Delicious." Billy reveled in what he did, "and he was good at it!" Because of his charm and ability to get accused murderers freed, Billy knew that he was special. James Naughton said that this was because the lawyer was essentially a showman, and that knowledge determined his "size" onstage: big, showy, and able to administer the "razzle-dazzle."

Composer John Kander said that the inspirations for Billy's music and song delivery were Ted Lewis, Harry Richmond, and Rudy Vallee, who was cast in the musical *How to Succeed in Business without Really Trying* by Frank Loesser. Mr. Kander noted that the entry songs from Chicago, "All I Care About Is Love," and "All That Jazz," are what he calls "extroverted" in delivery. Mr. Kander also noted that the original Billy in *Chicago*, Jerry Orbach, created a number of the conventions associated with the song, including the trademark cigar.

I've Heard It All Before

Shenandoah

"The audience feels his pain, but they should also be aware that Charlie is learning a strong, almost unbearable lesson about himself."

—John Cullum, the original Charlie

CHARACTER: Charlie Anderson

MUSIC: Gary Geld

LYRICS: Peter Udell

BOOK: Peter Udell, Philip Rose, and James Lee Barrett

BASED ON: Barrett's original screenplay for the 1965 film

SETTING: Virginia, during the Civil War

BROADWAY PREMIERE: 1975

CLASSIFICATION: Baritone up-tempo

RANGE: 

TESSITURA: Upper-middle staff

TME: 2:50

PLOT: See "The Only Home I Know."

CHARACTER: Charlie Anderson is "a strongly principled farmer of about fifty, who rules his large family with authority and tenderness." He is only interested in his family and land, but his world as he knows it is broken apart by the war. He is a widower and has six sons. The oldest, Jacob, is twenty-eight, followed by James (twenty-six), Nathan (twenty-four), John (twenty-two), Henry (seventeen), and Robert (the Boy), who is twelve. Jenny is nineteen, and James is married to Anne.

CONTEXT: It is Sunday morning inside the Anderson home. The breakfast table is set. Charlie, at the head of the table, is clearly the strong and stable presence in the house. Charlie detects uneasiness in his sons, and he encourages them to speak out. The sons do not see how Charlie can sit idle and not expect his sons to fight for what they believe in. "The people at this table are the only concerns I have in this world," he answers. "If those fools want to slaughter one another, that's their business, but it's got nothing to do with us! Not one damn thing has it got to do with us!" He immediately sings "I've Heard It All Before."

CONTENT: The accompaniment is very active, in an eighth-note arpeggiated figure. The strongly sung rhythms and delineated text, brashly sung, clearly articulate an antiwar message, with the words "I've heard it all, a hundred times, I've heard it all before" repeating in three verses. A key line is "They've always got a holy cause that's worth the dying for," sung during the second section of the song, as the melody begins to shift toward another key from g minor. Eighth-note triplet rhythms with half-note chord patterns are added to the texture in the accompaniment, while the declamatory style of the vocal line in the same rhythm continues. With "the trumpet sounds the call" the song continues to be energized with active rhythms in the accompaniment and the vocal line, as the dramatic message in the text continues with momentum. When the singer comes to the phrase "And always the ending is the same . . . the same" the music is marked "slower," and repetitions of text "the same" are separated by caesuras. The next section, "The dream has turned to ashes" (marked "andante-rubato"), is in the key of G major, and is marked "pianissimo," while the less active accompaniment (block chords) doubles the melody for most of this section. The tone here is more serious and heart-felt—no longer repeating the "call to arms." After "Upon my soul I swear," there is a short recapitulation of the opening measures leading to the final cadence, again in g minor. The orchestra punctuates the spaces between vocal phrases with accented chords for emphasis. At "I've heard it all before" Charlie slams his fist on the table, as sixteenth notes in the accompaniment (marked "accelerando") help to propel the song to the final cut-off release.

VOICE: The song requires a very strong delivery that projects the text and vocal line above a very active accompaniment. The performance could all be sung in an angry tone, but the singer could find many other available emotional colors appropriate to use in the song. There is sarcasm, discouragement, frustration, annoyance, determination—all examples of specific emotions that can color his singing. With his intense delivery, the sustained notes can become constricted, especially as the singer reaches high D and E. The singer should try to project Charlie's anger and conviction strongly through supported initial imploded consonants and keep the jaw free. The consonants, body language, and facial expressions can go a long way in expressing strong emotions. The throat will want to get involved, but low, deep inhalations and anchored breath support can help, with practice, to combat the instinct of tightening the throat when emotions run high.

BEHIND THE SCENES WITH THE ARTISTS: JOHN CULLUM, THE ORIGINAL CHARLIE

"Charlie Anderson is strong minded, tough, and determined to be a good man. He is heroic. But that gets him into trouble when he acts on his principals without taking into consideration his deep personal feelings. At the breakfast table he makes it clear that the war is wrong, killing is wrong, and he will have nothing to do with it. He is strong, determined, and bristling with righteous conviction. When his son James is killed and Robert is abducted he gets drawn in and kills a young Yankee soldier in a fit of rage," John observes. Charlie Anderson's world is compromised, and he feels he has lost his compass in life. "The fortress of his farm and his convictions begin to crumble, and he is filled with doubts and fears that he has lost his way. He expresses that in the second meditation. The audience feels his pain, but they should also be aware that Charlie is learning a strong, almost unbearable lesson about himself."

The Pickers Are Comin'

Shenandoah

"Charlie Anderson is a great role to play because he is strong minded, tough, and determined to be a good man"
—John Cullum, the original Charlie

CHARACTER: Charlie Anderson

MUSIC: Gary Geld

LYRICS: Peter Udell

BOOK: Peter Udell, Philip Rose, and James Lee Barrett

BASED ON: Barrett's original screenplay for the 1965 film Shenandoah

SETTING: Virginia, during the Civil War

BROADWAY PREMIERE: 1975

CLASSIFICATION: Baritone

RANGE: 

TESSITURA: A to top F

TIME: 3:06

PLOT: See "The Only Home I Know."

CHARACTER: See "I've Heard It All Before."

CONTEXT: Charlie overhears a young man sweet-talking his daughter, Jenny. Charlie tells his young son that Jenny is "ripe for pickin'," and then needs to explain to his boy what that means.

CONTENT: The song is marked "slowly," and is to be played in the four-bar introduction pianissimo as marked. After a fermata, Charlie begins to sing, the vocal line marked "faster." The accompaniment consists of a repeated quarter-eighth-note rhythmic pattern, as Charlie explains how he raised is daughter "from a seedlin'," and he repeats this eight-measure section two times, before singing: "And now I'm bothered by the feelin' that soon [ritardando] she'll be leavin' me" (caesura), followed by a spoken "You'll see." He then begins the chorus in a *valse rubato* (waltz with freedom) tempo in 3/4 meter, strongly in deliberately sung quarter-notes, accompanied by a bass quarter-note downbeat, which is then followed by quarter-note-value chord on beats two and sometimes three, in the waltz rhythm. Charlie is speaking to his son about the facts of life: "The fruit's on the vine now," Charlie sings, clearly about his daughter. There is a little bridge transition of eight measures to connect (*poco meno mosso*) "And though I know it's only right" to another repeated chorus with variations with the same charming lyrics. When he comes to the text "They're comin' for my little girl," the pitches are sustained to signal clearly that Charlie is finishing the song, and when he sings "my little girl" the second time, he sings it reflectively, as the word "girl" is sustained with a fermata, before finishing with the resigned: "My little girl [fermata] no more," on a sustained D at the top of his range, sung softly and tenderly.

VOICE: This is a great song for showing a number of emotions as indicated by the text and situation. In the opening verses, it is quite low, but conversational, with many accidentals and very little doubling in the accompaniment. Inflection of the important words is important, and not overvocalizing the song would be wise as well. The words "The apple of my eye" is clearly more lyric and tender, and can be sung with a little more voice by the proud father, with strong commitment and clarity of text. "My little girl [fermata] no more," should be sung with a soft (but supported) tone.

BEHIND THE SCENES WITH THE ARTISTS: JOHN CULLUM, THE ORIGINAL CHARLIE

John approached this great role in his own way, which he is convinced every actor does individually, "even though they may profess a method they have studied." He has never been able to express in words exactly how he does it, but he believes that he works from the "outside in." In other words, he doesn't try to feel what he would feel if he was the character. However, he does "empathize with the character," as he does when reading any story. "Once you know how the story unfolds you should have an idea of how to play each scene as it occurs." He admits that this is easier said than done. John clearly understands that the role of Charlie Anderson is a great one to play, because "he is strong minded, tough, and determined to be a good man. He is heroic. But that gets him into trouble when he acts on his principals without taking into consideration his deep personal feelings. At the breakfast table he makes it clear that the war is wrong, killing is wrong, and he will have nothing to do with it. He is strong, determined, and bristling with righteous conviction." John believes that this is the approach the actor should take while singing "The Pickers Are Comin'." The song "uses the imagery of the harvest—something that Charlie understands and appreciates. Intellectually he knows it is coming and that it is 'only right.' He accepts it in his head, but in his heart he can't, because his little girl is becoming a woman, and she will be his little girl no more. Charlie is heroic when he follows his principles and human when he follows his heart. When the two come into conflict Charlie has to make adjustments, and that keeps his character and the story interesting." John says that he uses his father and great uncle as examples of people with Charlie's good points as well as his bad ones, and adds: "My own experiences helped to shape Charlie as I played him."

Funny

City of Angels

"The essence of [Stine is that he is] . . . more cerebral than emotional."
—Gregg Edelman, the original Stine

CHARACTER: Stine

MUSIC: Cy Coleman

LYRICS: David Zippel

BOOK: Larry Gelbart

SETTING: Hollywood, late 1940s

BROADWAY PREMIERE: 1980

CLASSIFICATION: Lyric baritone

RANGE: 

TESSITURA: Begins low, syllabic; builds to top of staff

TIME: 2:35

PLOT: See "You Can Always Count On Me."

CHARACTER: The author, Stine, is a novelist, and is the "real" character in the play. He is adapting his book, which is entitled *City of Angels*, into a screenplay. As Stine struggles to preserve both his job and the integrity of his novel, his wife, Gabby, is fed up with his womanizing and leaves for New York. Soon after, he begins another affair. Gabby leaves him when the affair is discovered. Stine flies to New York in an unsuccessful attempt to reconcile with Gabby.

CONTEXT: "Funny" is sung in act II, scene 18, in Stine's office/writers cell. It is toward the end of the show. What should Stine do? His wife has rejected him, his lover (and secretary) Donna, he learns, has been rewriting his script. It is clear that he feels sorry for himself: "Try it sometime," he says. "Try doing what I do before I do it." Stine faces the collapse of his real and fictive worlds, and as his emotions take over, his wit turns bitter as he sings "Funny."

On returning, Stine discovers that his film's ending has been drastically rewritten. Reacting with anger, he tears up the script and quits. He is causing a commotion, and is about to be beaten by the studio guards. The detective Stone (Stine's creation) aids Stine by typing a new scene, which allows Stine to defeat the guards and win back both his wife and his self-respect.

The song "Funny" is preceded by dialogue between Stone and Oona, his secretary, as he is reading the Stine script to her. They are discussing the verisimilitude of the script. Stine, the creator of the script, is arguing a point with Donna, *his* secretary. The dialogue moves toward an escalating argument between Stine and his fictive alter ego Stone, with interjections by Donna, who finally says, "Funny, I *never* got that impression," which leads directly to Stine's singing the song.

CONTENT: The song begins in a cabaret-like style, with a four-measure introduction of staccato chord accompaniment and the voice entering in a half-sung/spoken *Sprechstimme* style the word/motive "Funny," on the low E-flat–F at the bottom of the staff. As the song unfolds it ascends and becomes more invested with emotion. The song's rhythm is active and not at all predictable, like the accompaniment and its written irregular rhythmic patterns. The text and tone are bitter, edgy, and sarcastic, with clipped words and notes, as Stine talks about "all the irony I missed, all the unusual twists," alternating short phrases with sustained tones that are powered by a strong emotion as the melody ascends. He alternates also in his language, flipping between the style of words he is using in the script and his own. He is at the point with his script when he is fed-up and cynical and bitterly ironic. As the song unfolds, many accidentals must be negotiated, especially in the transition section. At this point, Stine is revealing more emotion as he sings on higher sustained pitches ("forcing you into a smile"), and actually repeating the opening phrase ("Funny") one octave higher, at the top of the staff, in the song's melodic recapitulation. The song modulates from B-flat minor to G minor after "I always pick up the check," and then returns to B-flat minor for the octave-higher motive to the finish of the song, with more sustained tones written at the top of the staff.

VOICE: The singer needs to deliver the words in a cabaret style with a lot of words spilling out at the beginning of the song, building to a much more belt-like sustained finish, singing sustained Fs at the top of the staff. It has a desperate feel, as Stine is feeling like he is losing his creative soul in this work and needs to find it again. Consonants need to be strongly enunciated for a committed diction and attention to text without chewing the words, which creates throat tension.

BEHIND THE SCENES WITH THE ARTISTS: GREGG EDELMAN, THE ORIGINAL STINE

Gregg Edelman told me that "Funny" was a difficult song to sing because "it gave Stine a markedly different tone than at any other place in the show." Singing this song, he is not the Hollywood author; instead he is rejecting the seductive lure of Hollywood and comes face to face "with what he has become." The song also contrasts with the rest of the show, which is witty, humorous, and has a happy ending. Gregg needed to "find a take on the song that would accomplish the confrontation" of a man coming to terms with compromising his own artistic standards. Mr. Edelman is grateful the composer and lyricist for writing a special song that could dramatize a very smart man coming to terms with himself with clarity, and keeping the essence of a man more cerebral than emotional, "as a writer would be in a moment like that—helping to turn the song into a self-indictment and not an extended moment of self-pity."

I asked Gregg if he recalled anything he learned about the character in his work with director, Michael Blakemore, as the role was created onstage. The director reminded him numerous times that "Stine is not an actor; he is a writer." He said, "I would try to inflate moments in the play to be more than they were intended, because the character was sharing the stage with all these wonderful Hollywood archetypes which our book writer, Larry Gelbart, had lampooned so brilliantly. That is an easy trap to fall into when playing a writer, especially in a comedy," and this tendency was discouraged, with sensitivity and understanding, by the director.

Lullaby of Broadway

42nd Street

"Julian Marsh is the 'greatest director on Broadway,' but he's had a rough time lately between failed productions and financial losses in the Great Depression."
—Mark Bramble, author of the musical's book

CHARACTER: Julian Marsh

MUSIC: Harry Warren

LYRICS: Al Dubin

BOOK: Michael Stewart and Mark Bramble

BASED ON: The novel by Bradford Ropes and the 1933 film adaptation

SETTING: Broad Street Station, Philadelphia

BROADWAY PREMIERE: 1980

CLASSIFICATION: Baritone swing

RANGE: 

TESSITURA: Upper-middle staff

TIME: 3:50

PLOT: The show is about the (fictional) famous dictatorial Broadway producer Julian Marsh, and his efforts to bring a hit musical to the Great White Way at the height of the depression. There are many obstacles in the way of the production.

42nd Street, which premiered on Broadway in 1984, is a "nostalgia musical," based on a 1933 movie-musical, with songs from that time and set in that period. The song "Lullaby of Broadway" was originally published in 1935.

CHARACTER: Julian Marsh is a man in control, very savvy about the business, confident, experienced, and professional. When Broadway director Julian Marsh is doing a show, it means jobs (important during the depression). The 1929 financial crash "got him down for the count," but he's still Julian Marsh and will get back on top. He is not afraid to speak frankly to anyone, especially if it threatens to compromise his show. In response to his meddling in her affairs, the show's star, Dorothy, says, "You're the director of my show, not my personal life!" "When your personal life gets in the way of my show, I direct that too!" responds Julian. He is very good at motivating and knowing which buttons to push with the actors of the company. When chorus understudy Peggy walks out on her opportunity to star in the production in order to go back to her home in Allentown, he says to her: "Think of the songs that will wither and die if you don't get up there and sing them!" Broadway is in his blood.

CONTEXT: In the act I finale, Julian has fired Peggy because Dorothy has accused her of pushing her, causing her to twist her ankle so that Peggy, the understudy, can take the starring role. Because of this accident, Julian has to refund the audience's money at the intermission. Act II, scene 4 is set in Broad Street Station in Philadelphia, as Peggy is leaving town. Julian, having learned the truth about the incident, changes his mind about firing Peggy. He tries to convince her not to leave the show, which would sink the production for good. They are at the train station in Philadelphia. Peggy is sitting on her suitcases waiting for the train.

CONTENT: The opening of the song is signaled by three chords, setting up the dialogue as Julian is trying to convince Peggy not to leave. He is reminding her of her chance to "star in the biggest Broadway musical seen in 20 years." He further reminds her that if she does not perform, there will be songs never heard, scenery and costumes never seen, all wasted. He reminds her of the "kids" in the cast who will be "thrown out of work" if she doesn't perform. As the well-known melody unfolds (marked "freely"), and then is repeated in a steady moderate swing tempo with its signature rhythmic pattern of eighth- and sixteenth-note rhythmic combinations, she begins to soften and eventually is carried away by the seductive dance of the stage. However, she catches herself, coming to her senses. Members of the cast then arrive and take the melody from Julian to eventually transform the song into a large production number. If the song is sung as a solo by Julian, then the classic melody is repeated a total of four times, each marked with a different tempo, and the last two times it is sung the key will modulate up by one-half step both times the refrain is performed. As far as the musical form is concerned, the two sections of the song are the chorus and the bridge (the "good night, baby" phrase), which is simply whole notes followed by rhythmic tags. Most of the accompaniment in the song consists of sustained chord support, with occasional rhythmically syncopated patterns.

VOICE: The singer needs to embrace the collective syncopated and dotted rhythms to deliver the song energetically and persuasively. After all, Julian is trying to entice Peggy to come back to the theater, and at stake is his reputation as a well-known producer and musical theatre advocate. Although the song is a straightforward song and dance number, there are a lot of dynamics to observe that can help draw Peggy into the environment of the musical (e.g., "Good night, baby" begins piano, then crescendos on the whole note, and is followed soon by a decrescendo of two measures). At the line "Let's call it a day," with a marked rallentando, the vocal line ascends to high E-flat on the word "day." Julian needs to sing this high phrase passionately and persuasively, but cannot push or strain. The larynx needs to remain low and the support should be strong. And remember, Julian's focus should be on Peggy and her reactions to his message. It is also important to remember that Julian is an established producer and displays gravitas and a loyalty to the theater that is not trivial or taken lightly.

BEHIND THE SCENES WITH THE ARTISTS: MARK BRAMBLE, AUTHOR OF THE MUSICAL'S BOOK

"Julian Marsh is the 'greatest director on Broadway,' but he's had a rough time lately between failed productions and financial losses in the Great Depression. He is a martinet who, at the beginning of the play, is emotionally shut down. . . . As *42nd Street* begins, Julian is planning a new Broadway show called *Pretty Lady*. He casts a young girl in the chorus from Allentown, Pennsylvania, named Peggy Sawyer, and through the course of the play's rehearsals, Peggy's wide-eyed, joyous wonder while performing reawakens Julian's passion for the theatre as well as his heart. In the finale of act I, Dorothy Brock, the star of the show, falls onstage and breaks her ankle. Julian thinks Peggy is responsible for Brock's accident and fires her. After the rest of the company try to persuade Julian that it wasn't Peggy's fault and that she can replace Dorothy Brock as the star of *Pretty Lady*, he follows Peggy to Broad Street Station, where she's waiting for the train back to Allentown. He tells her, 'I want you to come back and take over Dorothy Brock's role in *Pretty Lady*.' Peggy isn't interested. 'I'm sorry, Mr. Marsh,' she tells him, 'show business isn't for me, I'm going back to Allentown.' Julian responds with a speech in which he reawakens his own passion for the theatre, until he can no longer speak and his emotions must be sung. The final line he speaks before he sings is: 'Think of musical comedy—the most glorious words in the English language! Sawyer, think of Broadway, dammit!' "

There Is a Sucker Born Ev'ry Minute

Barnum

"It's debated whether P. T. Barnum actually coined the phrase, but even if he didn't, everybody *thinks* he did, and the audience would be waiting for it."
—Mark Bramble, author of the musical's book

CHARACTER: P. T. Barnum

MUSIC: Cy Coleman

LYRICS: Michael Stewart

BOOK: Mark Bramble

SETTING: 1835–1880

BROADWAY PREMIERE: 1980

CLASSIFICATION: Baritone lyric

RANGE: 

TESSITURA: Middle of staff, some sustained D-sharps, some E after modulation

TIME: 3:50

PLOT: The show is about the life and times of P. T. Barnum during the years 1835–1880 in America and throughout the major cities of the world. Barnum was known as the first great American showman and promoter. His circus featured acts that included the "oldest woman," the "smallest man," and a number of sideshow acts. He also became entranced with the figure of Miss Jenny Lind, a singer from Sweden billed as the "Swedish Nightingale." To entice her to come tour America, Barnum promised her an exorbitant sum of money he did not have at the time, even before he heard her sing. The words "There is a sucker born ev'ry minute" have been traditionally attributed to

Barnum, though that has been disputed. Nevertheless, it makes for good musical theatre to have Barnum sing "There Is a Sucker Born Ev'ry Minute" to the audience at the opening of the show.

The show itself ran for more than eight hundred performances on Broadway, primarily because the production had the feel of a circus, and although Barnum was not a performer himself, this show portrays him singing, dancing, clowning, and riding a unicycle. This opening song displays his showman's personality from the opening measures.

CHARACTER: P. T. Barnum is brash and confident in his public persona. He is a showman and salesman, and he will risk much if the situation calls for it. In the musical he is lithe and flexible and a performer in the circus, as played by Jim Dale. In reality Phineas Taylor Barnum (1810–1891) was a showman in name only, and was the founder of the circus that became the Ringling Bros. and Barnum & Bailey Circus. Barnum was also an author and even a politician. However, he considered himself a businessman.

CONTEXT: The song is placed at the opening of the show, and it establishes Barnum's personality as a man who could sell anything to anyone. He is onstage in front of a tent speaking to an excited audience. He is building the audience's expectations, and is about to introduce the oldest woman alive, Joice Heth.

CONTENT: Barnum sings this energized melody syllabically, in a patter style, demonstrating his gift of gab. The accompaniment is notated in chords of eighth-note rhythms, in the vaudeville-based song and dance style. At the end of every phrase, the song has an upward interval that is high for the baritone. The singer should either approximate the E natural from a heightened speech pattern or sing it securely. It is not advised to attempt to sing the notes without success, as the result is that the top notes will be flat or sharp.

The song is written in the key of E major. Before the last verse, there is a modulation up one half step to the key of F, which entails a number of sustained tones at the top of the baritone range, including a final sustained F at the top of the staff. Much of the accompaniment is written in off-the-beat chords, which provide momentum for the vocal line. The form of the song is in an ABABCAB, with the final AB in the new key of F.

VOICE: This song requires a highly charged, energized delivery of the text. It can sound as if he has delivered the same speech before, because he has—

it is hardly extemporaneous or thoughtful in its delivery. The actor needs to focus on different folks in the crowd, not generalize the focus of the performance. It is also important to note that he is speaking in the vernacular language of the common man, the nineteenth-century equivalent of the used-car salesman, in an attempt to communicate directly with people. There are no interludes or gaps in the song. He doesn't give anyone the chance to comment or to question. The singer should be aware that this song is performed at the top of the show, and it is the audience's first exposure to this man's character, energy, and personality. Also notice that he ends the song by showing that perhaps he doesn't take himself so seriously, with the line "There is a sucker born every minute, and biggest one—excluding none—is... *me*!" The song is a tricky one to sing, with its rhythmic challenges, the many words—which need to be enunciated clearly and distinctly—in the patter style of Gilbert and Sullivan, and the accidentals and wide intervals (e.g., "born ev'ry min-*ute*," leaping between the lower E-sharp and the high D-sharp). The rhythms and text need to be sung with the confidence that befits one of the great legends of nineteenth-century showmanship.

BEHIND THE SCENES WITH THE ARTISTS: MARK BRAMBLE, BOOK WRITER OF *BARNUM*

Mr. Bramble says of the song's title, "It's debated whether P. T. Barnum actually coined the phrase, but even if he didn't, everybody *thinks* he did, and the audience would be waiting for it. It became the first song in the show, and Michael Stewart created a lovely payoff in the last lines of the lyric, "The biggest one / excluding none / is me."

Colors of My Life

Barnum

"I chose to play the spirit, not the man."
—Jim Dale, the original Barnum

CHARACTER: P. T. Barnum

MUSIC: Cy Coleman

LYRICS: Michael Stewart

BOOK: Mark Bramble

SETTING: 1835–1880

BROADWAY PREMIERE: 1980

CLASSIFICATION: Baritone lyric

RANGE: 

TESSITURA: Middle of staff

TIME: 3:50

PLOT AND CHARACTER: See "There Is a Sucker Born Ev'ry Minute."

CONTEXT: In this important scene, the couple is seated and Barnum's wife, Charity, is knitting. She urges her husband to get a real job, but Barnum resists. He shares his plans with Charity, which she dismisses as "schemes and dreams!" As he reveals his dreams, she reminds him that they only have "100 dollars to our name." She has to draw all of the plan's vital information from him; he doesn't want to reveal the details, because she will belittle his dreams. She wants him to have "sensible" plans, while he wants to reveal "miracles" to the masses. He is not thinking in practical terms; he is thinking in colors, and that idea introduces the song. She reminds him that he has two daughters and responsibilities, and there is a job open in the local factory. As the song begins, Barnum knows that he cannot use the old

Barnum charm to sway her. He has to sing to her about what drives him, his vision, while still showing that he understands his family responsibilities and cares about providing for his family.

CONTENT: The song is straightforward, honest, intimate, and vulnerably sung. It is a sharp contrast to Barnum's opening song, "There Is a Sucker Born Ev'ry Minute." Although his public manner is confident and brash, and he has a polished spiel, he is unable to pull the wool over his wife's eyes. He has to explain himself in a sincere and honest manner. Charity may not like what she hears, but this song expresses what he genuinely believes. It is not sung by the razzle-dazzle showman who is P. T. Barnum, but instead reveals a man who is above all positive in his outlook and appreciative of what he has been given. At the same time, the stakes are quite high for Barnum's character at this point of the show, for his reputation to continue to grow. The song begins without introduction with the refrain. After he sings one chorus of the song, there is an orchestral interlude while dialogue with his wife continues under the score. After a slowing cadence (in four) with a fermata, Barnum continues to sing ("faster, in two") the bridge section ("The splendor of a sunrise"), and, as staged, he exits as his wife, Charity, sings the last chorus in her own words. In a solo version, Barnum has a number of choices: singing one chorus, or singing a chorus followed immediately by the bridge, and then repeating the first chorus to finish, or singing the entire piece with her text.

VOICE: The song calls for a vocal delivery that is tenderly sung. It begins low, at the bottom of the staff, but quickly ascends in the melody line to E-flat and D at the top end of the staff, which is not easy to sing while communicating important, poetically nuanced text. These pitches, sung on the words "I'd put them all to shame," and "with rose and cherry red," need to have freedom of vocal production so that they are not constricted. The tone is honest and lyric, and belies the Barnum public persona that is established at the beginning of the show. It is nice if it is delivered with good tone quality, but what is most important is the warm sincerity that is revealed when Barnum drops his salesman personality and tries to explain why he dreams and what drives him in a thoughtful and sensitive manner. He finds it in a lyric melody without fancy footwork or sleight of hand rhythm. This is not a complex song, but it requires singing in tune and carrying a melody that is not doubled or assisted by the accompaniment. There are sustained notes that are written at the end of every phrase while the orchestra is moving. While the melody is attractive, the tempo marking (quarter note = 112) recommends that the vocal line moves without too much sentimentality.

BEHIND THE SCENES WITH THE ARTISTS: JIM DALE, WHO CREATED THE ROLE OF BARNUM ON BROADWAY, AND MARK BRAMBLE, THE AUTHOR OF THE MUSICAL'S BOOK

Mr. Dale says that he made a decision to "play the *spirit* of the man, and not the man himself. I tried to be the most sincere when singing 'Colors.'" Mr. Bramble told me what he thought the show was about: "The theme of the show was clear: follow your bliss and it's possible for your dreams to come true." He sees this as the "ultimate American Dream story." "The structure of the show," he pointed out, "would be an impressionistic look at the highlights of Barnum's life, starting in 1835 with Joice Heth, and on to the American Museum, Tom Thumb, Jumbo, Jenny Lind, and culminating with the creation of the Greatest Show on Earth in 1881. The libretto would have the effect of broad, vivid pointillism, with snapshots of the major events in Barnum's life, a valentine to the gaudy élan of nineteenth-century America."

The question was "What was going to hold all these snapshots together? Where was the conflict?" For this, Mr. Bramble focused on Barnum's life with his first wife, Charity. There is not a lot known about her, but, he said, "This could only come from a personal story, the story of his love affair with his first wife, Charity." The writer, "for the sake of drama," wrote about two characters who were in love but had two completely different ways of looking at things: "He was a dreamer and she was a realist. The story of Mr. and Mrs. Barnum would be the glue that held the whole thing together," Mr. Bramble explained. One of the key songs to underscore these differences was "The Colors of My Life": "It was Barnum's theme, and when Charity sang her version of the refrain, it clearly illustrated the differences between these two people."

Don't Go, Sally

Cabaret

"In creating the performance, I needed to throw off any preconceived notion of what a 'love song' sounds like and how it plays."
—Gregg Edelman, first actor to sing "Don't Go, Sally."

CHARACTER: Cliff Bradshaw

MUSIC: John Kander

LYRICS: Fred Ebb

BASED ON: John Van Druten's play *I Am a Camera,* adapted from Christopher Isherwood's 1939 novel *Goodbye to Berlin*

SETTING: Berlin, 1929–1930, before the start of the Third Reich

PREMIERE: 1966 (this song added to the 1987 version)

CLASSIFICATION: Baritone lyric

RANGE: 

TESSITURA: Middle of staff

TIME: 3:35

PLOT: See "Cabaret."

CHARACTER: Clifford Bradshaw, an American from Pennsylvania, is in his late twenties. He is described as "pleasant-looking," "intelligent," and "reserved" in the script. When first introduced in act I, scene 2, he is alone in his train compartment asleep, traveling in Europe en route to Berlin. A German passenger, Ernst Ludwig, enters the compartment and engages in conversation with the awakened American. Cliff describes himself as a "writer who gives English lessons." He is traveling to Berlin to live and write, but knows no one there. He does not have the means to support himself as a writer and is looking for a place to live that is inexpensive. Ernst, his "new friend," helps him find a room in Berlin.

CONTEXT: Cliff sings "Don't Go, Sally," added to the 1987 version of the show. The song appears in act II after Kit Kat Club entertainer Sally Bowles, who lives with Cliff, has told him that she is pregnant. She says that she is not sure who the father is. Cliff has no prospects for work in Berlin, and he insists that she come back to America with him so that they can raise the baby. Sally argues with him that life in Berlin is wonderful and she doesn't want to leave. Cliff tells her to look around and see that the mounting unrest in Germany is increasingly dangerous and they must leave. He wants a traditional relationship—in America. They continue to argue, and Sally puts a suitcase on the bed as she begins to pack.

CONTENT: At the opening, the accompaniment is in a treble-clef chordal pattern with a quarter-note half-note quarter-note rhythm. Accidentals abound in the melody, as if Cliff is trying to find his footing in choosing the proper words. After "con moto," he repeats the opening melody ("No, I can't wish you luck"). After some dialogue, the B section is repeated ("This life, This giddy, hectic life"), and finally one more chorus ("Well, I've spoken my piece") is sung, followed by a tag, in which Cliff literally cries out at the top of his range one last plea, followed by a final "Don't go, Sally. Don't go," sung plaintively, the dynamics marked "piano."

VOICE: The range of this song is wide, requiring the baritone to sing some low pitches (A natural) at the bottom of the staff, as well as the E natural at the top, with notes and vowels that will not "spread" and raise the larynx, resulting in a constricted tone. The singer will also need to tune many intervals that include accidentals and enharmonic tones not in the key of A major, the key in which the song is written. The performer should be aware of rhythmic delineation between quarter notes and the combination of quarter/dotted quarter followed by the eighth-note rhythm, and the many triplet rhythms, including those that open the piece. The song will have much more life when the singer has a strong sense of when to move the line forward with momentum, because his time with Sally is short and the stakes are high. It's good, for example, to move "This life, this giddy hectic life" forward with more urgency.

BEHIND THE SCENES WITH THE ARTISTS: ACTOR GREGG EDELMAN

Mr. Edelman was the first Cliff to sing the song "Don't Go, Sally," which was added for the Broadway revision in 1987. Gregg wrote me that when the show was revived in the late 1980s, Hal Prince and the original production team theorized that the theatre-going public was sophisticated enough to accept a Cliff who was in more of a modern, complex relationship than in the original, "a relationship between two desperate people trying to find their way in pre-WWII Germany." Unlike the original production, "they decided that the 'new' Cliff would be a homosexual man who was aware of his sexual attraction towards men but who was terribly frightened by that realization. In fact, the new book refers to homosexual encounters in Paris before his arrival in Berlin." John Kander, Fred Ebb, and the great book writer Joe Masteroff rewrote much of the Cliff/Sally relationship so that his secret is exposed as the show progresses. "When rewriting the scene in which Sally decides it's time she leave, due in large part to her belief that Cliff is gay, the authors decided that the original Cliff song 'Why Should I Wake Up?' did not capture the desperation that Cliff would feel at the moment. The original song was romantic in both music and lyrics. At that moment in the show, the authors felt that Cliff is confronted with the end of quite possibly his last chance for a 'normal' life, and that terrifies him." Fred Ebb's lyrics "You're more than just a girl. You are the only girl. And maybe my last chance," exemplify the desperately raw emotions that Cliff goes through as he begs Sally to stay. Gregg describes how he needed to think about the song: "In creating the performance, I needed to throw off any preconceived notion of what a 'love song' sounds like and how it plays. Cliff is desperate, but tries not to sound that way. He knows he is asking her to stay to save him from his fears, his perceived demons, and that is an awful thing to ask a lover and friend to do. When she relents after the song, he holds Sally, not as a joyous moment but as a grateful release. The inevitable, like the coming war, is held off for a while."

You Should Be Loved

Side Show

"Jake is the only principle character in *Side Show* not based on an actual person."
—Bill Russell, who wrote the book and lyric

CHARACTER: Jake

MUSIC: Harry Krieger

BOOK AND LYRICS: Bill Russell

SETTING: Carnival sideshow, 1930

BROADWAY PREMIERE: 1996

CLASSIFICATION: Lyric baritone

RANGE: 

TESSITURA: Middle staff

TIME: 1:26, with optional extension

PLOT: *Side Show* was inspired by the true story of Siamese twins Daisy and Violet Hilton, who were born in England in 1908. The sisters became stars on the vaudeville circuit, earning more than three thousand dollars per week during the Great Depression. It is also true that Violet Hilton was married in 1936 on the fifty-yard line of the Cotton Bowl for a paid audience.

The company in the sideshow consists of the bearded lady, the Reptile Man, and the Bride of Snakes, and the main attraction is to hear the "haunting song of the Siamese Twins." The company also includes an African American (Jake) who plays the "Cannibal King." The company of "freaks" thinks of itself as a family. Buddy Foster is a young man with aspirations of becoming a vaudeville musician, while Terry Connor is a talent scout for the Orpheum circuit. By the end of act I, Violet admits that she is in love with Buddy, while Daisy cares for Terry.

In the show it is made clear that the twins have markedly different goals in life: Violet wants a husband and home, and Daisy wants stardom.

CHARACTER: Jake is a member of the sideshow. His role is that of exotic Cannibal King from the dark jungles of Africa. Jake is good-hearted and kind, and he cares about Violet. He feels that the ambitious Buddy is not good for her, and she should be loved for who she is. Jake's emotions and persuasive energy will ensure the delivery of the text and the rhythmic variety of the song's vocal line with leadership and commitment.

CONTEXT: As the show progresses, the relationships of the twins and their feelings for Terry and Buddy deepen, and eventually, even though their act is a hit, they quit the sideshow and go on the vaudeville circuit. They think that on the vaudeville stage, away from the sideshow, they will be taken seriously, but the reporters ask them the same rude questions, and the twins wonder if they will ever be loved for themselves.

In act II, at a New Year's Eve party, Buddy unexpectedly asks Violet to marry him, but Terry is not interested in marrying Daisy. As time goes by, they all express their reservations about the marriage, and Buddy's separate confession is overheard by Jake. Trying to save her from disappointment and heartbreak, Jake confesses to Violet that he has always loved her, and he sings to her "You Should Be Loved."

CONTENT: A character that has not been front and center in the show sings a surprising declaration of love in this song. He could be interrupted by Violet (or Daisy) or Buddy at any time, so Jake sings the song with urgency. It is a dangerous confession, and it spills out of him, since has been holding the words and the song inside for a long time. The song begins quietly with a cello countermelody. The song is melodic, lyrically sung with care, and moves with momentum. It is telling the way he sings to her at the end of the first verse with an interruptive eighth rest: "You should be loved in the way [rest] I love you [sustained D at the top of the staff]." He continues (marked "a little slower") as he becomes more expressive ("broaden") in the B section to tell her that he has been holding his feelings inside for years, holding back tears, waves, "and the tide." He can no longer hide from his emotions, as the vocal line rises to a sustained E-natural (forte). In the next verse he explains that the two of them should be close, "coupled with a lifetime connection." He sings, "WE should be joined." The song comes to a cadence at the text "You should be loved [molto rallentando, quarter rest]—in the way I love you." Their "conversation" then continues with an exchange (in song) that expresses her reservations. His emotional declarations of love continue: "The world won't let us," she says. "We *are* close, like a brother and sister." Their discourse continues, and their vocal and textual counterpoint continue until they are interrupted by Buddy.

NOTE: the song can be sung solo and extended by adding Jake's last verse without Violet's counterpoint to complete the piece.

VOICE: The song requires a lyric smoothness, a legato to the vocal line, as Jake sings the opening melody with tenderness. Many of the notes at the top of the song's range at the D are uninflected syllables, which call for a lack of vocal tension even though the intervals may ascend. On the other hand, in the B section, which has more power and drama, the singer needs full breath support up to the climactic high E natural sustained at the top of the staff, and must continue to crescendo with expression through to the cutoff after eight beats. The final line includes the text "in the way I love you," with the "you" extended for the last sustained note on the D. It is not an easy vowel (*u*) to sustain on a higher pitch. Sometimes, when the performer is trying to support and get more sound, he or she may open up the vowel too much. advice good way to counter this tendency is to make some space in the jaw, giving some room in the throat, and round the lips, so that the integrity of the vowel is maintained.

BEHIND THE SCENES WITH THE ARTISTS: BILL RUSSELL, WHO WROTE BOTH THE BOOK AND THE LYRICS

Bill Russell told me that "Jake is the only principle character in *Side Show* not based on an actual person." Bill further explained: "For one thing, I love Henry [Krieger]'s score for 'Dream Girls,' and I really wanted to explore the African American sound, which Henry has in his soul, in the show. Jake's song 'The Devil You Know' does. 'You Should Be Loved' doesn't come from that musical tradition. As I remember, we had a hard time with that song, and we wrote several different ones for that spot. The first time Henry set this lyric he did it in 3/4 time. . . . I didn't think waltz tempo was right for Jake's character, so Henry tried it in 4/4, which is where it remained."

Mr. Russell offers some insight into the casting of Jake: "Because one of the themes is difference, since the Siamese twins are different, having an African American principal seemed important. I've always been fascinated how people who are in oppressed groups still seem to need to oppress others. So when Violet rejects Jake's confession of love because he's black, it's troublesome, since she's been considered an outsider her whole life. . . . But, of course, that's part of the reason—she wants to be like everyone else."

Shouldn't I Be Less in Love with You?

I Love You, You're Perfect, Now Change

"For me, the questions related to the couple's history and made the answer at the end of the song inevitable."
—Rob Roznowski, the original Husband

CHARACTER: Husband

MUSIC: Jimmy Roberts

BOOK AND LYRICS: Joe DiPietro

SETTING: contemporary suburbia

BROADWAY PREMIERE: 1996

CLASSIFICATION: Baritone/tenor rock ballad

RANGE: 

TESSITURA: Upper-middle staff

TIME: 2:32

PLOT: See "I Will Be Loved Tonight."

CHARACTER: Rob Roznowski, who originally created the role of the Husband, made the following observation about his character: "I don't think this character spends each day in heavy contemplation about his choices. This one moment of song is a rare occurrence in his life. As [someone playing] a character married for thirty years, I made specific choices about the fights and nights referred to in the song. I think the regrets he has are not about marriage, but more about the folly of his younger choices."

CONTEXT: The song "Shouldn't I Be Less in Love with You?" occurs toward the end of the show with the husband and wife at the breakfast table. She is reading the morning newspaper (frozen) and oblivious to his song.

CONTENT: This is the classic misdirection love song, yet it also displaying originality—a song that sums up the relationship from the husband's point of view and allows him to realize that he should love her less (not more). He is arguing with himself as he begins with an opening musing, which is recitative-like and fragmented, accompanied by a sparse figure in the piano, in half-note-rhythm octaves. The text declares that experts say that "love fades so fast" and doesn't last, so, he wonders, "Why is my heart [rest] still beating?" before he goes into the main melody of the song. The refrain is sung with rhythmic energy, accompanied by block chords in the piano. Shouldn't I go out and explore "what I can be?" Then, there is a two-measure piano interlude, with movement ("a little bit faster"), as he continues to question their relationship. Shouldn't he "confess a sordid fling?" "A little bit faster" and "with passion" are marked in the next section, a bridge, in which he says that "after thirty years together," with their fights, and seemingly at the end of his rope as he remembers all those "sleepless nights," it makes him wonder, why he doesn't love her less.

The song returns to the main melody ("with strong emotion"). Shouldn't he have quit the marriage, like his friends did? Shouldn't he love her less? he asks, as the song is marked "slower (emphatically)" and there is a dramatic rest (fermata). After the pause, over a final chord, he concludes: "No." He is silently staring at her now, as she sits at the breakfast table. The Wife looks up from her paper and asks, "What?" during the final chords as the song ends. The last moment is whimsical, and also real.

VOICE: Important in the delivery of this song is attention to text and rhythmic specificity, building from random musings to tough, targeted questions sung with emotion. Focusing in the song is important, to keep it from being an empty rant. He really wants to know the answers to these questions as the song unfolds. At the opening, where the tone is more reflective, the phrases should be sung with a lighter tone, so that the vocal production is not strained on the upper D and E-natural pitches. The first time the Husband sings the refrain "Shouldn't I be less in love with you?" he is moving from reflective to active, but still the vocal weight should be lighter, so that the vowel (*u*, set on the word "you") is also not strained and constricted on the high D on the staff. At the text of the bridge, "After 30 years together," the song moves with more momentum, passion, and feeling. When he recounts the "brutal fights, the futile fights, and the sleepless nights," the song is at its emotional peak. He continues with one more repetition of the refrain melody as he asks another question: "Shouldn't I have quit?" also sung with dramatic passion, wanting—needing to hear the answer to the question. He continues: "Shouldn't I profess it's time to go?" sustaining a high, strong E natural. The singer is singing strongly at this climactic point of the song. However, the throat must not be constricted, because the resultant tone would be thin and "straight," and the result is a loss of vocal power. It is advised that the performer attempt to crescendo on the high E, thinking more about strong breath support than just hitting the note with force. A passionate crescendo will create an exciting (and free) climactic point in the song. And it is impossible to crescendo on a high sustained tone when throat tension causes the singer to hold the note. After the sustained high E-natural ("go"), the song suddenly turns more reflective, evident in the musical marking, "softer," in the accompaniment, as the Husband asks himself once more, "Shouldn't I be less in love with you?" and he answers his own question on a sustained middle C as he sings: "No," softly but emphatically. As the song concludes, it is important for the Husband to not ignore his final brief space of silence and reflection before he sings the last "No." It is an effective dramatic moment, and it should not be rushed.

BEHIND THE SCENES WITH THE ARTISTS: ROB ROZNOWSKI, THE ORIGINAL HUSBAND

Rob feels that in a revue like *I Love You, You're Perfect, Now Change,* in which actors play numerous characters, "understanding a character's history is important." Before this song, the couple is silently going about their everyday tasks of reading the paper, pouring the coffee, setting the table for breakfast, and showing the rut that they are in. The musical introduction of "Shouldn't I Be Less in Love with You?" only starts, Mr. Roznowski observes, "when a casual glance between the two lingered. For me, the character was singing his inner monologue, and his wife was oblivious to the what-ifs the character was exploring." Rob feels that the lyricist, Joe DiPietro, had written such a great series of questions that the husband asks throughout the song, and composer Jimmy Robert's music so perfectly led the character into his emotions, that "the song really landed emotionally from the first rehearsal. For me, the questions related to the couple's history and made the answer at the end of the song inevitable."

It's Hard to Speak My Heart

Parade

"It is wrenching for him and he is struggling with the words, the emotions . . . the careful intervals."
—Brent Carver, the original Leo Frank

CHARACTER: Leo Frank

MUSIC AND LYRICS: Jason Robert Brown

SETTING: Atlanta, 1913

PREMIERE: 1998

CLASSIFICATION: Baritone

RANGE: 

TESSITURA: Middle of staff

TIME: 2:41

PLOT: See "Old Red Hills of Home."

CHARACTER: Leo Frank was an unpopular factory owner. He was cold and distant, an educated Jew from Brooklyn living in Atlanta, Georgia. He earned a degree in mechanical engineering from Cornell University in 1906. He was twenty-nine years old during the trial and was murdered at age thirty-one. During the trial the prosecutor was Hugh Dorsey, who eventually was elected governor of Georgia. During the politically charged four-week trial, Frank's cool demeanor and body language incenses the crowd inside and outside the Atlanta courthouse. Clearly, he will be condemned for this villainous crime, and he has no choice but to plead his innocence by the conclusion of the trial.

CONTEXT: The song "It's Hard to Speak My Heart" is sung by Leo Frank in the seventh and final scene of the trial at the end of act I. In reality, the entire trial lasted four weeks. Leo Frank's final testimony reportedly took four hours. Pictures of the trial show how crowded the courtroom was, and after witnesses recounted the circumstantial evidence gathered by the ambitious prosecutor, the room was filled with vitriolic hatred. It is against this emotional backdrop that Leo Frank begins to defend himself in the play. Preceding the song is the chorus singing (and shouting) "Hang him!," "Jew," "Take 'im down!" and other epithets.

CONTENT: The song is complex, with many sections and dramatic transitions. Basically, the piece unfolds, driven by the text, in a through-composed manner. The music at the beginning of the song is marked "with a sense of stillness." There is a vamp of a two-note "chord," the B and E (perfect fourth) together in incessant quarter-note beats, which is reminiscent of a clock ticking (building tension) in the introduction of one measure, vamped until a reluctant Leo is ready to speak. This open interval of B and E sounded together continues through the first section. Leo's entrances are not musically predictable, because they tend to start off the beat in the interior of the measures, making it sound as if his words are erratic and not articulations of clear thought. Leo explains that he is "not a man who bares his soul." "I know I hide behind my work, I must seem hard and cold," he says. "I never touched that girl," he insists, repeating the opening motive as the accompaniment, in arpeggiated sixteenth-note patterns, becomes more active. His lines gradually grow more intense, more emotional, and more agitated as the song unfolds. Leo's testimony begins with the same melodic motive in each of his lines, where rhythmic complexity and choice of interval (higher) creates more tension and dramatic crescendo. The orchestration becomes more colored and dense, too, as the song unfolds. And then, in the last section, the music is marked "still again," with the quarter-note two-note chords. Frank, exhausted, finishes pianissimo, a cappella, singing (rubato) "I pray you understand" (a cappella), for an extremely dramatic ending to the song.

VOICE: This is a challenging song to sing musically and vocally. Along with the tricky entrances, the singer also has a variety of rhythms to negotiate, also not predictable. There are many accidentals without doubling assistance from the accompaniment. The range is challenging, requiring low pitches at the beginning of the song and also a sustained high E as he cries out, and the singer must find all of the correct intervals through mild dissonance "against" the accompaniment. The sustained high Es are sung on the words "say," "said," and "hand" and are emotionally sung, but need to be produced without tension, because the voice at that pitch level without vibrato and freedom will sound strident and harsh, which is out of character for Leo. His character is more in control than that. The rhythms need to be sung sharply, with definition, for the express purpose of showing agitation because of the circumstances. At the end of song, Frank sings in a light, simple, plaintive tone. He has exposed himself by begging for mercy. One of the most challenging aspects of this song is for Leo to become more agitated and emotional (along with the music), while at the same time maintaining an eerily calculating presentation, which is part of Leo Frank's character.

BEHIND THE SCENES WITH THE ARTISTS: BRENT CARVER, THE ORIGINAL LEO FRANK

Mr. Carver says of Leo Frank: "He is a man of very few words, and this is the first time he speaks in public. He does talk with his wife and to himself to chronicle his character in the play, but it is very difficult for him to express himself, because his character is closed. He is always in control, in check. He is essentially a bookkeeper and makes lists and is comfortable with figures. So when he begins to sing this song in the courtroom, he is not sure at all how to express himself." Brent describes Leo's courtroom ordeal: "It is wrenching for him, and he is struggling with the words, the emotions.... The careful intervals, especially at the beginning of the song, mirror his own difficulty in getting the correct emotions out. 'It's hard to speak my heart,'" he repeatedly says. "The music is the door to him expressing himself, ultimately. But at the end of the song, he goes back into his protective shell again."

Love Who You Love

A Man of No Importance

"And that is where the poignancy is–that he is unable to follow his own words."
—Stephen Flaherty, composer of *A Man of No Importance*

CHARACTER: Alfie Byrne

MUSIC: Stephen Flaherty

LYRICS: Lynn Ahrens

BOOK: Terrence McNally

BASED ON: The 1994 film *A Man of No Importance*

SETTING: Dublin, Ireland, 1964

BROADWAY PREMIERE: 2002

CLASSIFICATION: Lyric baritone-tenor anthem with movement

RANGE: 

TESSITURA: Upper middle of staff

TIME: 2:30

PLOT: Alfie, a bus conductor in Dublin in 1964, directs an amateur church theatre group, St. Imelda's Players. Despite the church's objections, Alfie wants to stage a production of Oscar Wilde's play *Salome.* As Alfie reflects on the story in the show, the actors in his troupe become a kind of Greek chorus, and we basically have a play within a play, where Alfie is the leading character. The "play" includes "characters" in Alfie's life, including his sister Lily, the handsome bus driver Robbie Fay, and a woman named Adele Rice.

CHARACTER: Alfie Byrne lives with his sister, Lily. She would like to get married but instead watches over her brother. She acts as his mother, taking care of him and worrying about his well-being. Although Alfie leads a church theatrical group and is given rehearsal space by the church, he is not a religious man.

Alfie works in a civil service job on a London bus as a conductor. However, he has considerable imagination and is described as having his "head in the clouds." Alfie is the "man of no importance." He has a secret life, as he is immersed in the world of amateur theatre, and he is in love with his bus driver, Robbie Fay. Alfie greets those boarding the bus each morning, and as he takes their tickets, he "gives them a verse in return," and "a few simple hearts are thus warmed." Alfie, looking at himself in the mirror, remarks: "Hair getting thin and chin getting slack, an anonymous little man…and a poet's heart. Afraid of the world, afraid of myself and the love that dare not speak its name."

CONTEXT: In act I Alfie meets a young woman, Adele Rice, on the bus, and proceeds to become interested in her—as a potential actress in his amateur theatre group. He wants her to take the role of Salome in Oscar Wilde's play. After spending an evening drinking in a pub, Alfie returns home, confused about his sexual identity. As he looks into the mirror, he sees Oscar Wilde in a dream, and admits that he loves Robbie, the young bus driver. At the end of act I, after a rehearsal of *Salome*, while Alfie is walking Adele home she begins to cry and reveals a secret, telling him that she has a boyfriend in her hometown. Alfie, who understands secrets, sings "Love Who You Love" to comfort her.

CONTENT: The introduction of the song is a very simple twelve measures in 3/4 time, relaxed tempo, under the dialogue. The melody begins with very short phrases in the lower-middle voice (marked "simply, conversationally"), almost spoken in its free delivery, and the accompaniment is composed in block chords. The melody is not doubled in the orchestra until verse two. "You just have to love who you love" is the key melodic refrain, and it is a lovely, simple four-measure line that is then repeated. After another short verse, with more of an active rhythm in the accompaniment, the melody in the bridge moves forward in momentum to the top of the staff ("People can be hard sometimes"). There is an important countermelody in the flute. The last verse, "There's no fault in loving. No fault in shame," has a much more elaborate arpeggiated figure in the orchestral accompaniment. "I love who I love who I love" is the text finally placed in the cantus firmus of the short melodic phrase, at the end of the song, which is as much Alfie singing to himself as he is singing to Adele. The tag follows: "Then just go and love [quarter-rest pause]," and finally a spoken "who you love," for a poignant and heartfelt conclusion. The song needs to be delivered with a sincere and genuine simplicity. As he thinks of all of the circumstances, Alfie's life is complicated by his relationships—real and imagined. He dreams of producing *Salome* at the same time that the reality of life's problems confront him. The lyrics of the song are marvelous, and they must be delivered with care and warmth.

VOICE: Although the song has a charming melody with attractive harmony, the approach to its delivery should be intimately conversational. The bridge ("People can be hard sometimes") goes higher into the singer's range (to E natural at the top of the staff) and has more movement and passionate expression, with a settled rubato at the cadence before the next verse ("There's no fault in loving"). The lyrics at the top of the staff will need more yawn space, so that they are not constricted and difficult to understand. The words are mostly syllabically set, and the articulation of the important text must be accomplished with the lips, tongue, and teeth, without the jaw becoming involved.

BEHIND THE SCENES WITH THE ARTISTS: STEPHEN FLAHERTY, COMPOSER

The composer says that the person who is singing this song "should try to lovingly and freely offer advice to the listener who he is singing to [the scene partner, Adele]." The irony is this: "Alfie actually is unable to do this very thing himself. And that is where the poignancy is—that he is unable to follow his own words. That is, until act II, when Adele sings the song back to him—and he knows he must actually take his own advice and find his own way in the world. This is the 'extra layer that makes the experience of the song richer.' "

I Was Here

The Glorious Ones

"[Flaminio] found his truth in everyday life, in the streets."
—Marc Kudisch, the original Flaminio Scala

CHARACTER: Flaminio Scala

MUSIC: Stephen Flaherty

LYRICS: Lynn Ahrens

BASED ON: *The Glorious Ones*, a novel by Francine Prose

SETTING: A beautiful spring day in Venice, early seventeenth century

PREMIERE: 2007 (off-Broadway)

CLASSIFICATION: Lyric narrative baritone

RANGE: 

TESSITURA: Opening: low A to A (octave above); song proper: D to D

TIME: 4:26

PLOT: See "Absalom." I am grateful to composer Stephen Flaherty for suggesting this song for this book.

CHARACTER: Flaminio Scala is the leader of the commedia troupe called the Glorious Ones. At the beginning of the show, Flaminio describes the broad style of the commedia dell'arte. He tells us that many of their comic routines were improvised. In his early life, he was raised by monks and later thrown into the street. There, the endless parade of humanity inspired him to create a new style of theatre. A member of the troupe, Amanda Ragusa, a dwarf, is madly in love with the dashing Flaminio. She steals little souvenirs from him (buttons, stockings). The leading lady of the Glorious Ones, Columbina, is Flaminio's mistress. Flaminio Scala always gets the girl.

CONTEXT: Flaminio meets a talented young comic, Francesco, who is performing on the street. Flaminio takes him under his wing, and soon they are like father and son. He teaches Francesco how to be an actor. The next adventure for the troupe is a whirlwind trip to France to perform for the French court. Scala is convinced that their broad humor will enchant the king and ensure their fortunes. They perform their bawdy pieces. During the course of the skits Flaminio informs Columbina that she is too old to play opposite him, and she is later replaced. In turn, a trick is played on Flaminio, as the clown Arlecchino (Francesco) becomes the leading man, replacing Flaminio, as they tell him that *he* is too old to be the leading man. The troupe then presents "The Moon Woman," improvising a skit which soon turns into reality. Flaminio always pretends to kill himself with a fake sword when performing this skit, but this time a real one is used, which kills him. Since this is a play within a play, Flaminio rises and looks back on his life and the reward of creating something of worth. He sings, "I Was Here."

CONTENT: The song is in two parts, and the singer may leave out the introduction if the song is presented alone for an audition, showcase, or recital. The beginning, which introduces the song, is marked "freely" in the music, and is recitative-like, with block-chord-triad dotted half notes for accompaniment. Flaminio tells us what he has had to face in his life: he's gone without food and housing, and he's begged for any "chance to perform." The vocal line begins very low in the baritone range, below the staff. The next section modulates up one half step, as he continues to talk about the specific trials of waking with "my guts in a knot," and he remembers all of his sacrifices, what he has given up for his art, "and for what?" He has given them up for show business, for his silly costumes, makeup, and "a pitiful tent in a storm." There is very little that he earns ("tempo, with motion"). He's always on the move, always packed, just for "this madness to act!" he sings, as the accompaniment's rhythm becomes more active and the vocal line rises in pitch. Since he is Flaminio, in seventeenth-century Florence, a center of knowledge, he has a theory about what he calls this "disease we contract," and he believes most men who act are "equally crazy." And so concludes a lengthy introduction, which is a nice setup for the song proper, which begins after an attractive, up-beat eight-measure introduction.

The song that he sings is an irresistible melody with accompaniment, insistently moving forward with momentum, as Flaminio seeks answers to his questions. He asks why a boy will "carve his name on a tree," and then why a sculptor dedicates his life to carving stone. "Kings build tombs," he proclaims, and fools write books and poetry (here there is a rallentando). Why do we aspire to this immortality? The key modulates up one half step, as Flaminio unveils his revelation: we need to leave something behind. Men give their sons his name. Others leave something "in song or in story, something in blood or in glory," he says—"something that will last," and here he sustains the tied over-the-measure notes for two full measures. He exclaims that his memory will not "die like an ember." He will leave something behind; don't ask him why, he says. He will not leave sons or carved stones; he can only leave a name and his skill, and possibly make them known. This is the only way that he can leave "something immortal." Time will not make his legacy disappear, and "my name and reputation" will prove that he was here.

VOICE: Flaminio, as leader of the Glorious Ones, is summing up his life and ambitions in this song. It is at the "end" of his life (and the show), but he summons the strength and desire to tell his story. It is with no small amount of pride that he discovers the vocal resonance and richness to sing these many sustained tones of D and E at the top of his range. Because he is a leader, his character will also take charge in this song, for it is important that the singer is very clear about ritardando and tempo changes. The introduction is quite low, as he sings mostly between A below the staff to E, the lowest line. However, Flaminio is reciting as much as singing, as previously described in the "Content" section, and he does not need to fully vocalize the lower tones. The opening of the melody is in the key of D-flat major, while the second melody section ("I say we yearn to leave something that lasts") modulates up to the key of D major. Before the last chorus, at the bridge, the singer needs to follow carefully the directions for this all-important transition to the last section. At the words "Somehow I must!" there is a crescendo to poco rallentando to a freely sung, subito piano "Don't ask me why," which is at the very top of the staff at F-sharp and can be sung in a supported falsetto, since it is marked to be sung softly and freely. After the final chorus, Flaminio finishes with a last "I was here!" sustained on half notes, with "here" sung on the final note for six measures, marked "forte." The singer needs to form the *i* vowel with the tongue and not set the vowel with the jaw. The final note should be delivered with strength, meaning with a jaw that is not locked, with full abdominal breath support, providing a desired crescendo on the final sustained pitch.

BEHIND THE SCENES WITH THE ARTISTS: MARC KUDISCH, THE ORIGINAL FLAMINIO SCALA

Mr. Kudisch learned that the real Flaminio Scala (1547–1624) "wrote the Bible" for the commedia dell'arte in Italy during the Renaissance. The leading man in the commedia is also the director. Flaminio found his truth in everyday life, in the streets. He felt that the written word was deaf, and "I Was Here" represents the last moment of reality, the last moment of his life. "In fact, the place that the song was eventually placed [the song was written before the rest of the show], after Flaminio had killed himself and then stands to deliver the song, becomes his truth. The song was not always in its present form, for there are two parts that are separable." The first part, which Marc prefers to include when he performs the song, is a monologue with music, so to speak.

The piano introduction is the beginning to the second part of the song, the melody proper. Marc prefers to sing the final passages intimately, softly. He quoted Stephen Sondheim: "The more intimate you get, the more universal the communication."

INDEX OF SONGS

INDEX OF SHOWS

GENERAL INDEX

Made in the USA
Columbia, SC
03 May 2021

37292678R00207